PRAISE FOR *DATA AND ANALYTICS STRATEGY FOR BUSINESS*

In my experience, taking people somewhere they've not been before requires leadership and trust, whether that's climbing Everest or making a success of your business through the use of data and analytics. In *Data and Analytics Strategy for Business*, Simon Asplen-Taylor cuts through the jargon and provides a clear route for success.

Kenton Cool, 15 successful Everest summits, one of the world's greatest high-altitude mountaineers and leaders, expedition leader behind Sir Ranulph Fiennes's north face of the Eiger ascent and Everest summit

One of the benefits of going digital is that organizations can collect, review and analyse enormous quantities of data. Correctly interpreting this data provides the intelligence which enables a business to understand the consumer and marketplace in a completely new way. Successful organizations require a clear data strategy and a disciplined set of operational processes. Simon Asplen-Taylor shows in practical detail how to make this happen in the real world. He demonstrates that data is key but reveals that an effective data officer never loses sight of the commercial application and human element of the intelligence created.

Kevin Gaskell, serial entrepreneur, and former MD, Porsche GB and BMW GB

Brilliant book! Genuinely the best and most readable book for existing and aspiring CDOs. Every CEO should read the first chapter. Simon Asplen-Taylor has shared his significant expertise to create the go-to data guide for business and data leaders. *Data and Analytics Strategy for Business* uses examples from a wide range of organizations to explain why data can revolutionize a business. A genuinely good read, the book's structure superbly guides the reader through all aspects of delivering a data and analytics strategy with vital tools and tips. Whether your organization is struggling with trust in its reports or ready to launch the bots, this book is for you.

Nina Monckton, Head of Data, Just Group plc

Businesses operate in an increasingly complex and fast-moving environment, where making the right decision at the right time can mean the difference between winning and losing. Key to this is the successful management and use of data, underpinned by a robust data strategy. *Data and Analytics Strategy for Business* provides a structured approach to show how you can succeed – whether you are just embarking on your journey, part way through or just fine tuning. The book is full of practical advice, anecdotes and experiences to help you win and not lose.

Carl Bates, former Senior Partner, Data and Analytics, and leader of the Ventures practice, Deloitte

One of the ways we can encourage women into data leadership roles is to provide the advice and methods to help remove barriers, while sponsoring next-generation leaders. In *Data and Analytics Strategy for Business*, Simon Asplen-Taylor does just that. He has shared his experiences and strategies for success to create a level playing field for all data leaders. He also talks specifically about how to build and leverage the strengths of a diverse team.

Roisin McCarthy, Founder, Women in Data

As we strive to gain more value from our data assets, we create more risk, opportunity and motivation for breaches. Simon Asplen-Taylor's new book, *Data and Analytics Strategy for Business*, provides amazing insight on how you can create more value in your organization's data while also ensuring its security! Highly recommended.

Ned Finn, CISO, Currys

A very interesting book in such an important and contemporary area of knowledge and skills. Data analytics is not just an area of knowledge that you need to learn more about, but it is considered to be a crucial skill that is required for every business. Therefore, this book is a great addition to the intellectual body of knowledge that can help students, especially those studying post experience executive programmes, such as MBAs and DBAs, to gain clear insights of the key elements of business analytics and to acquire the required set of skills to compete in the changing world of practice.

Amir Michael, Professor of Accounting and Associate Dean (MBA, DBA), Durham University Business School, UK

The world of a chief data officer (CDO) requires a full understanding of how a business operates, the sector it works within and the people involved. Simon Asplen-Taylor's book gives a fine insight into the approaches, decisions and specific actions a CDO can use to bring real value to an organization and make it a critical part of business strategy.

Helen Crooks, Chief Data Officer, Ofgem

Beyond his remarkable expertise across all the complexities of today's data sphere, this book clearly demonstrates Simon Asplen-Taylor's mastery of the art of data storytelling. Yet, what makes it even more compelling is that it is so helpfully structured in waves that align to the variety of levels across the entire data maturity spectrum – making it instantly transformative regardless of where an organization currently finds itself in its data journey. This book is an absolute essential for anyone who wants to successfully leverage the abundant value that can be derived from data and analytics.

Edosa Odaro, Chief Data and Analytics Officer, Tawuniya, and author of *Making Data Work*

Data and Analytics Strategy for Business

*Unlock data assets and increase innovation
with a results-driven data strategy*

Simon Asplen-Taylor

KoganPage

First published in Great Britain and the United States in 2022 by Kogan Page Limited

2nd Floor, 45 Gee Street	8 W 38th Street, Suite 902	4737/23 Ansari Road
London	New York, NY 10018	Daryaganj
EC1V 3RS	USA	New Delhi 110002
United Kingdom		India
www.koganpage.com		

Kogan Page books are printed on paper from sustainable forests.

ISBNs

Hardback   978 1 3986 0607 4
Paperback   978 1 3986 0605 0
Ebook   978 1 3986 0606 7

British Library Cataloguing-in-Publication Data

A CIP record for this book is available from the British Library.

Library of Congress Cataloging-in-Publication Data

Names: Asplen-Taylor, Simon, author.
Title: Data and analytics strategy for business: unlock data assets and
    increase innovation with a results-driven data strategy / Simon
    Asplen-Taylor.
Description: London, United Kingdom; New York, NY: Kogan Page, 2022. |
    Includes bibliographical references and index.
Identifiers: LCCN 2022008088 (print) | LCCN 2022008089 (ebook) | ISBN
    9781398606050 (paperback) | ISBN 9781398606074 (hardback) | ISBN
    9781398606067 (ebook)
Subjects: LCSH: Management–Statistical methods. | Strategic
    planning–Statistical methods.
Classification: LCC HD30.215 .A87 2022 (print) | LCC HD30.215 (ebook) |
    DDC 658.4/033–dc23/eng/20220222
LC record available at https://lccn.loc.gov/2022008088
LC ebook record available at https://lccn.loc.gov/2022008089

Typeset by Integra Software Services, Pondicherry
Print production managed by Jellyfish
Printed and bound by CPI Group (UK) Ltd, Croydon CR0 4YY

CONTENTS

About the author xiv
Preface xv
Acknowledgements xvii

PART ONE
How data and analytics can help you grow your business 1

01 How can this book help you? 3
Introduction 3
CDOs hold the future of their organizations in their hands 7
Task: Ten questions to ask about your business 7
Are you worried? 19
References 20

02 The business case for data 22
Introduction 23
The cost of doing nothing 24
The value of data is only as good as the value of your business case for it 26
Identifying the most pressing data problems 28
Keep it simple 30
Aligning the business case with the business 31
References 32

03 Your data and analytics strategy 33
Introduction 33
What is a 'data and analytics strategy'? 35
Defining the CDO role 36
Task: Setting priorities using the data periodic table 37
Task: Using the data periodic table to design projects 42
Five waves of transformation 44

Value, build and improve 47
Task: share the story 48
References 50

04 A team game 51

Introduction 51
Cracking the code as a CDO 53
The résumé problem 55
Discovering problem-solvers 56
Task: Recruiting for PQ and AQ 57
Beware of ready-made data teams 60
Diversity 61
Data and analytics capability model 63
References 70

PART TWO
Wave 1: Aspire 73

05 A quick win 75

Introduction 75
Anatomy of a quick win 77
Task: Identifying the right project 79
Make sure it's a quick win for everyone 83
Quick wins are not strategic wins 84
References 85

06 Repeat and learn 86

Introduction 86
Why build a repeat-and-learn culture? 87
Listen to what data is telling you 89
Task: Define a data process 91
Task: Develop a business change process 92
Learning and innovating through experimentation 93
References 95

PART THREE

Wave 2: Mature 97

07 Data governance 99

Introduction 99
What is data governance? 102
The importance of accountability 105
Data stewards, data owners and the data executive 107
Task: Implementing data governance 111
References 115
Further reading 115

08 Data quality 116

Introduction 116
The risks of low-quality data 117
The upside of high-quality data 119
The four principles of data quality 122
A data quality strategy 124
Task: Setting a baseline and a target 125
Task: Build a data quality team 129
Task: Improving data quality in the short term 130
Task: Improving data quality in the long term 132
References 134
Further reading 134

09 A single customer view 135

Introduction 135
What is a single customer view? 137
Benefits of the SCV 143
Other single views 144
How do you build an SCV? 146
Shadow data is the enemy of the SCV 148
Ownership of the SCV 149
References 150

10 Reports and dashboards 151

Introduction 151
Task: A report audit 152
From static to dynamic decision support 156
Task: Designing your dashboard 158
Task: Dashboard implementation 160
From reporting to insight 162
Task: Information architecture 163
Avoiding short-termism 165
References 167
Further reading 167

11 Data risk management and ethics 168

Introduction 168
Five pillars 169
Task: Working with a regulator 174
References 176

PART FOUR
Wave 3: Industrialize 177

12 Automation, automation, automation 179

Introduction 179
What can we automate? 180
How much can we automate? 182
Task: The business case for automation 184
Task: Manageable automation projects 187
Will I use a tool? 189
References 191

13 Scaling up and scaling out 192

Introduction 192
From quick wins to big wins 193
Be dull and repetitive 194
Task: Choosing how and when to scale 195

Use your resource multipliers 197
Task: Implementing your hackathon 200
The dividend from scaling 202
References 203

14 **Optimizing** 204

Introduction 204
Best intentions are not optimal 205
Task: Plot a path to optimization 206
Task: Overcoming resistance 208
The limits of automation 209
This is a tipping point 210
References 211

PART FIVE
Wave 4: Realize 213

15 **The voice of the customer** 215

Introduction 215
Hearing their voice 216
Reasons to use other sources of data 218
Understanding competitors 219
Customer behaviour 221
Social listening 222
Task: Applying insights from social listening 223
Task: Creating a reliable Net Promoter Score 226
Integration 229
Hear the bad news 229
References 230

16 **Maximizing data science** 232

Introduction 232
Data science, not data magic 233
How *not* to do data science 234
Task: Integrating data science 236
Task: Sustaining data science 238
Embrace the potential for failure 240
References 241

17 Sharing data with suppliers and customers 242

Introduction 242
Widespread exposure 243
Exposing data to business partners and suppliers 244
Blockchain in the supply chain 246
Sharing improves markets 247
Exposing data to customers 249
Task: Prepare to share 250
Exposure is inevitable, so do it your way 252
References 253

PART SIX
Wave 5: Differentiate 255

18 From data-driven to AI-driven 257

Introduction 257
What does AI do? 260
A hierarchy of data value 261
The AI journey 263
Task: Detection 264
Task: Process automation 266
Task: Improved clustering 268
Data bias 269
Task: Complex analysis and prediction 270
The limits of AI as a guide or manager 273
Task: Creating commitment to AI for independent real-time decision-
    making 274
From data-driven transformation to AI-driven business 275
References 276

19 Data products 278

Introduction 278
What is a data product? 280
A data and analytics centre of excellence (CoE) 281
Task: Creating a data CoE 283
Three functions of research 284
A continuous improvement life cycle 284
References 285

20 Right leadership, right time 286

Introduction 286
Leading a sustainable data culture 287
Which leader are you? 288
Reference 288

Epilogue: Data success 289
Glossary 291
Abbreviations and acronyms 298
Index 300

ABOUT THE AUTHOR

Simon Asplen-Taylor is one of the most experienced and successful data leaders in Europe, having served as chief data officer for several FTSE firms and led some of the largest data-led transformations in Europe.

He specializes in transforming businesses through the use of data, analytics and artificial intelligence whilst delivering significant upside in revenue, customer satisfaction, organization efficiency, cost reduction and reduced risk. He has a unique depth and breadth of data experience covering more than 30 years across many industries, having led the data capabilities at Lloyd's of London, Tesco, Rackspace, Regus, BUPA, UBS and Bank of America Merrill Lynch and been a data consulting leader at IBM and Detica.

His major achievements include:

- For a UK FTSE 100 financial services organization, delivering a $1 billion per annum contribution to the bottom line and also generating a significant uplift in share price.

- For a FTSE 250 business, delivering a 64 per cent improvement in the company's margin through the use of data.

- Troubleshooting and fixing the data capabilities of two organizations under direct threat from regulators.

- Being a leader in the data and analytics consulting practices of BAE systems and IBM – advising clients across financial services, telco, retail, entertainment, media and insurance.

- Designing and leading the implementation of the data ecosystem for the UK's financial regulator, which in turn supported the first prosecution of insider dealing in the UK.

He has an MBA from Durham University, is a Fellow of the British Computer Society and a Fellow of the Royal Statistical Society. He has studied artificial intelligence at MIT.

His awards include being shortlisted for Data Leader of the Year (2019) and DataIQ100 top 100 influential people in data (2020 and 2021), the only fully curated list of influential people in data and analytics. He is a frequent data blogger and regular speaker, panel member and chairman at data events. He is a keen sailor and an avid rugby supporter.

PREFACE

Why *Data and Analytics Strategy for Business*?

Whether you're a CEO, CFO, CIO or indeed any C-level role, whether you're a businessperson who wants to understand more about data strategy so you can decide how to manage it in your organization, or just want oversight then this book will greatly help you not only to understand the challenges of those in your data and analytics teams but also your role in supporting them. If you're a chief data and analytics officer, data scientist, data engineer, MBA or business student wanting to understand the growing role of data and analytics in business, or just data curious, then there is much to be found in this book for you.

This book has been written by a practitioner who's seen it work and, just as importantly, seen it fail. As the author I only wish this book had been around when I started out, and that's part of the motivation for writing it.

What makes this book different from other data books?

I've thought carefully about the content and at times I feel I've given away the 'crown jewels'. So rest assured I've not held back from giving the best advice I can.

Key features include:

- Artefacts that will bring significant value to you. I draw your attention to the data periodic table in Chapter 3. It looks simple but it is the culmination of years of experience and something I use almost daily.
- Real case studies that bring the strategy to life.
- Ideas underpinned by solid business theory – with references to relevant research. If you're a businessperson you'll want to know that it's based on proper research. If you're a student you'll want to follow up on the research.
- Key concepts highlighted throughout the book making it easier to remember and use, and assuming no prior knowledge in the subject.

- I've followed a maturity model with five waves throughout the book, to give you a practical approach to follow and to help you measure your progress.
- The book is written from the perspective of data being a key business enabler, not a technology capability – the way it should be done.
- It's written by someone who's made mistakes and is willing to share the learnings so you don't make the same ones, and who's seen all elements of data and analytics – consulted, delivered, owned the capability and been responsible to the board.

I hope you won't just read this book. I hope you'll use it!

Follow up

- If you have feedback on this book please do share it with me: feedback@datatick.co.uk.
- If you're interested in having me consult to your organization or provide coaching and mentoring services please do get in touch. There is more information available at www.datatick.co.uk.

ACKNOWLEDGEMENTS

Along the way I've had the privilege to work for some great firms. They've had blood, sweat, tears and I hope a lot of value from me. I've had some smart colleagues and we've had mostly fun times with a few, inevitable, bumpy patches, but we've all learned a lot along the way.

I'd specifically like to acknowledge the help and support of:

- Kogan Page for believing in me, enabling this to become real, and for all the support you've provided.
- Tim Philips for his support, knowledge and experience, and Catherine Walker for making my illustrations work.
- Durham University for giving me the best education I could have had, and for giving me the desire to keep learning.
- My friends and family – you know who you are.
- My three boys William, Alexander and Matthew, who are the main motivation in my life, without whom this would not have happened. I dedicate this book to you.

PART ONE

How data and analytics can help you grow your business

01

How can this book help you?

The data your business holds, and acquires through doing operational and trading activities, is the key to its future. You may be surprised to discover how much you can use that data to drive increases in revenue, reduce costs, improve operational efficiency, reduce risk, and improve customer and employee satisfaction.

KEY CONCEPTS

- Chief data officer (CDO)
- Digital transition, digital transformation
- Data and analytics strategy
- Single customer view (SCV)
- Single source of truth
- Shadow data resource
- Data leakage

Introduction

'The world's most valuable resource is no longer oil, but data' (Economist, 2017). The article pointed out that Alphabet (Google's parent company), Amazon, Apple, Facebook and Microsoft were (and are) the world's five most valuable listed firms.

The assumption that data-equals-oil is broadly true, but not new. It is casually tossed about in meetings or announced with great portent at the beginning of hundreds of conference keynotes.

Before we discuss the value of data, let's start by defining what data is for our purposes. You have a business, and that means customers have transacted with it. Every transaction creates data: contracts, orders, invoices, and perhaps refunds and credits. Storing this information means that you have created a database of your customers, containing their names, addresses, mailing preferences, and much more. You have employees too, and so that means another database containing their remuneration, the hours they have worked, where they live and the office they work in, their skills and experience. At some point you purchased goods and services for your business: raw materials for manufacturing, stationery, energy and water; you spent time on the telephone and rented an office. Records of what you did all become your data. You launched your own products and services that were researched, developed and released to the market. You wrote press releases, published your accounts, and updated your websites. That has generated even more data. Your competitors did the same, and you have stored data about that too. Your customers and journalists reviewed your products and commented on them on social media, which created even more data that you can use.

This, and hundreds more items of information that you capture every day, is what we mean by data. It matters how we manage and store that data, and also how we use analytics, artificial intelligence (AI), and machine learning to extract the value from it.

In this book I'm not going to make the case for data in itself as an asset – because at this point, I'm assuming that you get it. At this stage, it's like making the case for railways, or the internet. But despite the fact that every leader in every business implicitly knows that the company is sitting on a potentially game-changing asset, not many of us really know how to turn that data into value.

Seventy-three per cent of data kept by companies is unused for analytics (Gualtieri, 2016) because most of its potential lies dormant; it is either locked up somewhere it can't be easily accessed, or it isn't business-ready.

We will discuss both of those problems at length in this book and outline how to solve them. But think about this for a second: three-quarters of data is kept, and never used.

If data is oil, your chief data officer (CDO) will locate the reserve, estimate its value, and extract and refine it. Not only that, but if you stick to your strategy to create value from data, your CDO will make sure you get better at it. Unlike oil reserves, which are ultimately exhausted, you will never run out of data or, in my experience, ways to use it to help your business. In fact, the volume and variety of data available to a business are growing rapidly. In 2021 it was calculated that the volume of data created, captured, copied and consumed worldwide would be 64 zettabytes (Zb) (Holst, 2021). That's 64 billion terabytes, or 64 trillion gigabytes – 10 terabytes for every person on the planet. By 2025, this number is expected to triple.

This book is a guide to how your business, channelled through a data executive led by the CDO, can leverage its data assets successfully. But, be warned: however tough you think it's going to be... it's harder.

There's a reason why so few businesses do this well. It's easy to get distracted, misallocate scarce time, resources and investment, or get stuck in the weeds. This book will also give a structure, five waves of innovation, that can be a template for using data in your business.

CHIEF DATA OFFICER (CDO)

The person responsible for enterprise-wide governance and use of information as an asset. This involves data collection, governance, processing, analysis, business intelligence, data science and key elements of data-driven AI and other techniques. A CDO usually reports directly to the chief executive officer (CEO).

The chances are that your business is not handling any of its data processes as well as it could. Right now, there's no shame in that. But it's costing you lost earnings today, and potentially your future. Your teams today are wasting time finding, correcting and managing bad data; they have missed opportunities because they didn't know they existed; they have made bad decisions because they didn't know the facts or didn't trust the data; they are formulating bad strategies or drifting because they have a limited ability to predict what will happen next; they are even risking censure or fines from regulators because of poor data management.

You know your business can do better. This is a great opportunity. It is inspiring and fascinating, but it is also stressful. If data and analytics can make a difference, the window in which to do that is rapidly closing.

The title of this book is *Data and Analytics Strategy for Business* because you have one of the greatest challenges that any business executive can face: the once-in-a-generation shift to a new way of doing business. The data and analytics-driven digital transformation, not least due to the impact of the Covid-19 pandemic, is happening much faster than we expected, and it requires a strategy to *Unlock Data Assets and Increase Innovation*.

There is no holding pattern. This is both thrilling and extremely stressful. As I will mention many times, this book is not a guide to writing code, or a shopping list for technology. It is intended to be a guide to the projects that

---

DIGITAL TRANSITION, DIGITAL TRANSFORMATION

The process of taking analogue information and translating it to a digital environment. The accompanying transformation involves changing business processes underpinned by data and analytics to take advantage of the opportunities.

---

your business can launch and complete. Like any executive with a 'C' in their job title, a CDO can't do everything at once or keep everyone happy. This transformation will need to demonstrate results at every point and change the culture of the business, and that will sometimes cause conflict.

It is daunting. Part of the reason I wrote this book is so that you can learn from my mistakes as a CDO – and hopefully avoid them – while sharing in my successes.

If you cannot use your data optimally, firms that have mastered the ideas in this book and go on to complete the five stages in our journey will challenge your business, and with data to help them, they are likely to win. Data and analytics will help them build better products and services, take your best customers and make them happier, run processes at a lower cost, defend themselves against new competitors, and innovate better, quicker and cheaper, with happier employees.

Your smartest competitors will get on with solving their underlying business problems using data and analytics. They may also be able to invent entirely new ways to do business. Already, the world's biggest provider of transportation does not own a car. The biggest provider of accommodation does not own a hotel. Supermarkets provide banking services. Our economy is changing, driven by the success of data-driven innovators.

CDOs hold the future of their organizations in their hands

The strategies to get through this are not secret. There is a community that I have found universally inspiring and supportive who are eager to share their insight: other experienced CDOs. We've been there, and we have the scars to show it. This book would not have been possible without the conversations I have shared with them.

When first-time or would-be CDOs ask me for advice, perhaps the most useful thing I can tell them is not to get lost in the weeds, and that applies to everyone who gets involved with a data and analytics strategy. Step back, plan, think about how you are going to prioritize, and communicate what you are doing and why. And so before we get into what you could do, how you can do it and what you stand to gain, let's confront the problems you face head-on.

Below are 10 questions that I ask the board, directors and senior managers when I start a data transformation process for a company. The answer to each is either 'Yes', 'No', or 'I don't know'. Keep track of the answers, and then I'll explain why I'm asking the questions.

Task: Ten questions to ask about your business

1 Do you invest more than 1 per cent of your revenue in data (excluding the cost of IT infrastructure)?

2 Can you describe a product or project driven specifically by data that had a measurable positive impact on the business?

3 In meetings, do participants use expressions like 'in my experience...' or 'what I feel is...' as a way to make decisions?

4 Do your colleagues argue about whose version of the data, or report, is correct?

5 Have you checked that your customers' experience of your organization matches your assumptions?

6 Recall the last time there was a crisis in your business. If you had been given an hour to pull some numbers together for an emergency meeting, would you have been able to find and access the right data?

7 Do you know how much you are paying for data across the whole business?

8 Is there a revenue-generating opportunity that your colleagues could tell you about that isn't captured in data?

9 Is the collection of data functionally isolated from the process of creating value with it?

10 Can you explain to your customers everything that you do with their data, and would they approve if you did?

Do you invest more than 1 per cent of your revenue in data (excluding the cost of IT infrastructure)?

The exact amount of your investment doesn't matter as much as whether you know what you are investing in. I suspect that many managers answer 'I don't know' to this. One obvious reason is that the cost of data is often wrapped into the cost of IT in general. Historically, this made sense: in the early years of the information technology boom you could imagine that somewhere there was a fixed lump of data, an inventory of every piece of knowledge your organization could assemble, that just had to be interrogated. The constraint was the investment in systems that could process it.

This is not a useful way to think about the world we now inhabit. On one hand, with the emergence of cloud computing, computing power and storage are services that are as elastic as the need you have for them. Digitization has also created the potential to acquire almost infinite amounts of data to analyse. The data and analytics strategy determines the investment in IT, not the other way round. In fact there is an absolute need to decouple the costs of data and technology.

DATA AND ANALYTICS STRATEGY

The choices and priorities that create a course of action to achieve the high-level goals of the organization. Through the use of all aspects of data – including data generation, data storage, governance, quality, analysis, business intelligence and data science – these goals will create returns or competitive advantage for the business and support its wider goals.

And, of course, high spend does not mean a high return, although some of the numbers invested by data-driven companies are extraordinary (Krauth, 2018). Google, for example, invests $3.9 billion in data science every year. UPS spends $1 billion. Amazon spends $871 million.

If you don't know how much you are investing in data, would you know how to find it out? Who would you ask, and do you think you'll get an informative answer if you do? Often this is a useful exercise. Many businesses have many pockets of data activity that are ineffective because they are buried in silos. Adding up the cost of all these activities may lead you to think: could we be investing this money more effectively?

Which brings us to the next question.

Can you describe a product or project driven specifically by data that had a measurable positive impact on the business?

Note the emphasis on measurable results that are attributable to data, rather than technology or improvements in general. If you answered 'no', why do you think that is? It might be that there weren't any projects of this nature. Or it might be that you don't know about them yet.

We often implicitly know that data will be, or has been, valuable to delivering results – think about a project to cross-sell, or to increase customer satisfaction that increases your share of that customer's wallet. But often we don't structure these projects as data-driven, even when they are. We tend to attribute the success to people, products, or an improved process. And, often, that's part of the story. Being able to tell a story of how data was the catalyst to create value, and being able to quantify that value, has three benefits:

1 It is a way to work out whether you are successfully using data. Can you isolate the role of the data in the business success, and can you express the return on that investment?

2 It is a way to think about how we can innovate. Often it takes a long time, or is not practical, to change a product, process or service. So instead, reframe the question: can we apply better data to existing decision-making, or can we make the data more relevant, to improve a process?

3 Finally, storytelling is a way to share stories of data that will help others buy into what you want to do. So, if your answer to the question was 'I don't know', this will be the most valuable first step. These do not have to be complex stories – often, the simpler the better, to inspire our imagination.

An example: in 1999, a major UK bank acquired an investment and pension provider. In 2010, the data team was given a strategic goal to use data to increase the size of the business. The bank had 30 million customers, and the investment and pension provider 30,000. And so, by using customer data from bank customers to identify those who would potentially want investment and pension products as well, our team was able to identify and convert 30,000 new customers for the investment and pension provider, doubling revenues accordingly. Data-driven cross-selling doubled the size of that business.

In meetings, do participants use expressions like 'in my experience...' or 'what I feel is...' as a way to make decisions?

You're not alone if they do: Forrester Research reports that only 12 per cent of companies use data-driven intelligence to guide key business functions or corporate strategy (Little, 2016). Listen to two psychologists describe the limitations of what psychologists call heuristic decision-making, but what we know as 'gut feel'. Gary Klein, a senior scientist at MacroCognition who has analysed the way people make decisions in high-pressure jobs like firefighting, describes it like this: 'You need to take your gut feeling as an important data point, but then you have to consciously and deliberately evaluate it, to see if it makes sense.'

Daniel Kahneman, who won the Nobel Prize in Economics for his work on decision-making, trusts his gut even less: 'Overconfidence is a powerful source of illusions, primarily determined by the quality and coherence of the story that you can construct, not by its validity. If people can construct a simple and coherent story, they will feel confident regardless of how well grounded it is in reality' (Kahneman and Klein, 2010).

Kahneman concedes there are two contexts in which gut feel has some validity. The first is a predictable situation that is familiar from experience. We all do this every day without noticing: we don't have time to research every tiny choice we make, so our brain fills in the gaps. Most of the time our instinct makes a good decision for us and if we get it wrong (for example, picking a film to watch on Netflix and finding it's rubbish) it doesn't matter. But this is not the case for most business decisions.

Kahneman agrees with Klein that gut feel is a reasonable starting point in a situation in which the statement is inviting feedback and qualification. What is important is that you test that intuition with data. Think about the opinion as a hypothesis, one that the CDO can support or dispel by using data. Gut feel is based on past experience, but high-quality data can show that it was based on assumptions that no longer apply (a different market, different customers, different macroeconomic conditions), or one that adds more detail to what we all assume (showing that the business actually is underperforming in a region, but that this is driven by one office, for example).

Remember, in your data and analytics strategy no decision-making meeting is held without relevant data. You should not trust narratives that overconfident minds have constructed that will lead to bad choices.

Whether you call it heuristics, intuition or gut feel, these instincts are always with us, and shouldn't be ignored. They just shouldn't be used as a way to decide – although our data limitations mean that's often what we do. Which brings us to our next question.

Do your colleagues argue about whose version of the data, or report, is correct?

In a recent job, I was called in to adjudicate an argument. My CEO had sat in a meeting in which two of his managers fought over some figures for their business unit. The best we can say is that neither of them was trusting his gut: they both brandished reports, with numbers, relating to the same part of the business. But the bottom lines were completely different. He set me the goal of discovering who was telling the truth.

It took four weeks to find the answer that nobody wanted to hear: neither of them. When we dug into it, both had missed out some important costs and made some incorrect assumptions, and so both, in their different ways, had given a too-optimistic picture of the real state of the business, slanted in ways that made them look good. They hadn't set out to deceive and weren't aware that that was what they were doing. Neither report was an effective basis for decision-making but by looking into it we identified some flaws in the business processes and by fixing them, we generated real business value.

This often happens when systems are not integrated, or when there are too many manual processes involved in creating the output. Perhaps the people who create the reports don't know what the numbers they are adding up really mean. Or people in different parts of the business interpret numbers differently or use the output of different IT systems.

But that doesn't excuse the practice. Doing this for internal meetings is bad, but having no authoritative source of truth for financial reporting can literally be criminal. The most destructive example of this must be the bankruptcy of WorldCom. By June 2002, the United States' second largest long-distance telecommunications company confirmed it had overstated its earnings, mainly by classifying as capital expenditures those payments it was making for using the communications networks of other companies. It reclassified money it held in reserve as revenues, making it appear it had profits of $1.38 billion. As the SEC reported, the improper accounting entries were easily accomplished because 'it was apparently considered acceptable for the General Accounting group to make entries of hundreds of millions of dollars with little or no documentation beyond a verbal or an email directive from senior personnel'. In total, WorldCom made more than $9 billion in erroneous accounting entries to achieve the impression it was making profits (International Banker, 2021).

At a more mundane level, Gartner Group calculates that poor-quality data drains $15 billion annually from businesses which miss opportunities to sell, or waste cash without realizing it (Moore, 2018).

As a CDO, you might have gone to work at a business that already has good-looking dashboards and elegant presentations. But does anyone know for sure they can trust the data in them to make decisions, or is it what Sir Alan Sugar, a market trader in London's Petticoat Lane before he founded Amstrad, used to call the 'mug's eyeful' of technology: good-looking but ultimately irrelevant decoration?

Or, worse, do people create a single truth by averaging several different reports, in the vain hope that they are all equally wrong? Remember, an inaccurate graph will look just as good, and appear just as precise, as an accurate one. Without a single source of truth, you can't act with confidence on what one piece of data is telling you.

Have you checked that your customers' experience of your organization matches your assumptions?

Pointillist, a firm that specializes in customer experience, surveys businesses every year to discover how well they are doing. In 2020 its survey of 1,050 analytics and customer-care professionals found that 48 per cent thought that lacking a single view of the customer was their number one challenge (Pointillist, 2020).

SINGLE CUSTOMER VIEW (SCV)

The process of collecting data from disparate data sources, then matching and merging it to form a single, accurate, up-to-date record for each customer. It is also known as a 'Golden ID' or '360-degree customer view'.

A single view of all the transactions and contacts and communications that you have with a customer is possible if you have a single source of truth about your business, but it is not easy. One of the problems is that what might look like a single, consolidated and complete view of the customer might be missing some vital pieces of data. You cannot discover this by looking only at the data you have. So systematically surveying your business units can help you find out whether your data represents the whole of the customer's experience of your business. You might be optimizing the customer experience that your data captures but failing to achieve your wider goals for the business.

SINGLE SOURCE OF TRUTH

Every data element is stored and edited in only one place, with no duplicates. Updates to the data propagate to the entire system.

This isn't just about customers: there are two equally important dimensions of business relationships that you can treat the same way. Do you have a single employee view? A single supplier view? You might think you do, but often you are relying on what your systems tell you, without examining the underlying experiences.

The employment contract is 'incomplete', in that it doesn't tell us much about what makes an employee work hard or be loyal because few of us work in an environment in which our employer can see everything we do. Therefore, a view of the employee based only on what the contract captures is going to be incomplete. As we move towards a culture in which more employees work from home or wish to work flexibly, being able to structure their contracts and incentives efficiently depends not just on what they can do for their employer but on the full picture of their circumstances, needs, motivations and abilities.

If you have a single view of each supplier, you can identify when that supplier is servicing many parts of your business or where you have multiple suppliers that could be consolidated with a bigger volume discount. Consolidation means you have a huge opportunity to save costs.

One of the achievements of a successful data and analytics strategy is a no-surprises culture. No customer, employee or supplier relationship is perfect, but you can aim for an environment in which none of your colleagues can respond to a problem by saying 'I had no idea that was a problem'.

Recall the last time there was a crisis in your business. If you had been given an hour to pull some numbers together for an emergency meeting, would you have been able to find and access the right data?

We all know by now what it is to nurse a business through a crisis. Everyone whose employer was affected by Covid-19 can recall the scrambling and off-the-cuff decision-making. Every day involved rapid replanning, most often around protecting cashflow. And so suddenly people are asking for different data, because there are different decisions to be made. They want it now, because tomorrow is too late.

So, imagine that you need to analyse one of these ideas, and to do that you need data about the current performance of the business. How much detective work do you need to do to find the numbers you need? Will you need to ask someone else to locate it? How many manual processes will you go through to extract and consolidate those statistics?

Often, it is quite a lot of work to locate this data. This happens because we too often get used to the tedium of assembling and curating data. Each quarter, season or month there are routine or repeated tasks that you and your colleagues complete that require the same types of data, just with different dates or product codes. Learning the steps to find and clean that data by hand is often an unwritten part of learning the job. It's inefficient and wastes time, but it is never a high enough priority to create a more efficient process.

That small inefficiency is replicated across hundreds of tasks, month after month. When you ask, people will tell you with a shrug that sure, it's a pain, but it's only once a quarter, and they are used to it now, and they have all the steps written down on this sticky note.

Or you might have a centralized data function: a team of gatekeepers who can find the data you need, but they're busy right now and is it OK if they get it to you tomorrow?

Hard-to-find data is an unexamined cost of doing business. Pre-Covid, you might have heard that we'd all like to fix it, sure, but it's the end of the quarter and so for the next week we'll be busy on the report, so could we discuss it later?

Take a minute to imagine the avoidably dull experience of reporting in your job. If you have the back of an envelope handy, calculate the cost of hard-to-find data in wasted time (after all, finding the data on that cost would probably take too long). And that cost is a lower bound: it assumes that the data you eventually compile is accurate, and that no one ever decides to blow off a potentially transformative piece of analysis because it would take too long to do it. And anyway, the cleaner put the sticky note with the instructions on it in the bin.

Hard-to-find data is a constant drag on your business: you can't respond to change, you make worse decisions under time pressure, it wastes everyone's time every day, and it strangles good ideas at birth. This book will deal with these issues, ensuring your data is easily accessible and well managed.

Do you know how much you are paying for data across the whole business?

One of the understandable responses to the scenario above is that a bright, resourceful employee thinks, 'I could put this data together', and creates a small resource for the team or department. One of the reports is now less of a problem, and response times improve.

But this is a shadow data resource, of the type that most businesses have, and those costs may be buried in departmental expenses, credit card bills and overtime costs. In my experience, as they proliferate, shadow data activities across an organization increase the costs of acquiring, holding and using data by a factor of two or three for no additional benefit over a centrally planned resource. And, of course, shadow data resources are created by people who are not skilled and might not understand the data or know how to update it. They drag down the quality of the data in that report, despite the well-meaning efforts of everyone involved – more hidden cost to the business.

> **SHADOW DATA RESOURCE**
>
> The collection, processing and analysis of data without explicit approval of the data function, usually funded by departmental budgets or corporate credit cards.

Another reason that few organizations know how much they are paying for data is that it is subsumed within an IT budget, which skews the cost-benefit analysis of the value that data delivers to the organization.

Data is a remarkable asset. For the cost of staff, for example, we assume a trade-off: pay less, and you get lower-quality work. The same goes for raw materials, or advertising space. But data need have no trade-off. You can bring down the cost of acquiring and using it without affecting the quality of the data itself. In fact, the relationship might work the other way: automating data acquisition and eliminating rekeying usually drives up data quality, for example, so you get more for less. But if you don't know what you're paying at the outset, and where that money is being spent, you can't even start this process.

Is there a revenue-generating opportunity that your colleagues could tell you about that isn't captured in data?

Between 2017 and 2018, I was CDO at a global commercial real estate services. It is a fantastically complex, fascinating and data-rich business. It is one of the world's largest commercial real estate services firms, with annual revenues of $8.8 billion in 2019.

A single property may have several separate teams to deal with tenants, landlords and maintenance staff. And then there's the sales team, using another application. This is normal, but often we missed out on simple but powerful ways to capture data. For example, when one team met a commercial tenant, there was a customer relationship management (CRM) application for the reporting of that meeting. Staff filled in the fields on a standard form: what the meeting was for, who with, and so on. Every meeting had its form to capture the relevant data for that team.

But the system did not capture all the important data for the business as a whole, because the form was a series of fields that could not, for example, tell the sales team whether the commercial tenant was happy or unhappy, an extremely important indicator of future revenues, or whether the tenant mentioned other business opportunities outside the scope of the meeting.

There was a simple way to remediate this: add a field, with free text, asking if there were any other potential ways to help the client, and make sure that data was communicated and followed up.

This is a simple example that you see every day, in every business. We call it data leakage. In essence, everyone can do their job well, and you can still miss out on countless ways to improve business performance.

DATA LEAKAGE

The failure to take advantage of potentially useful data generated by the business process in a way that can create an advantage for the organization. This can be a failure of acquisition, silos or business processes, but it creates a persistent leak of value that needs to be plugged, or data that is captured with a quality that is too poor to use.

How to measure data leakage

Data leakage is really three problems in one:

1 **Do you need to ask better questions to get more data?** Your business processes may be restricting data capture rather than enhancing it. The tell-tale sign is that when a crisis hits, many people at the customer-facing end had known there was a problem but didn't have a way to communicate their knowledge.

2 **Do you need to create new ways that the data can be retrieved?** Leakage can happen at the next stage. The data is there, but it is not being shared with the people who can act on it. An example may be social media data that is used to analyse sentiment for customer relations, but which contains important feedback on a problem with a product or service that demands action.

3 **Do you actually retrieve that data and follow up on it?** Surprisingly often, data is collected and shared, but there is no mechanism by which it prompts action. It is in the system if you look for it, but it's no one's job to look.

No one wants to miss opportunities through data leakage. But every time we are wise after the event, we are acknowledging its corrosive effect.

Is the collection of data functionally isolated from the process of creating value with it?

I recently spoke to someone in a financial services firm who confided that progress on creating the data warehouse was going well – and had been going well – for four years.

One problem: no one had actually used it yet.

Capturing data is only half the story. Creating an integrated data-driven culture that seeks to optimize the return on that data, by designing data into the organization at the point it is collected – rather than just inconsistently employing data to solve today's problem – is the other half. The two halves are entirely complementary, but you wouldn't know it when you peer inside many organizations.

Of course, there are always quick wins or tactical improvements that better data can create. But optimizing the business to use data has a far higher return.

What's the difference? You might have one of those, a beautiful, expensive and under-used data warehouse that causes the CFO sleepless nights. But this money is wasted if a series of teams have been set up in different parts of the business, independently aggregating, analysing and reporting this data for their line managers. This often happens because data-generating IT projects are focused so much on how to acquire and process data that we forget to think about how that data can optimally be used and that it needs to be cleaned up before it can be used more widely.

Maybe other departments continue to languish in a data-lite twilight, because no one has explained that the value in the data in other parts of the business downstream depends on what they are doing today.

Meanwhile, the data team looks on in exasperation, wondering, why isn't anyone using these wonderful things we build for them?

This way of working treats data as a stock of resources, adjacent to the business. It is something that just makes existing processes marginally more efficient or, worse, is deployed as a weapon to win internal turf wars.

Yes, we all want to democratize the use of data, and that often requires adoption to be driven from the bottom up. Yes, different departments, locations and job functions have different needs and definitions of success. The stock-of-data vision views it as something like food for the body: the organization eats when it is hungry, but often you need to prepare it and cook it before it is palatable. The organization I am imagining uses data as an integrated flow, like a nervous system enervating every activity in the business.

One of the major disadvantages for a business that thinks of data in this disjointed way became obvious on 25 May 2018 – the day that the General Data Protection Regulation (GDPR) came into effect.

Can you explain to your customers everything that you do with their data, and would they approve if you did?

One of the impacts of the GDPR was that it forced businesses to build data protection safeguards into products and services from day one.

Under the GDPR, consumers have the right not only to know what you are storing, but how the data is used. It forces any organization to have a narrative about how the data was acquired, why it is necessary, how it is held and used, and what the result of that process is.

But the GDPR, extensive as it is, doesn't tell the full story. Think of a bigger story: yes, there is risk, but there is also opportunity and value. And that value does not accrue only to the business but is shared with the customer. Furthermore, it goes deeper: how are you using machine learning (ML) and artificial intelligence, and how can you explain it to people who are worried about being discriminated against by a technological black box?

There are many reasons to make these policies explicit. Clearly there is regulatory risk, and reputational risk. But it is also a tool to explain to yourselves and the business why you do the things you do, and what is operationally and ethically right. Just because something feels like a good idea in a meeting doesn't mean the idea should be implemented. Your data and analytics strategy isn't just about how much you can do, but why you do it, and whether it fits in not just with your employer's targets but also with its social purpose.

Are you worried?

You will have noticed that the least reassuring answer is usually 'I don't know'. So many of these questions arise because the hundreds of data-generating processes in any organization have grown organically and independently. Often, they contradict or duplicate one another. Often, they go on, unmanaged, for years, sucking up more and more resources. It seems sometimes that the people in a business are working for the data, rather than the other way around.

This book shows you a process, based on the work that I have been doing with organizations like Rank Group, Tesco, Lloyd's of London, BUPA and Rackspace, to change this. In the next section I will introduce how you create a strategy to do this, and briefly outline the stages. It might seem hard work, because it is. But it is also some of the most profoundly interesting, enjoyable, creative work you could do.

These 10 questions might inspire your colleagues, or they might make them uncomfortable. I wouldn't argue with either response, as long as it creates a desire to act, to improve. In the rest of this introductory section, we'll find out how to create, resource and communicate the strategy for that plan of action.

SUMMARY

- Extracting value from data is fascinating but incredibly challenging, because it has an impact on every part of the business.

- It is important not to try to do everything, for everyone, at the same time, and so finding out which problems require attention is priority one.

- There is no hiding place today. If you lose, you lose money, lose customers, or lose your job. On the other hand, if you succeed it will be transformative.

- You don't need geeks to diagnose data problems. Ask questions of the people you work with about how they do their jobs, how they make decisions, and where they see opportunities to improve processes.

- It's often surprising, and a bit scary, to find out how little your business knows about itself, its products, its markets, and its customers. Providing certainty in these cases, even if it uncovers bad news, can present a huge opportunity for growth.

References

Economist (2017) Regulating the internet giants: The world's most valuable resource, https://www.economist.com/leaders/2017/05/06/the-worlds-most-valuable-resource-is-no-longer-oil-but-data (archived at https://perma.cc/KPA2-FVT6)

Gualtieri, M (2016) Hadoop is data's darling for a reason, *Forrester Research*, https://www.forrester.com/blogs/hadoop-is-datas-darling-for-a-reason/#:~:text=Hadoop%20thoroughly%20disrupts%20the%20 economics,enterprise%20goes%20unused%20for%20analytics (archived at https://perma.cc/FH8D-PU4X)

Holst, A (2021) Amount of data created, consumed, and stored 2010–2025, *Statista*, https://www.statista.com/statistics/871513/worldwide-data-created/ (archived at https://perma.cc/EP66-DT8D)

International Banker (2021) The Worldcom Scandal 2002, https://internationalbanker.com/history-of-financial-crises/the-worldcom-scandal-2002 (archived at https://perma.cc/V3JR-DGA3)

Kahneman, D and Klein, G (2010) Strategic decisions: When can you trust your gut?, *McKinsey Quarterly*

Krauth, O (2018) The 10 tech companies that have invested the most money in AI, *Techrepublic*, https://www.techrepublic.com/article/the-10-tech-companies-that-have-invested-the-most-money-in-ai/ (archived at https://perma.cc/A64H-JB34)

Little, C (2016) Where are you on the road to customer insights maturity? *Forrester Research*, https://www.forrester.com/report/Where-Are-You-On-The-Road-To-Customer-Insights-Maturity/RES53622 (archived at https://perma.cc/V8MK-J9UP)

Moore, S (2018) How to stop data quality undermining your business, *Gartner*, https://www.gartner.com/smarterwithgartner/how-to-stop-data-quality-undermining-your-business (archived at https://perma.cc/CMZ5-C6U8)

Pointillist (2020) State of customer service journey management and CX measurement report, pointillist.com (archived at https://perma.cc/9AQA-EPN9)

02

The business case for data

It takes time and trust, the willingness to work in different ways and to cooperate with other departments in order for any investment in data to be transformational for your business. Your fellow executives need to be taken on the journey with you. Therefore, you need to be able to demonstrate the value of investing in data.

KEY CONCEPTS

- Data inventory
- Tangible value of data
- Intangible value of data

FIGURE 2.1 The investment in data and analytics leverages your other investments

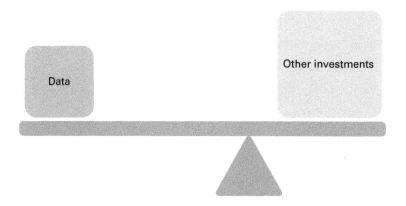

Introduction

Our first thought is that we shouldn't have to make a business case for the value of data. Trivially, no business can function without data. We all know that those businesses that know more about their customers, their market, or their products and services have always outperformed their rivals.

But that's not *your* business case.

Before we can start the data transformation, before we can even make a detailed strategy, we need to make an argument that investing in data, *rather than investing in any other part of the business*, is justified. This is why Figure 2.1 shows a balance: you are probably not investing enough in data at the moment, but that argument needs teeth, because it inevitably means (at least in the short run) diverting funding that might have been earmarked for business-as-usual projects. However, in my experience, any investment in data and analytics leverages your other investments, but it's often hidden. In the short term we will focus on revenue-generating projects that stand up in their own right, to prove the value of data and analytics. In the medium term the data projects will help pay for the data infrastructure required. In the long term, after the transformation, there will be no trade-off between the data and analytics strategy and any other case for investment; the data and analytics work will be embedded in everything you do. Later we will look at how you prioritize projects or decide what not to do. But first, we have to make the case for data in general.

Someone – and certainly the CDO – needs to evangelize the value of data. I would argue that everyone who manages a team or process should be doing the same.

Compare this to evangelizing ethical conduct. If this is your responsibility, clearly you would want to praise a whistle-blower policy, or a specific diversity initiative. But you also want to make sure that people understand that acting ethically in every situation is important, that these values are baked into the business.

The same applies to data. We should all internalize the idea that business decisions made without data are worse than decisions made using data, in every part of the business, at every level of the hierarchy. You are not evangelizing a project but a way of thinking, a data culture.

Perhaps your colleagues at the moment are correct to be sceptical of the value of data. Hype and confusion are normal. It's probable that last year someone else was making exaggerated claims for an ambitious data project that never achieved its goals. Many people, some in the C-suite, will naturally assume that it's pointless to try again, or that all data evangelists are obsessive geeks. The risk is that if you jump in and start driving changes without making the argument for data in general, you will fail too.

The cost of doing nothing

We can make this argument in many ways, but the most immediate one may be a competitive argument – you need a *Data and Analytics Strategy for (your) Business*. In 2018, look at the sums that these companies invested in data science alone (Krauth, 2018):

1 Google – $3.9 billion
2 Amazon – $871 million
3 Apple – $786 million
4 Intel – $776 million
5 Microsoft – $690 million
6 Uber – $680 million
7 Twitter – $629 million
8 AOL – $192 million
9 Facebook – $60 million
10 Salesforce – $33 million

These companies are built on data. They thrive by being able to generate value from it, and it is the engine of their growth, used to optimize processes such as putting the most suitable advertisements in front of us, pushing the boundaries of design, or encouraging us to spend just a little more on the things we care about.

But their growth is not just in becoming better at one thing. Today, data is the way in which fast-growing companies can quickly enter and dominate other sectors. Amazon Prime or Uber Eats are examples. So the first point to make is that doing nothing is not an option. If you cannot use the value of data to grow your business, it is more than ever likely that someone else will enter your market and use their superior capabilities to take your customers or win the profitable parts of your business.

CASE STUDY
Amazon Prime (Del Rey, 2019)

Challenge: How do we grow?

In 2005, Amazon had the same market capitalization as its rival eBay, but eBay looked the likely winner in a fight for market share. Amazon was known as a niche retailer of books and CDs that shipped in four or five business days at best. It wanted to expand into general retailing and was investing in better logistics to do so. Its data advantage was that it was tracking the behaviour of its loyal shoppers and realized that it could use its control of logistics as a competitive level against rivals.

Analysis: Simplify and add benefits

The data showed that a significant proportion of regular Amazon customers were voluntarily paying for premium shipping on each order. So Amazon decided to offer a fixed fee of $79 for year-round premium delivery. It would save this valuable segment money. Once they had paid up-front for shipping, this provided an incentive for them to consolidate their shopping with Amazon, which was, in turn, an incentive for suppliers to pay to use the company's logistics capacity.

Action: Amazon Prime was launched in 2005

It was used as an asset to reach new markets. For example, data showed that in the first year of study, students changed their shopping habits, so they were given a free year of Prime. To win customers from other retailers, Amazon bundled video, photo storage and music for the Prime customer base. This, in turn, attracted more occasional customers to dedicate a larger share of their spending. Amazon later added a credit card and food retail.

Outcome

Amazon, more than probably any other retailer, has used data to grow market share. Prime contributed to horizontal expansion and increased share of consumers' spending in its core markets. While Prime has not been the only driver of Amazon's growth, using the data from its customer base to cross-sell on the promise of no additional shipping costs has been a significant factor in taking business from rival online retailers. Market capitalization in 2020: eBay $35 billion; Amazon $1.59 trillion.

The value of data is only as good as the value of your business case for it

Note that the cost of doing nothing is expressed in business lost, markets missed. On the upside, the benefit of your business case is in expanding the potential of your business, and this can be measured in many ways. But what's common to all of them is that the value of data cannot be sensibly measured when it is at rest. It's how you leverage the data that counts.

This measurement problem doesn't stop many smart people from assigning an arbitrary value to data. Even the *Financial Times* got in on the act in 2013, giving us the opportunity to 'Explore how valuable your data are with this interactive calculator' (Steel et al, 2013).

This implies that data has some kind of fixed value as an asset, and that more data always has more aggregate value for the business. This leads us to the conclusion that any activity that generates or organizes data for your organization is intrinsically a valuable thing. This is not true. This doesn't mean that you shouldn't capture data that you can't use yet, just that it has no value (and potentially some cost) until you do use it, and so if you capture masses of data that you have no intention of using, that data can be argued to have a negative value.

We can think instead of data (and this is how accountants tend to think of it) as your inventory, a raw material, stored in a warehouse somewhere, waiting to be used in those processes. Too much inventory is bad, the wrong type of inventory is worse, and poor-quality raw materials are the worst of all.

Making a formal record of that data inventory is one of the tasks of data governance that we will complete in the next section. It's not easy to do this, as data resides in so many places: accounting systems, customer records, sales data, email archives, research, social media, the list goes on and on.

DATA INVENTORY

A fully described record of the data assets that you maintain. An inventory should record basic information about a data asset including its name, contents, update frequency, owner and source.

Whereas most raw materials are straightforward to value because they have a market price, measuring the value of that data inventory is not so straightforward for two reasons:

- **Your data inventory is of value mostly to your own business**

  It refers to your products, was generated by your processes, and is focused on your customers. This means it is of less value to anyone else, but regulations like the General Data Protection Regulation also mean that much of it cannot be freely traded, so there is no market price. Therefore, you usually have to value data by what it achieves for your organization.

- **It's not easy to grade the quality of your data until you try to use it**

  We'll see that many organizations overestimate the value of their data assets for many reasons: the information might be too old, or incomplete, or stored in different silos, or simply incorrect. That's not obvious until you try to use it. It may not be obvious even when you use it: often the reality dawns when you improve the quality of the data, and results improve dramatically (this will be one of your first tasks, and one that will not be completed in a few weeks).

So we can think only about the value of data in terms of what it allows us to do. This can often mean that we don't explicitly calculate or recognize the full impact of more complete, more accurate, or more timely data. Often this value is attributed to IT systems that use the data, for which there is a long and not particularly rigorous history of estimating returns on investment (ROIs). These are used to justify the cost of the acquisition and development of software and hardware, but often not to invest in the data.

But, of course, the same IT application can create extraordinary value in one location, and none at all in another (often inside the same company), depending on the data that it uses. So that ROI is really a function of two variables: one is the IT system's potential ability to create value, the other the quality of the data that's used as an input to it.

So do we throw our hands up in the air? Quite the opposite. While it is almost impossible to measure the value of data as an asset when it is at rest – treating it as what economists would call a 'stock' variable – we can say quite precise things about how it can create value as a 'flow', that is, when it is used to solve our problems.

Identifying the most pressing data problems

While the messenger who is pitching the business case for data might not be popular, most managers will accept that they have a real problem to solve. According to the KPMG CIO Survey 2019 (KPMG, 2019), digital leaders are more likely to maximize the value of the data they hold (35 per cent) versus only 9 per cent for other firms. Considering the huge potential of data to generate returns across every part of the business, this amazes me. But part of the problem is that those of us whose responsibility it is to extract that value will fail when making our case to the business.

Data ROI

Done right, your business case can promise incredible returns, whether you measure financial or capability benefits. These benefits can be quite precisely measured, because the return is incremental business. When I was working for a large global consulting firm, I developed a business case for a major UK bank to generate £1 billion of incremental revenue per annum by using data and analytics, which was agreed and signed off by the board. It was at the time and, as far as I'm aware, still is the biggest business case made for data in Europe by a non-tech firm. The up-front investment was (only) £64 million.

Data as an engine of transformation

In 2008 I led a transformation programme for the UK's financial regulator, which meant we could generate the data that was sufficiently compelling to achieve the UK's first criminal prosecution for insider dealing. Remarkably, insider dealing had been a criminal offence since 1985 (Dean, 2009).

Note two things about these examples: they focus on an important business problem, and they have a precise goal. In my experience, many so-called business cases are based on hope, rather than sound business logic, for several reasons.

If we build it, will it work?

Many companies are wasting money on collecting and storing data in the hope that something good will happen later, without reasoning how that will come about. This is as likely as alchemy. Much of the data that organizations capture could be recorded as a liability: it costs money to acquire it, secure it, and keep it, but it is extremely unlikely that it can ever be used for any revenue-generating purpose. We are all aware of data warehousing initiatives that have failed to deliver any value. Gartner, another technology analyst, estimates that four out of five projects of this type fail (White, 2019).

Are you trying to build a buzzword?

Often data evangelists make the mistake of describing what they will do, rather than what the data will do. When I speak at conferences, I'm sometimes asked how to make a business case. For example, I recall the CDO who was having difficulty trying to explain to their CEO whether the business case was for a data lake, or a data warehouse, maybe a data vault, or perhaps a data swamp. My immediate response to this is, that's not a business question. You should be talking about solving business problems to a CEO in their language, not using technical buzzwords they are uncomfortable with.

Do you know what the business values?

It's not whether you think what you are delivering has value. What matters is whether the business agrees with you. As leader of a data transformation, if you don't deliver value to the business, you will be viewed as a cost, rather than a benefit. There are two types of value we can get from data: tangible and intangible. The large UK bank example creates tangible value. The FSA experience is intangible value.

TANGIBLE VALUE (OF DATA)

Comes from increasing revenue and reducing costs. Both combine to increase the margin of the business.

INTANGIBLE VALUE (OF DATA)

Comes from reducing risk and from improving productivity, automation, customer satisfaction and employee satisfaction. Perhaps the business can do something that it could not do before.

Keep it simple

But beware, it's easy to overpromise in your business case, based on a grand design that is impossible to implement. Let me admit something to you about the business case I made for the large retail bank. It almost didn't work.

We based the business case on an existing project that had been successful for another bank in the United States, so we knew that it *could* work. The opportunity was theoretically simple. The organization had many brands, products and services, but was not cross-selling between brands, even though in some cases it had very high customer brand loyalty.

The core product – retail banking – had 30 million customers, but only tens of thousands for the other products. Grab the back of an envelope, and if the bank could convert one in 150 customers, they would double the business for the other products. Finance agreed. It was like discovering a rough diamond. Everyone was getting excited, and of course we made the fatal error: we imagined the final product without recognizing the work that needed to be done to get there.

When we started to do the work, we discovered it was tougher than I expected. The systems in the organization had grown organically in many firms and across different brands, creating a sort of technology spaghetti, and my business case depended on untangling it. Also, the people who understood the data structures and processes had moved on to other companies. We didn't understand the quality of the data, and what data we could access, or even how to access it in some cases.

The CIO unhelpfully admitted it was all 'complex', and suggested that I'd fail. The lead IT architect told me it was 'complex' to do overnight processing, so there were no time slots to access the data.

I'd created the business case, and the pressure from the CEO and the board was immense. This was one of the flagship initiatives that they hoped would revive the bank's growth. It's at times like these that you have to grit your teeth, become more resolute, and think out of the box.

The key to success was, as with Amazon Prime: *simplify*. We exported the key data from the production systems we needed on a public holiday. We didn't try to reform the structure of the data or build new software applications. In a matter of days, we had done the analysis of which customers we could cross-sell one of the niche products to, and 12 months later, the customer base for that product had grown by 80 per cent.

The moral: a business case isn't a business case until you can make it work.

Aligning the business case with the business

Remember at the beginning of the chapter we learned that the majority of organizations are not effective at maximizing the value of their data? Ideas on what to do with data aren't the problem. It is more likely that they don't have a clear idea of how to decide what to prioritize, what to leave for later, and what to ignore.

For that, you need an enterprise-wide data and analytics strategy. This will be our next step. It's an essential one: in that same KPMG CIO survey (KPMG, 2019), only 18 per cent of organizations claimed they were 'very' or 'extremely' effective at maintaining an enterprise-wide data management strategy. In the next chapter we will look at what should be in that strategy so that it is possible to maintain it and use it to maximize the value of your data.

SUMMARY

- The idea that data can help the business is not a business case by itself. Data has value only when it is used to solve business problems.

- An analysis of the threat from competition is an essential element of the business case. If you don't use your data, you will lose.

- Data can be valued as an asset, but that valuation is not based on the volume of data, the number of records. It is based on the value creation of the processes you build using it.

- Do not be distracted by buzzwords and grand technology projects without a clear return on the investment.

- Do focus on solving well-defined business problems with a clear definition of value.

- Data and technology are different things and their budgets (and capabilities) need to be decoupled.

- Make your business case to do this in the simplest way possible, and use the return on the investment to build the enabling data infrastructure that will create scale and automation.

References

Dean, J (2009) The FSA guide to insider trading, *Financial Times*, https://www. ft.com/content/eea1c701-3e1e-302b-96c8-e9086ce731f5 (archived at https:// perma.cc/5LLQ-9MDR). Christopher McQuoid knew that Motorola was planning a takeover bid for TTP, where we worked. He told his father-in-law, who bought shares and made a profit of £48,919, which he shared with McQuoid. Both were sentenced to eight months, with his father-in-law's sentence suspended.

Del Rey, J (2019) The making of Amazon Prime, *Vox Recode*, https://www.vox. com/recode/2019/5/3/18511544/amazon-prime-oral-history-jeff-bezos-one-day-shipping (archived at https://perma.cc/KA2B-WU5M)

KPMG (2019) Harvey Nash/KPMG CIO Survey 2019, https://assets.kpmg/content/ dam/kpmg/kz/pdf/2019/09/CIO-Survey_2019_ENG.pdf (archived at https:// perma.cc/4FBZ-JUFM)

Krauth, O (2018) The 10 tech companies that have invested the most money in AI, *Techrepublic*, https://www.techrepublic.com/article/the-10-tech-companies-that-have-invested-the-most-money-in-ai/ (archived at https://perma.cc/JX4X-CAG6)

Steel, E et al (2013) How much is your personal data worth? *Financial Times*, https://ig.ft.com/how-much-is-your-personal-data-worth (archived at https:// perma.cc/5ANU-25AZ)

White, A (2019) Our top data and analytics predicts for 2019, *Gartner*, https:// blogs.gartner.com/andrew_white/2019/01/03/our-top-data-and-analytics-predicts-for-2019/ (archived at https://perma.cc/4NSA-2CCQ)

03

Your data and analytics strategy

The business needs a common understanding of how it will create value from data. This means creating a strategy for the business, with priorities and goals that are hardwired to that strategy. But it is easy to lose focus or try to do too much, too soon.

KEY CONCEPTS

- Sunk cost fallacy
- Data and analytics strategy
- Data periodic table
- Five waves of transformation
- Value, Build, Improve (VBI)

Introduction

While you were reading the last chapter, you probably thought of many possible ways to use data to generate value for your business. Once you start thinking about them, it's hard to stop. You want to start fixing things, today.

But beware: without a strategy, you may be building a bridge to nowhere.

The original 'bridge to nowhere' is now a century old. The case of *Rockingham County* v. *Luten Bridge Co.*, decided in the Circuit Court of Appeals, Fourth Circuit on 15 October 1929, is taught to every law student in the United States (Richman et al, 2006). On 7 January 1924, the board of commissioners of Rockingham County, Tennessee, awarded the contract to build a bridge to the Luten Bridge Company. But many citizens of Rockingham County didn't want the road that was to pass over the bridge to be built. The board decided to cancel the contract.

But the Luten Bridge Company decided that it had been contracted to build a bridge, and so it was darn well going to build it, whether the county wanted it or not. It sued when the board of commissioners refused to pay up.

It lost. 'The bridge, built in the midst of the forest, is of no value to the county,' noted the judge. The builders should have used their sense and stopped work, he added, because you don't just keep spending money because that was what someone decided at the start. This is the sunk cost fallacy, and billions of pounds, euros and dollars are wasted on it every year because bad or unfeasible ideas aren't killed off.

SUNK COST FALLACY

When we don't ask, 'For each pound, euro or dollar we spend on this from now on, will it return a pound, euro, or dollar in value?' and instead say, 'Look at all the money we spent and it hasn't generated any value for us yet; we'd better keep going until it does.'

In data, this usually happens because the investment is not guided by a clear view of what actions will create value. Even when a project is obviously a bad idea, there often isn't a mechanism to evaluate it, give it the thumbs down, and kill it. Quite the opposite.

Recall, at this point, the Gartner statistic that 80 per cent of data warehouse projects fail. Often, the IT department, or the data science team, or those people over there who have been building your data warehouse for the last two years can seem like the Luten Bridge Company: doggedly ploughing on with something that almost everyone has lost faith in, because that was what they were told to do.

Or, I have many times stepped into a situation after someone has recruited a head of data science without a plan and found themselves halfway through a project that has no chance of success:

Executive: Welcome, data scientist. Go and fix our data problems, because there are many and you are brilliant at your job.

Data scientist: Where do I start?

Executive: I rather thought that was your job.

[six months pass]

Data scientist: I have created a cunning algorithm to extract insight from data, and it tells me that if we were to launch a driverless car, I could optimize our market penetration.

Executive: But we sell stationery.

So resist the temptation to act without strategic direction. It is the surest way to ensure that you will fail to achieve the important things you want to accomplish using data. A year from now, you'll be lost in the weeds, or fire-fighting multiple crises, or trying to do everyone's job for them – and then going home and complaining that no one understands how hard you work, because nothing ever seems to quite get finished.

You're going to need to set priorities, and for that you need a data and analytics strategy.

What is a 'data and analytics strategy'?

Creating, sharing and achieving buy-in to a strategy is not optional if you are to succeed. This is your statement of what you want to do, and how you intend to do it. It is also, importantly, about what you *do not* intend to do.

The data and analytics strategy is the key to all this. It brings together all aspects of data generation, data storage, governance, quality, and analysis. It defines how you use data to learn about your customers, and what is most important to do for all your stakeholders with this data.

DATA AND ANALYTICS STRATEGY

The choices and priorities that create a course of action to achieve the high-level goals of the organization. Through the use of all aspects of data – including data generation, data storage, governance, quality, analysis, business intelligence and data science – these goals will create returns or competitive advantage for the business and support its wider goals.

The strategy has many practical uses:

- **It defines success in your context.** You can demonstrate to stakeholders that you are delivering against objectives.

- **It defines failure.** You know when projects are not delivering and take swift action to either improve them or cut funding for them.

- **It keeps you on track.** You may start with a clear idea in your head about a project but, in the words of Field Marshal Helmuth Karl Bernhard Graf von Moltke, 'No battle plan ever survives contact with the enemy' (Oxford Essential Quotations, 2016). When a crisis hits, we often act before we think through whether the solution to the problem is aligned with our strategy – or is an emotional reaction to what happened yesterday. We sometimes need a document to remind us that 'we agreed not to do that'.

- **It makes the best use of scarce resources.** If you have funding for one project but two requests, you need to know which one receives your backing. Lots of people, many of them senior to you, have ideas for things that we can do to extract value from data. It is tempting to evaluate, pilot or invite presentations on bright ideas. When your board asks for yet another indicator on their dashboard, you can ask yourself, 'Is this what we decided would create value?', pull out the strategy, and decide that no, we're not going to spend time and money on it.

- **It forces the data transformation to support strategic goals.** It also has to be cohesive and support the broader strategy of the organization, rather than merely presenting a list of projects to tick off.

- **It defines roles and responsibilities.** Everyone wants to see the data transformation happen, and to take credit when it does. But not so many people will want to be accountable or to take responsibility when there are challenges to face. Part of this is a more formal definition of the reach and role of the CDO.

Defining the CDO role

The CDO is this strategy, walking around. That is why the strategy and the CDO are co-dependent: one cannot be a success if the other is not. As Gartner (2019) points out:

> For many organizations, the CDO role is still new, untested and somewhat amorphous. In these circumstances, the scope, priorities and responsibilities of the CDO's role can quickly become inflated. It seems that once a CDO is hired, regardless of how small the associated budget, resources and team, every data problem that crops up, however minor, seems to fall into their lap.

One disadvantage with making the business case for data successfully is that every problem can, in the eyes of the board, become a data problem. Later you never seem to make progress on the big problems, the ones that you were supposed to fix as a priority, and the things that will really move the needle on those dashboards that sit on everyone's desks. It can be dispiriting to be working 100-hour weeks but still have the CEO wondering aloud when all this activity will begin to show a result.

Therefore, part of the data and analytics strategy is to make it clear what the CDO's role is. Clearly there are some fires that simply must be fought.

Others can be parked, delegated, outsourced or even ignored. Having an agreed list of priorities and goals, and a roadmap to achieving them, can save everyone involved from the very real risk of burnout.

This also extends, of course, to the data team. When making changes is a strategic priority, having a formal approval of what needs to change can reduce conflict at every level of the organization. Though, it must be said, probably not eliminate it.

Task: Setting priorities using the data periodic table

FIGURE 3.1 Data periodic table

Where to get value from data

A-E Business activities	A Increased revenue			B Decreased costs			C Risk	D Strategy	E Compliance
	A01	A02	A03	B01	B02	B03	C01	D01	E01
	A04	A05	A06	B04	B05	B06	C02	D02	E02
	A07	A08	A09	B07	B08	B09	C03	D03	E03
	A10	A11	A12	B10	B11	B12	C04	D04	
	A13	A14	A15	B13	B14	B15	C05	D05	
	A16	A17	A18	B16	B17	B18	C06	D06	
	A19	A20	A21	B19	B20	B21	C07	D07	
	A22	A23	A24	B22	B23	B24		D08	
	A25	A26	A27	B25	B26	B27			
	A28	A29	A30	B28	B29	B30			
	A31	A32	A33	B31	B32				
	A34	A35	A36						

F Enabling activities											
F01	F02	F03	F04	F05	F06	F07	F08	F09	F10	F11
F12	F13	F14	F15	F16	F17	F18	F19	F20	F21	F22
F23	F24	F25	F26	F27	F28	F29	F30	F31	F33	

Data toolkit	Dashboards	Reports	Data feeds and APIs	Data science, ML & AI	Alerts & notifications

Figure 3.1 is our data periodic table, and is based on my experience of thousands of projects across many firms, in 30 years in the data business. I use it when I start a new engagement, and you can too. I have outlined the detail in the tables below.

The point of the table is to set out a list of everything you can potentially achieve, and the ways in which you can approach it. You're a problem solver, and so your instinctive response when you see a business problem that data can solve is to think, 'We could do that' or encourage new ideas. It's broken down into the buckets of revenue increase, decrease costs, reduced risk, strategy and compliance.

TABLE 3.1 Revenue increase

A01. Increased number of customers through acquisition	A02. Increased share of wallet (number of products or value of product)	A03. Improved lead generation	A04. Improved lead conversion
A05. Improved revenue-generating processes	A06. Improved customer retention	A07. Improved customer experience	A08. Improved customer loyalty rewards
A09. Improved customer lifetime journey	A10. Increased loyalty / customer satisfaction	A11. Develop new products	A12. Increased suitability of products
A13. Improved customer / product pricing	A14. Increased cross- / up-sell	A15. Improved proposition selling	A16. Improved demographic targeting
A17. Improved real-time offers and interventions	A18. Improved media coverage	A19. Product placement optimization	A20. Improved alignment of brand image to next generation of customers
A21. Improved customer service	A22. Increased ease and reliability of service	A23. Increased sustainability culture	A24. Improved individual customer messaging on contact
A25. Improved style and channels of customer communications	A26. Improved next best action	A27. Increased ease of customer feedback	A28. Improved complaint resolutions
A29. Improved customer autonomy	A30. Improved customer knowledge	A31. Improved skills and knowledge of staff	A32. Improved staff satisfaction
A33. Improved staff retention	A34. Improved alignment of staff incentives with group strategy	A35. Monetization of data	A36. Marketing performance management

TABLE 3.2 Decreased costs

B01. Reduced cost to serve	B02. Increased automation of repetitive tasks	B03. Reduced fixed / operating costs	B04. Improved proactive intervention to minimize costs
B05. Reduced credit, risk and fraud losses	B06. Increased collections and recoveries amount recovered	B07. Improved bad debt forecasting and detection	B08. Reduced bad debt
B09. Reduced claims leakage	B10. Improved cost processes	B11. Decreased cost of data and analysis infrastructure	B12. Increased operational efficiency
B13. Improved credit and risk insight	B14. Improved credit and risk early warning	B15. Improved credit and risk capital adequacy	B16. Improved credit and risk channel optimizations
B17. Improved credit scoring	B18. Improved standardized reporting and measurement	B19. Supplier optimization	B20. Improved fraud detection
B21. Reduced 1st-party fraud	B22. Reduced 3rd-party fraud	B23. Reduced claims fraud	B24. Reduced application fraud
B25. Reduced card fraud	B26. Increased customer self-service	B27. Improved incentives for customers to reduce costs	B28. Reduced number of high- / medium-cost accounts
B29. Reduced non-profitable customers	B30. Reduced dormant accounts	B31. Distribution optimization	B32. Improved stock management

TABLE 3.3 Reduced risk

C01. Improved risk decision-making	C02. Improved cross-group relationships exposure	C03. Improved identification of corporate / sector risk exposure	C04. Reduction in data privacy risk
C05. Reduction in insurance risk	C06. Reduction in regulatory risk	C07. Improved data ethics	

TABLE 3.4 Strategy

D01. Improved risk decision-making	D02. Deeper macro-economic insights	D03. Improved identification of opportunities	D04. Improved understanding of impact of emerging customer behaviour
D05. Improved identification of macro trends	D06. Deeper insights into attitudinal sector trends	D07. Improved insights and forecasting on emerging trends	D08. Insights into competitor trends

TABLE 3.5 Compliance

E01. Reduction in compliance claims	E02. Better compliance insights	E03. Better compliance risk detection

TABLE 3.6 Enabling capabilities

F01. Increased use of external data	F02.Increased use of internal data	F03. Increased use of all onboarding data	F04. Incentives for customers to provide more data
F05. More consistent data capture	F06. Improved quality of customer data	F07. Increased use of structured data	F08. Increased use of unstructured data
F09. Improved data methods and processes	F10. Improved data governance	F11. Increased understanding and insight of customers	F12. Increased no of contactable customers
F13. Single customer view	F14. Improved use of historical dialogue customer data	F15. Improved modelling accuracy	F16. Reduced modelling development and production time
F17. Improved use of data science models	F18. Data science models embedded in downstream systems and op processes	F19. Improved analytics tools	F20. Real-time streaming data architecture
F21. Improved use of artificial intelligence	F22. More accessible data	F23. Improved use of machine learning	F24. Reduced time taken to access data
F25. Improved transactional data analysis	F26. Improved event detection for rules-based decisioning	F27. Improved real-time decisioning	F28. Improved data team skills

(continued)

TABLE 3.6 (Continued)

F29. Stronger analytics community	F30. More knowledgeable data community	F31. More data-aware exec	F32. Improved data ethics
F33. Improved data sets for teaching models			

> **DATA PERIODIC TABLE**
>
> A method to assign strategic business goals to data activities. The table highlights those business activities that can, through the use of data, generate business value. It then links those activities to enabling data activities and the data toolkit, and can be used to align data and organizational strategies.

At first, the data team will almost certainly have a limited budget, be small, and have little natural authority. It also has a limited window to demonstrate its effectiveness. If after six months a CDO can show only 20 half-finished projects, it will soon find its resources being reallocated.

Imagine company A. It is a 'digital native' fintech start-up, it has generated a lot of buzz for its first product, and now it needs to convert that into sales. But its data-handling processes haven't scaled with the company and are chaotic.

It is competing against company B. This is the market leader. But it has noticed that too many customers are defecting to company A. It doesn't know why, and its Net Promoter Score is plunging.

Company C has been in the sector a long time and has thousands of mostly happy customers and a solid brand. But it has just launched the first product for this particular market – and is worried that it is not making an impact against A's disruptive marketing.

And finally, company D has a wonderful product and cool brand, isn't losing customers to the others, but can't seem to make a profit on sales. And its figures don't add up.

Now look again at the periodic table, and list the priority projects for each of A, B, C and D. Imagine you have been tasked to find the five most important projects, based on what you know. When you look at your four lists, the chances are there will be little overlap.

- **Company A** has a short history, was born digital, and has only one product. It is unlikely to have masses of confusing or incomplete information.

It needs to boost sales, though. Most other activities can wait. But it looks like it may have all sorts of compliance and risk problems with its data that present an unacceptable risk. So, your priority may be to lead conversion and processes that generate revenue, as well as data compliance.

- **Company B** urgently needs to prioritize customer feedback and service.
- **Company C**'s priority, meanwhile, is likely to be to find ways to cross-sell.
- **Company D** might have fraud, high costs of serving customers, or too many bad debts. It doesn't seem to have effective processes to minimize costs. Until it has this under control, the sexy projects that it is naturally drawn to can wait.

This is the exercise you can perform for yourself, based on your business strategy. You can try asking your colleagues and your team to do the same. You are likely to have some differences, but hopefully the process of debating those differences in itself adds value.

Task: Using the data periodic table to design projects

Your data and analytics strategy does not mean simply pick two or three things from each category of business activities. So how do we create a coherent plan?

Describe data problems/solutions in business language

To get the business to buy into the work the data team needs to use language they understand, not technical speak that will alienate them. An example might be, 'Customer data quality is currently 30 per cent – if we increase it to 40 per cent we'll have 1,000 more contactable customers.'

Relate to business activities

An example might be, 'If we identify those customers likely to churn then it can help protect our revenues at a time when we have just lost significant revenue due to Covid.'

Sense-check for non-strategic choices

It's not easy. All business activities are, by definition, good for some business, somewhere. Which organizations would not want their customers to have a better experience, know more about their customers, or find new ways to cross-sell? So use the test of alignment with broader business strategy. Your strategy might not focus on increasing revenues at all (this is unlikely, but possible) because there is a complete focus on cost cutting. If there is, it doesn't matter how much you want to increase your share of what customers spend, it's not your job.

How will you deliver desirable outcomes?

This uses the enabling activities in the periodic table. Let's assume you want to use data to increase the number of customers. How will you do that? Employees will not act differently overnight. It needs to be easier for them to accomplish an existing task. Or they need information to identify new prospects. Or they simply need higher-quality data on customers who might leave. Some of these activities your organization might do well already. Others may need investment.

Link each outcome to specific, achievable projects

In this case, an example would be to find out which customers interact with you both in person and online, understand why, and create a model based on that insight to identify those customers who are similar but do not buy from you online.

Match to your data toolkit

There are surprisingly few ways in which you can use data to create action in the business, and not all of them will be relevant. In the toolkit: dashboards, reports, models, data feeds and alerts. And let's say that in this case, you'll need a model to find which customers to approach, and a dashboard to show how successful the marketing and sales teams are at converting them. (Note: you may be under- or over-invested in elements of that data toolkit, especially the most visible elements. For example, everyone loves having a dashboard, and organizations spend a lot of money on creating them. But a dashboard has to be the most appropriate tool in that context. Sometimes an automated alert when a data item reaches a threshold would be cheap, simple, and more likely to solve the problem.)

Define success

Using this method, you can take the organization's strategic vision and distil it into definite activities with measurable outcomes drawn from the business case. Not every project will have an impact on profitability, for example, because it creates the conditions that make a direct revenue-generating innovation possible. Indeed, some of the most important and powerful projects that you can undertake are in this category. But it is still important to have a meaningful benchmark of success.

You can communicate this back to the board and to the business as a whole, of which there will be more discussion later. But first, it's useful to think about the narrative of what will happen during the data transformation. As we just stated, some projects can't be a success until the groundwork has been done. Some goals aren't achievable without cultural or process change. The data and analytics strategy isn't a list, it's a roadmap.

Five waves of transformation

FIGURE 3.2   The five waves to data maturity

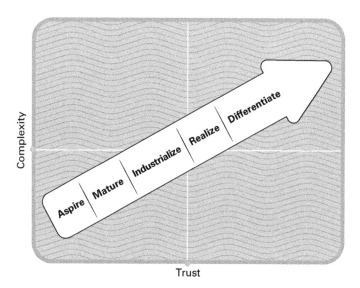

While every data and analytics strategy is different, it is still possible to think of common structures and sequences to get things done. This is the path you and your data team will take, overcoming increasingly difficult challenges, learning as you go.

FIVE WAVES OF TRANSFORMATION

A strategy for guiding the data transformation of a business. It posits that you start with projects that are foundational or less complex, and don't require trust from the business or customers. Success in these enables complex activities that generate more value, and require more funding or more trust. The waves give a time dimension to a data and analytics strategy.

Challenges like the quality and governance of your data will need to be sorted out before you can start on more ambitious projects. If you want to make a success of artificial intelligence or data analytics, you need to solve other problems first. That is why I have organized the rest of this book into these five waves that represent a typical order of priority. Figure 3.2 shows those five waves and you'll see that as complexity increases you'll need to have more trust in your data and analytics capabilities. That takes time.

To work your way through all five waves may take months or years. But as the periodic table showed us, executing a well-planned data and analytics strategy is not a box-ticking exercise, grinding through your to-do list project by project until you collapse exhausted on your CEO's desk.

A workable strategy uses a coherent set of goals. Motivation comes from knowing that each little success and improvement contributes to a greater whole, unlocking value along the way but also preparing the ground for the next stage.

It also has a narrative that your colleagues in the data team can understand and buy into. They know why they are being asked to do a task, or to use data in a different way, because it is both contributing an outcome today and laying the groundwork for improvement tomorrow, next week, next quarter.

The same goes for the whole organization. Once your data and analytics strategy gives you a narrative for change, it shows them that data is something that helps them work better, achieve better results, and avoid frustrations or stress. Technology is something that helps them, rather than something that is done to them. They can imagine their future selves, freed from repetitive tasks, more efficient, more productive, or doing a job they have begun to enjoy for the first time.

Note: this is not a rulebook. Your order might vary.

Aspire

Think of this as the programme for the first 100 days of the data transformation. It doesn't have to be completed in 100 days; it can be your first month (unlikely), or six months. Some projects will never be fully completed. In this time, you have many challenges. You have to demonstrate that you are making a difference, creating value. You have to build confidence in what you do at board level, and also among the business as a whole, where your actions will help people to appreciate that you are working in their interests. You need to connect with the stakeholders in the business who will help you to get the job done. And, importantly, you are going to learn about where the problems that you didn't know existed are, helping you to improve the strategy or allocate resources.

Mature

Having made some quick, tactical improvements, you will have learned where the deep-seated problems are. At this stage you will prepare the important groundwork for more ambitious projects further down the line. You will establish the most important principle of data: that there is a single, consolidated source of truth, from which reporting and risk management flow.

Industrialize

Having improved the quality of existing processes, it is time to optimize the way in which data is used in the organization. This means automation where possible, which eliminates inefficiencies like re-keying data. It means scaling up processes that generate value in one part of the business or scaling out to all offices.

Realize

From this point you put in place constant feedback, so that quality improves consistently. You will use data to improve decision-making and find new opportunities.

Differentiate

The final stage is for the business to become a leader, and innovator, with the tools to systematically outperform competitors. Data has created organizational and behavioural change. It is at the heart of innovation and new products and services, and you can create a wider ecosystem of data-sharing with other stakeholders.

Value, build and improve

FIGURE 3.3 Value, Build, Improve (VBI) content of each wave

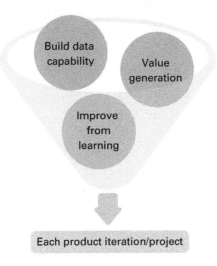

There is another reason not to think about each project as a tick-box. Each wave has three components that overlap. I call it 'VBI', for Value, Build, Improve. This is shown in Figure 3.3. When you start the wave, it is mostly about creating value. By the end, you will be building a better business.

VALUE, BUILD, IMPROVE (VBI)

The dimensions that measure the positive impact of each wave of transformation: creating value, building capability, and creating improvements in the business from the learning.

Value. We never lose the principle that we established when we considered the business case for data. Each project has to generate measurable value, a value that we can articulate at the beginning.

Build. Nothing stands alone. Every project at each stage builds some foundations. Nothing you do is entirely tactical. The success of each task contributes to other projects, improving their quality or outcome, making them easier to implement and use.

Improve. Finally, you are constantly reviewing, learning and making improvements in the next wave of the strategy. Take care to allocate time to learn from what you have achieved at the end, and to apply what you learn. It's useful to formalize this process because business processes tend to encourage what psychologists would call a 'bias to action'.

Task: share the story

If your data and analytics strategy tells a good story, and it inspires you (it should – if not, I suggest you get someone who can tell the story well and write it), then the next step is to share it. This is an exciting time. It is your opportunity to stand up, in front of the whole organization, and tell them how you plan to improve their lives. It's a great privilege. How do you make everyone aware that there is a strategy?

Use senior management as endorsement

I prefer to do it with the CEO present, or even better, to follow the CEO's presentation at a company meeting. 'I'd like you to meet Simon,' the CEO says. 'Could you please tell us what you're planning to do with data?'

Describe the destination

You're on a path, not a bridge to nowhere, so there's a destination. You have a vision. Don't be shy about starting off with that.

Make it relevant to everyone

It is also stressful, and so you will be tempted to tell them about your data and analytics strategy in management jargon. Don't. You must talk like a human person who has the same hopes and fears as they do. Remember, this might be the first time that some of your colleagues have given serious thought to the idea that there is such a thing as data, let alone that it can improve their lives. So describe real things they see and experience, real problems that they recognize, and how you can make those better.

Use passion

Passion about data? No, about what data can do for your audience. The energy that comes from knowing you can transform their jobs may inspire people in the business at every level to want to help you, to ask you questions and listen to the answers, and to have their own ideas. These are good reactions, because you will need all of these things later.

Show them what's possible

There will be cynics and nay-sayers. Many people you are working with might not even understand there is a problem with how they do their jobs. Others may know that things are wrong in some way – but they have seen people like you before, and nothing ever seems to get better. Tell them about the best companies in your industry, or even the household names that have used the techniques that you are going to use and that have transformed their businesses as a result, but also acknowledge their cynicism.

Money talks

If you're at a public company, show how success could move the share price. If your audience has incentive pay, show them how increased productivity gets them a bonus. If you are dealing with partners, show them that you're going to make them wealthier. Hard cash might not be the only motivation they have to support you, but we'd be foolish to assume that it's never a motivation.

Don't outstay your welcome...

These are early days. Your audience might be seeing a lot more of you in their day jobs, so it's best to leave them wanting more. Don't describe the entire data and analytics strategy, five waves of innovation, lovingly detailing every project. Give them your best 10 minutes.

... because you'll be back

Another reason not to be too precise is that you haven't achieved anything yet. Instead, promise your adoring audience that you will return in two months to show them what value you have managed to create. This is exciting for all of us, even for the people who want to see you fail.

There's only one problem with promising success in this way: you actually have to achieve something tangible in those two months. We'll deal with that soon, but first we have to talk about who will be with you on this path.

SUMMARY

- You can't do everything, so you will constantly need to prioritize. This starts before you create a data and analytics strategy that aligns with the business strategy.

- Use the periodic table (collaboratively, perhaps) to match potential projects and methods to the areas in which data will add most value to the business. Do not get side-tracked by cool projects.

- Create a coherent strategy based on these priorities. Some projects are groundwork that will unlock huge amounts of value later.

- Lots of people will pitch their pet projects to you. You will want to help them. Resist the temptation.

- Tell your story to the whole business to set them thinking about how data can help them – and never miss an opportunity to remind them of how your efforts are helping to grow the business and improve their day-to-day work.

References

Gartner (2019) 10 Ways CDOs Can Succeed in Forging a Data-Driven Organization, https://www.gartner.com/guest/purchase/registration?resId=3920325 (archived at https://perma.cc/Y374-XWK8)

Oxford Essential Quotations (2016) https://www.oxfordreference.com/view/10.1093/acref/9780191826719.001.0001/q-oro-ed4-00007547 (archived at https://perma.cc/6QNE-3Y2F). Helmuth von Moltke (1880) was quoted as saying, 'No plan of operations reaches with any certainty beyond the first encounter with the enemy's main force: *Kriegsgechichtliche Einzelschriften.*'

Richman, B D, Weinstock, J and Mehta, J (2006) A bridge, a tax revolt, and the struggle to industrialize: The story and legacy of 'Rockingham County v. Luten Bridge Co.', 84 North Carolina Law Review 1841–1912, https://scholarship.law.duke.edu/faculty_scholarship/1638/ (archived at https://perma.cc/U2TL-J4WY)

04

A team game

The most important qualification to be successful in a data transforma-
tion is a willingness to do things differently. The entire team requires
creativity and a problem-solving spirit. In turn, this may require creativity
in recruitment.

KEY CONCEPTS

- Practical quotient (PQ)
- Adaptability quotient (AQ)
- Retention quotient (RQ)
- Cognitive diversity

Introduction

How do you find the team to deliver your transformation, what talents does
it need, and what will motivate them?

In my experience, the standard recruitment process, which focuses on
acquired skills, has not been successful. For example, I never planned to do
this job: the job found me.

In June 1991, as an enthusiastic young techie, I spotted an advertisement
in the *Sunday Times* that grabbed my attention. Smith New Court, at the
time Britain's largest independent stockbroker, was looking for someone to
manage its trading systems.

I got the job. I arrived promptly at 8 am on my first day and was shown
to the office of the person who would be my manager. There was also someone there the same age as me. We made some conversation and discovered

we were starting in the same department on the same day. We had been employed to do the same job. At first, this seemed like a coincidence – but there was only one job, and twice as many people to do it as Smith New Court needed.

My new manager arrived two hours later, following car trouble. Now she had new-job trouble as well.

'I've screwed up,' she admitted.

She had advertised one job and had employed two people to do it. Our new employer couldn't decide between us at interview, so she had the idea to bring us both in. There was perhaps an additional job, she explained, but not the one advertised.

'I suggest you go and talk to the people here and decide which one of you does which job,' she told us, and left us to it. This was to be the first problem to solve in our two-hour careers at Smith New Court.

John and I looked at each other, thinking, 'Wait, what?' Both of us were thinking that one of us might have to take a second-choice job. We had both left our previous jobs, so we didn't have a choice.

Discouraged, I went to speak to the head of trading, and some of the key traders. Then I found the head of UK research, the head of European equities, and the head of brokerage. Sure, there was an IT job managing the trading systems, they said, but they needed a job done that I quickly realized could be far more valuable, and much more exciting. The job I had applied for was a challenge, but the job they described was an adventure, something entirely new.

They described to me the potential of vast data sets, aggregating up-to-the-minute financial information, that would deliver better insights than the competition in investment research. Using those insights, Smith New Court could systematically make better decisions than the competition.

The trading systems were machines that made trades. The original job – building and managing them – was important work. But this project would give me the chance to build a machine that would make *better* trades.

This, I instantly knew, was the job I really wanted, and that was the job I asked for. Over the next four years I got to be part of the firm's data journey. Using data better helped the firm to post a return on equity that would average 25 per cent.

I was lucky to discover that opportunity, but it wasn't all luck. John, my job-seeking twin, was equally pleased to take the more structured job that had been offered – it was what he had applied for, after all. I chose data because I was seduced by the idea of building something new, solving a problem that hadn't even been fully defined. It wasn't just an interesting puzzle. I was able to build something for the business that created far more value than anything else I could have done at that time.

This is the fundamental skill. You are solving problems that the organization can't quite define or doesn't know it has. Knowing a programming language or having experience with a particular piece of software is marginally useful, but those are the skills that anyone at this level can learn or teach. Focus on those alone and you, and your team, will underperform.

Cracking the code as a CDO

If you were a chemist, an entrepreneur, or an engineer, your job would have a lineage stretching back more than a millennium. The medieval craft guilds of apothecaries or merchants or stonemasons defined your skill, and created a system of apprentices and journeymen to improve it and pass it on.

The role of a chief data officer (CDO) doesn't have a long history to draw on. Cathryne Clay Doss, who you've probably never heard of, was the business world's first known CDO (*Forbes*, 2019). She was appointed to the job only in 2002, by Capital One. The second company to award the title was Yahoo, in 2005, and Gartner reports that a mere decade ago there were only 15 CDOs in the world (though, we must assume, there were thousands more people who did the job but without the title, power or status of the modern CDO).

By 2018, however, two out of three large companies had appointed a CDO, so there's clearly a need. But a need for what?

The CDO leads the data team. In my experience, that team needs certain problem-solving attributes that the CDO may not possess and would certainly be uncommon in the rest of the business.

With such a short history, who can you look to for inspiration? One candidate, though it's unlikely that he would have flourished at Capital One or Yahoo, is Alan Turing. Turing was a brilliant mathematician, the creative thinker whose insights helped to break the German Enigma code in World War II, and the genius whose ideas gave birth to the computer and are at the heart of artificial intelligence 80 years later.

His eventual suicide and the mythologizing influence of his representations in film have blurred the boundary between Turing the man and Turing the idea, so we should be selective about which elements of the concept of Turingness we choose to adopt. Whether you're taking your inspiration from the biography by Andrew Hodges (Hodges, 2014) or *The Imitation Game*, the subsequent movie that the book inspired and which took some liberties with the source material to simplify the narrative, we can never the less extract three elements that I look for in team members.

He could link abstract ideas to real life

While studying at Cambridge before the war, Turing also joined in Wittgenstein's classes on the philosophy of mathematics and helped build gears for a machine designed to calculate the Riemann zeta function. That's about as abstract as you can get, but he always thought about his insights as the way to solve real-world problems.

This is the first skill that your team needs, because people will come to you with a problem that they usually can't express in terms of data. If only we could do *this*, they will say, can you help?

He didn't follow rules if they didn't make sense

In *The Imitation Game*, Turing memorably goes behind the back of his immediate superiors and confronts Winston Churchill with his ideas and demands for resources. This didn't happen as it did in the film, but he was one of a small group of codebreakers who upset the military hierarchy by writing to Churchill, a move that was successful in getting attention for their ideas.

A large part of the job of achieving a data transformation will be to break down conventional structures and silos that stop data being shared. I know from bitter experience that data people are condemned to spend a lot of time listening to people who say, *but we always do it this way*, while you think, 'and how's that working for you then?' But it's part of the job to convince people that the better solution is *not* to always do it that way, and possibly to never do it that way again. Of course, this means finding a better way. And so…

He thought in terms of processes and automation

Turing didn't get bogged down in hierarchy, but he did understand systems. In the 1930s, he proposed the idea of the Turing Machine, a machine that could be adapted to do any well-defined task if you gave it the right instructions. This was the first formulation of our concept of the modern programmable computer. While at Bletchley Park during the war, this way of thinking helped take the artisanal manual processes and systems the brilliant early codebreakers had developed and use them to create a machine that automated codebreaking. As the journey develops, we will move from solving individual problems into scaling and automating them.

So the data team member is part chemist, using knowledge to mix elements in new ways; part entrepreneur, cutting through the constraint of conventional wisdom to find a better way; and part engineer, seeing the structure of the data, and how that can be used to create new sources of insight and value, finding ways not just to solve the problem today but to deliver value for months or years.

The résumé problem

The popular image of the geek is someone who sits alone in a cubicle wearing headphones and churning out code as an alternative to social activity. The sort of problem-solving that you generally encounter when working with data isn't a solitary activity, though like any project it has some tasks that are best done wearing headphones, on your own. The rest you can't do alone. The business needs a team with the sort of problem-solving attributes that you don't find every day.

Technical people are generally recruited as being 'an SQL developer' or 'I can do JavaScript'. They often do these things astoundingly well, but equally often in an environment in which the problem and its parameters have been predefined for them. Very little in the day-to-day work of data transformation is predefined.

If you are recruiting, you have probably been given a pile of résumés that don't tell you much but satisfy the criteria of external recruiters or the HR department. I have never found a résumé, ever, that has the things that I want in it. Not once.

The problem has not been solved by machine processing of résumés designed to make the process of recruitment more efficient. In 2019, a survey of 1,000 jobseekers found that two-thirds of them were gaming the system by using 'optimization strategies', like a particular phrase that will be picked up by a recruitment algorithm, and one in five deliberately adds buzzwords to a résumé so that it will make it through a machine sort (Tribepad, 2019).

The résumés you are likely to see are optimized for this bland recruitment process and so they focus on learned skills, like a programming language. You can learn those on a two-week course. But does that correlate with being able to solve the problems that the data transformation process requires? We know it means the candidate can solve the problem of polishing a résumé to get to an interview, but that's not a skill that's likely to pay off for us.

Discovering problem-solvers

I first discovered the thrill of solving problems when I was nine: my father was in the RAF, one of the officers in charge of recruiting. When he used to travel to evaluate potential recruits, I used to tag along. To stave off the boredom, I did the same Airmen Selection Test (AST) as the applicants. It was designed to evaluate their problem-solving and lateral thinking skills (RAF, 2021). I found that I loved solving those puzzles. They made so much more sense than what I was doing at school. I understood the value of IQ, the intelligence quotient – but I appreciated that IQ is not everything. Meanwhile, in class, we learned facts by rote, and never applied our knowledge to anything except an exam.

Then I discovered team sports. For a while I was good enough to row at international level. Beyond the physical challenge there was the thrill when you feel your contribution as part of a human machine in which you are expected to perform to your maximum ability, setting and keeping a tempo, responding as one to a challenge, interpreting the conditions and feeling how the rest of the boat is performing, working together with discipline. Also, the stopwatch measures how effective your problem-solving has been every time you get in the boat.

When I later qualified as a skipper on a sailing boat, I realized the value of practical problem-solving skills. When a problem arises at sea, you need to improvise, use what you have available on board. Impressive as we discovered Amazon Prime to have been, we can't call on it to deliver a new part. I discovered how many people were not practical; they may have had a high IQ, but were missing something – that ability to fix real things.

Teamwork under time pressure, improvisation, the ability to recognize the fundamental nature of a problem and deliver a result that can be measured are what I look for. When you are guiding a team through a data transformation, there's probably a lack of technical skills, but that's not usually the constraint to success. That would more often be that no one is prepared to rethink, pivot, or break habits. That ability to adapt, rather than do what you've always done before, to innovate.

Bad previous attempts to run data projects have a scarring effect. People will have tried and failed to solve data problems before, usually because they had good technical skills – so that is what they focused on. When they saw the problem, their first thought was that it required something like Power BI or Microsoft Azure. They assembled a team, started writing lines of code or configuring something, and made no progress at all because they weren't sure which problem they were solving, or how to go about it.

The scarring effect is that there is little trust from the business that a new CDO and a new data team can do a better job, and the practical problem that a half-cocked project might just have made a mess worse. Chances are the 'solution' will just add another layer of dysfunction that will make solving the problem even harder a few years down the line when the next person takes over.

If you are doing the recruiting, you must acknowledge that many of the people you will be encouraged to recruit think in this 'code-first' way. I'm not looking for that person in my team, and neither should you. So I'd recommend that you look for employees with a wider skill set: specifically business focus, the ability to share and discuss the problem with other team members, and probably more holistic decision-making.

Task: Recruiting for PQ and AQ

Some recruiters look for IQ, RQ or some other measure of intelligence. Of course, we want smart people transforming our enterprises. I've argued that it takes a couple of weeks to learn a programming language, which is of course not true for everyone. Put it this way: you prefer to recruit people who can learn a programming language in a couple of weeks if that's what you need them to do. The job does not wait for us to be ready, so the ability to learn to code in a different language is a low bar for adaptability.

RETENTION QUOTIENT (RQ)

The ability to store and recall information easily. Many people who have traditionally done well at exams are good at retaining information but these skills, whilst dominant in CVs, are less useful in a problem-solving environment than PQ, EQ and AQ.

In some jobs, the focus is more on the EQ, replacing the narrow focus on whatever 'intelligence' is with emotion. And yes, we want people who can empathize. That can help us understand how the people in the business have found a way to work together, what motivates them, what gives them satisfaction. It can also help to understand that it is often not the technology that stops people working together, because if you are going to fix the problem you will have to deliver the data, and then discover incentives for people to use it. It's a huge advantage if your team can relate to other people in the business, get on with them, find out what they need to know, and encourage them to cooperate.

IQ, EQ and RQ are important but not sufficient attributes, and we need some additional way to discover who can contribute to your data team. Traditionally in technology-focused interviews, young geeks are tortured with a whiteboard challenge. They are given a problem and have to write the code to solve it in real time. You can imagine what I think of that.

I prefer to recruit for PQ and AQ instead: a practical quotient, and an adaptability quotient.

PRACTICAL QUOTIENT (PQ)

The ability to think about problem-solving in a way that directly relates to the business, especially the ability to problem-solve using the mindset of other personas, such as an engineer or entrepreneur, without a prescribed solution or approach. High PQ relates to a high ability to conceptualize and solve data problems, and get on and deliver the solution, or get things fixed.

ADAPTABILITY QUOTIENT (AQ)

The ability to adapt your thinking from one domain to another. For example, if you're an SQL programmer being able to program in other languages, such as Python, and you accept that your skill is programming and not SQL. High PQ relates to a high ability to adapt your skills to new problems and not to solve every problem with the same skill.

When I interview, I'll ask you to solve problems, but not to write code on a whiteboard. For example:

The heaven and hell problem

'There are two doors. Through one of them is the solution to our problem (heaven). Through the other is the six months of hell trying to fix it, followed by failure (hell). There's one person in front of each door, one always lies, and one always tells the truth. You don't know which is which. You can only ask one question. What is the question?' See reference (Asplen-Taylor, 2021) at the end of the chapter for the answer.

What matters is how you break down the problem. It's almost impossible to solve if you just go through a list of questions in your head. What matters is to think of how you would extract useful information from someone.

Or, we can be much more concrete.

The 'describe a car' challenge

'How would someone who works with data describe a car?'

A BAD ANSWER

Many people with excellent programming skills will shrug and say, 'Well, it's just something that gets you from A to B.'

This is the outcome that a car delivers. Sure, it solves the problem of being at A and wanting to be at B, but the answer isn't interesting. Read the question again: 'How would *someone who works with data...*'

This is a very rich question, and there are many good answers. Here are some of them:

GOOD ANSWER 1: PURPOSE

'There are different types of cars. Some are four-wheel drives. Some are sports cars.'

GOOD ANSWER 2: CLASSIFICATION

'You've got different makes and models. You've got different colours, sizes. Different uses.'

I'm impressed, because that person understands how data can define things in the real world in many ways, thinking how the definition affects the use to which it can be put (and how choosing the wrong car means it won't do the job well). It also prevents them from giving a rehearsed answer.

GOOD ANSWER 3: HOW DOES IT WORK?

'It's a combustion engine.' Some people are data engineers. They become excited describing how an engine turns wheels. This, too, can be good.

There's a rare, and very interesting response:

GOOD ANSWER 4: IT'S GOT A DASHBOARD

'The best thing about a car is you've got a dashboard inside. It tells you about the fuel consumption, and whether it's what you expect. It will tell you whether you have enough fuel to get you where you're going, and whether you will arrive on time. It tells you whether there are any problems, and what to expect on the road ahead. Your car is solving your overall problem (getting from A to B), but a car's dashboard is successfully giving the driver the detailed information to decide how he or she should act, or how to respond if the driver needs to make a decision.'

And that's the sort of problem-solving that your team will be building for the business.

If you are very lucky, you will find one of the rare people who will take your simple question and run through all of these possible ways to think about it, and some more as well. If you hear that, your new recruit absolutely gets what makes data special. You know that when you give that team member a new problem that they've never ever had to solve before, they can do the most useful thing: they can describe what the problem really is. Overall, you want diversity of thinking in the team – that's why there is no one correct answer.

Beware of ready-made data teams

On day one in your job, you will probably be presented with the people who the business thinks you will need. And you will need some of them, because you know less than you think about the business and the way it is organized and the systems used.

And every time I start a new role, HR helpfully tells me that it will transfer a few people across from IT, because they have the skills I need. Beware, for two reasons:

Ask: why are they available?

The best people in the organization are normally absolutely maxed out so they won't be made available. They might be doing very helpful things, but the person they are working for isn't letting them go anywhere. More likely you are being given specialists. Which leads to:

Inheritance is not always a blessing

Resist being given people with skills that are too specialized. These people might be extremely capable. But when all you have is a hammer, everything looks like a nail. You might have inherited the highly paid data scientists who were hired last year, and no one can quite work out what they're doing. If they are to continue, they need to be able to deliver to your goals and approach and not just carry on as they were.

Embrace those who think differently

HR or an external agency might, in an attempt to be helpful, ask, 'What are the key words you're looking for to describe your next hire?' This will not help unless you make it clear that you are looking for PQ, not describing skills. This might work out well: some of my most interesting team members have turned out to be people who had not found a niche elsewhere. Encourage diversity of thought and the ability to challenge conventional wisdom. Embrace those who think differently.

Diversity

The technology industry has taken justifiable criticism for its lack of diversity, for its tech-bro culture. One of the ways in which this happens is that technology skills are not equally distributed throughout the population. But in my experience, if you focus on cognitive diversity in your recruitment, you will almost certainly get a mix of race, culture, gender and background without explicitly setting out to do that.

Diversity of background

If you're recruiting for those tech skills, you're going to get proportionally more applicants who are young, white males from a middle-class home. This can lead the data team to narrow thinking about how it designs products and how they are presented to customers. A variety of cultural, educational and racial backgrounds can help to prompt more challenging questions when designing and evaluating data products.

Diversity of thought

This is a fundamental aspect of diversity. The Herrmann Whole Brain model is one example of how to categorize it (Herrmann Global LLC, 2021). You may have a team with wonderfully diverse backgrounds and experience, and great problem-solving skills, but if that team agrees on a single answer to every problem, this is not a sign that it is getting the right answer all the time. It is a warning of a lack of cognitive diversity.

Cognitive diversity is more about the differences people have in how they prefer to think, and focuses on how we like to visualize and solve problems.

COGNITIVE DIVERSITY

The differences people have in how they prefer to think, rather than a diversity of genetics or background. There are many models, but Herrmann refers to analytical, practical, relational and experimental skills. Teams may contain members with all four preferences, or some individuals can change their way of thinking depending on context, making them talented problem-solvers.

This is the idea behind my interview questions. There are some answers I really don't like, but there are many that I do like (especially the ones that never occurred to me). In any team it's important to have more than one way to visualize the daily challenges they meet, but this is fundamental to the success of a data team.

HOW TO MEASURE: COGNITIVE DIVERSITY

If we narrow this down to Herrmann's four modes of thinking, then it's transformative in itself to have problems solved and decisions taken by people who have a mix of analytical, practical, relational and experimental skills.

Analytical: These people know how things work, understand money, are rational and mathematical.

Practical: These are data collectors, likely to be conservative, articulate and detailed.

Relational: These people are more talkative, intuitive and interpersonal.

> **Experimental:** While also intuitive, these people like to synthesize, be holistic, and think spatially.
>
> There are many tests (and other models) for this. But the ultimate test is that when there is a problem, you are hearing about more than one way to solve it.

So, for example, if you've got a data governance role in your team, some-one who has worked in law enforcement may have the skills that are hard to find. Identifying new data sources is primarily about analytical skills: curiosity, research and detection. You will also need people who under-stand not just the structure of the business but the motivations of the people within it and so would be comfortable seeing the problem through a people-focused lens.

An example: at a large investment bank where I worked, the success of one project relied on sharing brokers' data. Technically, this was not hard to do. But my team had to understand that we were not solving a technology problem here, we were solving an incentivization problem. If we took their client data and shared it, what was in it for them? We couldn't change their incentives, but we had to work both with the brokers themselves and HR to creatively align incentives to make them happier to share. That takes both doggedness and sensitivity.

So in the quest to find a team that is not stereotyped in terms of race and gender, focusing on the mentality of the recruits, their problem-solving abil-ity, will help you to find a much more diverse group of people than if you target existing skills. A team that has a good mix of IQ, EQ, RQ, AQ and PQ. What you're then getting is a group of people who will come with an open mind as to how to solve a problem. That's motivating for you – and may be a pleasant surprise for the rest of the business.

Data and analytics capability model

We have already talked about the diversity of thinking of the data team but I wanted to talk about the key capabilities of the team, their focus and how they work together. It's a recurring theme of this book that teams cannot work in silos, and so it becomes critical that the team works as a coherent whole. The capabilities themselves may suggest a team structure but you don't need to organize this way. These are mapped out in the data and analytics capability model shown in Figure 4.1.

FIGURE 4.1 Data and analytics capability model

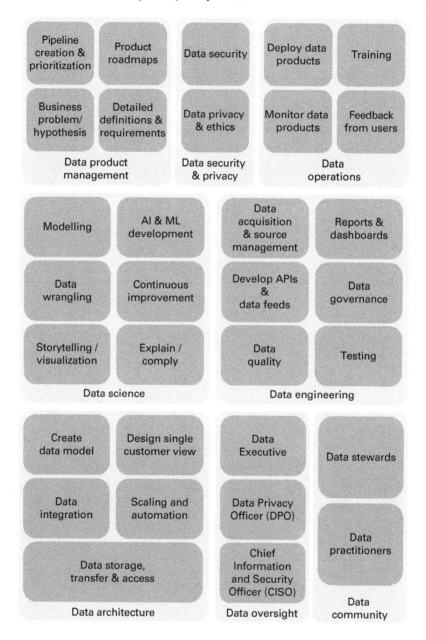

In my experience, one of the biggest reasons that data teams fail to deliver value is that they are not structured for success. The limiting factors are lack of alignment of roles to creating business value, clarity and purpose of roles, and making sure nothing falls through the cracks between different roles.

There are five key learnings from my experience on many occasions of building and fixing data and analytics teams. In running these teams I also had to face the consequences if I didn't get it right. I'm happy to share those learnings with you here:

- I would recommend that you create one data and analytics team initially. In time, when the data team and business as a whole have achieved a high degree of maturity, perhaps during the *Realize* wave, you could consider embedding certain capabilities across the business. However, I don't recommend you do it too soon.
- You need to ensure that all the capabilities are represented in your overall structure. Ensure there are no capability gaps.
- Make people explicitly responsible for the things that matter. I say explicitly because if something is not the key focus of their job, in my experience, it won't get done.
- You need to have a clear data process that enables the teams to know how they work together.
- With a clear structure you can define the success criteria for the teams, the job roles and descriptions, and their co-dependencies.

I'd like to spend some time explaining the capabilities, why they matter, and how the teams need to work together. Please refer to Figure 4.1, the data and analytics capability model.

Data product management

This team owns the data products (something we cover in more detail in Chapter 19) and that means they manage the pipeline of work for business and customer-facing activities, which includes most data science, reports and dashboard development, and APIs.

Key activities:

- Business problems are clearly expressed and understood by the business.
- Detailed requirements are written and signed off by the business.
- Pipeline of all work is managed and prioritized.
- Roadmap for each product is managed and roadmaps are aligned to the overall business strategy.
- Data roadmaps are communicated to customers, suppliers, exec, business sponsors, data stewards and practitioners, and they buy into it.

Key interactions with other teams:

- Data science: develop and manage the product roadmap for data science activities – models, AI, ML, etc.
- Data engineering: develop and manage the product roadmap for reports and dashboards, APIs, etc.
- Data operations: incorporate their feedback into the product roadmap.
- Data architecture: align their priorities to product roadmaps.

Data science

Develop and continuously improve the models, AI and ML capabilities that deliver value to the business.

Key activities:

- Best practice data science capabilities are developed.
- The 'art of the possible' use of DS is understood and explained.
- Data models, statistical models, and algorithms are developed.
- Models and algorithms are kept up to date.
- Latest data sets from data engineering are used.
- Business recommendations are made based on data models.

Key interactions with other teams:

- Data quality/governance: report any quality or governance issues to be fixed.
- Data operations: plan deployment of models.
- Data product management: develop according to their roadmap, and provide input to the roadmap.
- Data engineering: use the sources of data developed by them.
- Data architecture: provide requirements to them for data science infrastructure and to use the data model designed by them.

Data engineering

Source and provide access to data for the organization, ensuring it is properly managed and of a high quality.

Key activities:

- Product roadmaps are followed for capturing data sources and integrating with the data model and data infrastructure.
- Data quality and data roadmaps are used across the organization.
- Quality and governance of all data is managed to a high standard, including clear and consistent data definitions.
- Data products such as warehouse, data lake or APIs are developed.
- APIs and data feeds are built.
- Dashboards and reports are developed in line with product roadmaps.
- 'One source of the truth' is developed and shared across the whole organization.
- Data products are certified for quality, definitions, and trusted data sources and timeliness.

Key interactions with other teams:

- Data science: ensure they have access to the data they need.
- Data product: ensure development is in line with product roadmaps.
- Data exec: ensure governance and quality progress are reported.
- Data operations: plan deployment of data products.
- Data community: assist them in the testing and adoption of data products.
- Data architecture: provide requirements to them for data engineering infrastructure and to use the data model designed by them.

Data security and privacy

Ensuring that the company's data assets are protected, secure, and used ethically.

Key activities:

- Data privacy and data security policies are written and maintained.
- Data is properly classified and used in line with company privacy and data security policies.
- The GDPR, and other data regulation from relevant geographic jurisdictions, is understood and implemented.

- Privacy and security are designed into all data products and across the whole data infrastructure.

- Representing the views of the customer in terms of the storage and processing of their data.

Key interactions with other teams:

- Whole organization: provide advice, training and education on data privacy and security, as well as the GDPR and other data regulation.

- Data privacy officer (DPO): work with them to ensure privacy and ethics in all data activities. The DPO is an independent role representing the interests of the customer (ICO, 2016).

Data operations

Ensuring that data products are deployed, accessible and properly supported across the business, customers and suppliers.

Key activities:

- Data products are accessible by the intended audience during agreed operating hours in line with agreed service level agreements (SLAs).

- The environment for operating data products is stable and performant.

- Data products are supported in line with SLAs.

Key interactions with other teams:

- Data science and engineering: work with the teams to ensure products are fit for deployment and not just caught as they are 'thrown over the fence'.

- Data practitioners: manage relationships with the business, suppliers and customers to collect feedback on data products that have been deployed.

- Technology: ensure that the technical environment provided by technology is meeting SLA needs.

- Provide feedback from business, suppliers and customers to data product management.

- Manage problems and issues with products that have been deployed, through to resolution.

Data architecture

Design the end-to-end data environment for developing and operating data products, design the end-to-end data process and ensure accessibility and performance in line with SLAs.
Key activities:

- All data activities have the right environment to capture, store, transmit, manage and access data in an efficient and timely manner.
- All data tools support an integrated, end-to-end data process.
- The data model is designed and used as the single view of data across the whole organization, as well as potentially suppliers and clients. It's understandable and independent of the underlying data sources.
- The tools and data process support the volume, variety and velocity of data across the organization.
- Data across platforms and applications is integrated using APIs and data feeds, using one source of the truth.

Key interactions with other teams:

- Data science and data engineering: ensure the data environment meets their development needs.
- Technology: ensure the technical environment/cloud is fit for purpose.
- Chief Information Security Officer (CISO): ensure security across all data storage and transmission.

Data oversight

Ensure independent oversight of data capabilities and operations.
Key activities:

- The work by data teams specifically covering alignment to business goals and objectives, quality, governance, privacy and security is independently scrutinized.
- Data teams are supported and roadblocks removed.

Key interactions with other teams:

- Board and executive leadership: provide feedback to them on data risks – security, privacy, quality and governance, and 'value for money' of work.
- All data teams: feedback on progress of delivering data strategy.

Data community

Ensuring data is at the heart of everything they do and that the work the data teams are doing is given relevant and specific feedback.

Key activities:

- Specific and relevant input to products, product roadmap and projects.
- Data teams' output is tested.

Key interactions with other teams:

- Data engineering: raise quality and governance issues.
- Data product management: raise requirements.
- Data architecture: raise performance, accessibility, integration and timing requirements.

In the next section – the first wave – we will start by finding a problem to solve.

SUMMARY

- The limiting factors for success of a data team are lack of alignment of roles to creating business value, clarity and purpose of roles, and making sure nothing falls through the cracks between different roles.
- Working in a data team – and especially leading it – is not about technology skills. Coding can be taught much more easily than problem-solving ability.
- It's about problem-solving, and the ability to think in unconventional ways.
- When recruiting, cast a wide net. Make sure that recruiters don't restrict your options.
- Encourage diversity of thought and the ability to challenge conventional wisdom – and be ready to embrace those with a different mindset.
- Remember this is a job in which interaction with the entire business, not just those who understand data, is vital to your success.

References

Asplen-Taylor, S (2021) This is a question of programming logic: 'You ask either person what the other would say, then do the opposite.' The question will always give the correct answer

Forbes (2019) Rethinking the role of the Chief Data Officer, https://www.forbes.com/sites/insights-intelai/2019/05/22/rethinking-the-role-of-chief-data-officer/?sh=572cdd7c1bf9 (archived at https://perma.cc/6MHZ-NEVN)

Herrmann Global LLC (2021) Maximize your talent by harnessing cognitive diversity. https://www.thinkherrmann.com/ (archived at https://perma.cc/27WZ-TZMM)

Hodges, A (2014) *Alan Turing: The Enigma*, Penguin. If, on the other hand, you want just the bare facts, you can find them at https://www.turing.org.uk (archived at https://perma.cc/QRB2-5XXW) maintained by the same author

ICO (2016) Independent role of a DPO, https://ico.org.uk/for-organisations/guide-to-data-protection/guide-to-the-general-data-protection-regulation-gdpr/accountability-and-governance/data-protection-officers/#ib1 (archived at https://perma.cc/8XG6-MN27)

RAF (2021) If you have 25 minutes to spare, you can take a sample airmen selection test: https://www.raf.mod.uk/recruitment/how-to-apply/ast (archived at https://perma.cc/DT7Y-BSS3)

Tribepad (2019) Hiring humans vs Recruitment Robots. This is problem-solving of a sort, but 'gaming a weak system' isn't an attribute that is highly valued when you're dealing with risk or governance, for example. You can find the report here: https://www.tribepad.com/hiringhumanrecruitmentrobots (archived at https://perma.cc/HBB6-WUZ3)

PART TWO

Wave 1: Aspire

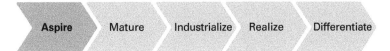

In Chapter 3 we talked about the five waves of transformation. We've now laid the groundwork with a business case, a data and analytics strategy and a team. This first wave is called *Aspire* because we know what we want to achieve, but it's all ahead of us. Now the real work begins.

We need to move forward and deliver some quick wins. The first projects are both a test and an opportunity.

They are a test, because they demonstrate that it is possible to find unrealized value in the data your organization holds.

But they are a once-only opportunity to establish credibility and prepare the business for a radical transformation. Get this right and we are on the march towards *Mature*.

Value, Build, Improve content of this wave

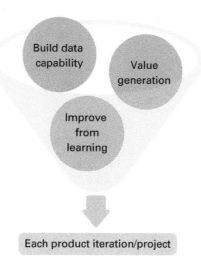

The activities for our VBI model in this wave are:

Value. A set of quick wins with measurable returns for the business. Quick wins show employees and the board that progress is real, releasing additional budget for next steps.

Build. Creating standardized, repeatable processes is a model for the future.

Improve. Early results will tell you a lot about the data in the business, its data strengths and weaknesses, and the organizational blockers to progress.

05

A quick win

A data transformation needs to demonstrate that it can create results in under three months. This means that some early activity must focus on a quick win to create value for the business. But project selection is critical.

KEY CONCEPTS

- Quick win
- The quick wins paradox

Introduction

In 2009 the Corporate Executive Board surveyed 5,400 leaders who were new in their jobs. The survey asked these leaders what they were focusing on. Cleverly, they also asked the bosses of these leaders to rate their performance so far.

The responses were sorted into two groups: those whose bosses thought they were succeeding, and those whose bosses thought they were struggling. What was the difference?

The outcome of this research was written up in the *Harvard Business Review* (Van Buren and Safferstone, 2009). 'Among the high-performing new leaders, one attribute stood out,' the authors wrote, 'a strong focus on results.'

Item one on every new manager's to-do list is a quick win. The new leaders who had found themselves a quick win were rated 20 per cent higher by their bosses than those who had not. As the article points out, a quick win reassures your boss that it was the right decision to give you the job, and it also sends a positive message to the people who are working for you (it's OK to follow you because you know what you're doing), and the people who work alongside you (you're going to make a difference).

QUICK WIN

An immediate improvement that delivers obvious value to the business. Because of the short deadline (two to three months), quick wins tend to be easy to implement but limited in scope. The best quick wins can be built on or repeated at a later date.

But – and we will get to this later – those who struggled in the survey didn't do badly because they didn't target a quick win. They were failing in the eyes of their bosses because they were going about it the wrong way.

We have made a lot of progress so far. You have identified data weaknesses in your business. You have used that knowledge to outline a data and analytics strategy that establishes priorities. You have started to recruit or appoint the team you need or identified more clearly the strengths and weaknesses of the team that's already in place.

These are three things that many CDOs never do, even though in my experience it means their data transformation would have a much greater chance of success if they did.

We finished off the process of creating a data and analytics strategy by communicating it to the business. This is a necessary step, a positive step, but it creates expectations. Given that some of them will have heard it all before, given that people have short memories, and given that the board has probably been burned before by people who promised to fix data, anyone in charge of a data transformation needs to demonstrate that they can create tangible value quickly.

I was recently recruited for a short-term project by an oil company. I was the third CDO they had tried. The first one knew how to speak inspiringly about what was possible, knew all about technology, but achieved very little in practical terms. The second was an internal promotion who understood finance, but not the data. Both had failed to deliver a quick result, and the company soon tired of them. It was a wonder they gave me any budget at all – but it was a strictly limited budget, with the not-very-coded message that I needed to demonstrate value from my first day on the job. This isn't an insult, it's a challenge.

Anatomy of a quick win

You will need to show the board, your team and your colleagues that you do make a difference. This might be small at first, but that's probably more than your predecessor achieved. So how do we pick the right project?

A quick win must be quick

Rule of thumb: unless the CDO can demonstrate progress in less than three months, there will be awkward questions about where the data transformation is going. This will rule out many dream projects or, ironically, anything that is truly transformational. That's maybe not a bad thing. The most important projects can't be rushed and will probably need much preparatory work anyway.

Think small

Target one area of the business, or one office, or one project. Resist the temptation to say, 'it's only a little more work to do this for the other offices as well'. It isn't, and at the minimum it will delay the time to get a result.

Think about scalability

Delivering value in your quick win should be the start of your story. So pick a project that allows you to repeat your win in other business units, or more locations. This restriction isn't just to make sure you don't overextend yourself. If you can go back to the leadership team and say, 'we saved $50,000 in one office as I promised, but you have 99 other offices that we haven't looked at yet', they can do the maths. If you had promised to save $5 million but only in one office, and couldn't apply it in the other 99, it's the same saving, but not transformative.

Target what you know

Remember also that, at this point, we know much less about those data problems we identified than we would like, which means that somewhere there will be a nasty surprise in the data or the office politics. Restricting ambitions to one relatively well-known process or office, or one for which the CDO can do due diligence in a day or two, reduces the risk that you will run into complications.

Beware of pet projects

When casting about for your first project, a CDO should be suspicious of the overly warm welcome in someone's office. Often, in my experience, your suitor will want to pitch a solution to a business problem that this person thinks is very important, but for their colleagues it doesn't matter. It might be a way to recruit you on their personal journey to the top. It might be a way to promote their idea of success at the expense of a rival that you have never met. It might be that this person just likes to be at the front of the queue. None of these is a good reason to take on this project as your quick win.

Don't throw away the data and analytics strategy

Whatever you choose, it must align with your data and analytics strategy, which is, in turn, aligned with the aims of the business. One of the reasons that you might be pitched someone's pet project is that it is being ignored for the very good reason that the company is focusing on other priorities. For example, if you have a priority to cut costs, and everyone knows this, every business unit will want to look heroic. In which case, the first thing that sales will want is a quick way to increase sales, so that jobs are protected. This is understandable, but it is – unfortunately for them – a distraction that could derail a data and analytics strategy.

Do something repeatable

There is also the temptation to perform magic by crafting a special piece of eye-catching analysis, for example, identifying one group of neglected customers in one location, or finding one superstar salesperson. After the applause dies down, it will soon become obvious that there is no benefit to anyone else. This is often the problem that occurs when the business hires a data scientist. We value data scientists because they are experimental, restless and creative, but these attributes are sometimes their greatest weakness. A successful insight prompts most CEOs to immediately consider how this can be applied elsewhere. But if the CEO asks, 'what's next?', a data scientist may interpret that as the signal to move on to a completely different project.

Task: Identifying the right project

FIGURE 5.1   Quick wins

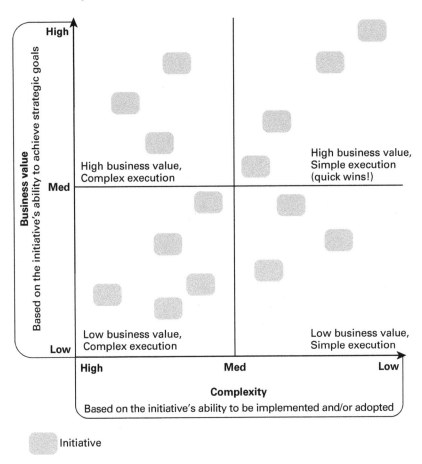

Let's look now at what qualifies as a quick win, and how to find it. Refer to Figure 5.1. The ideal project will have a high value to the business, and be relatively simple to implement (or, if changing the way that something works, to adopt). Quick wins are in the top right quadrant of the figure.

This is easy to say, but harder to identify in practice. Here are some pointers to help you filter the projects you will hear about.

Don't lock yourself away with the data

The best way to find what needs to be fixed is to talk face to face with people outside the data and IT functions at every level, and find out what is making them fret, or needling them. This will usually not be what the IT department tells you is wrong.

Don't focus on the first thing you hear

There will be some company-wide gripes, but that alone may be disqualifying, because it indicates a much larger project. When you talk for longer, you will often hear about a small failure, a minor frustration, or a longstanding mystery that is undermining someone's best efforts to achieve the strategic goals of the business. That is a better candidate.

Search for a problem that represents a bigger goal

You might hear about a product line that is mysteriously bleeding costs, or one group of customers that is making a disproportionate number of complaints. These are intriguing because any solution to these problems is likely to be repeatable and can give some insight into an issue that is probably pervasive.

Small data, not big data

We fetishize large amounts of data. For a quick win you need enough data to know what's going on, but not so much that cleaning and analysing the data may require months. If this project can make headway by comparing only two pieces of data or finding why one number doesn't seem to add up (or adds up in different ways, in two different places), this is enough. Trying to overanalyse at this stage is not a good idea.

Don't listen to ambition

Too many CDOs want to make a splash by immediately discovering a magical new source of revenue, or creating a dashboard, or unearthing lasting value from social media sentiment. This is aiming far too high. All of these things may be in the data and analytics strategy, and they may transform the image of data in the company as well as deliver business benefit. But there are good reasons, which we are yet to discuss, why day one may not be the time to kick off these splashy projects.

CASE STUDY
The mystery of the Singaporean photocopier

Challenge: A quick win on costs

In July 2014 I was on day one of working for a flexible shared office provider, as global head of data. They run 3,000 serviced office locations around the world. Many start-ups work on one floor or in one room of one of their buildings, many growing companies expand into new cities by finding office space provided by them, and other companies that just want to run a meeting or a training session off-site hire a room by the hour. Asking around the business, I discovered that everyone was worried about the costs that were depressing margins.

Analysis: Service costs hold the key

Their customers get access to a full range of business services, from sandwiches to printing. Some basic services (electricity, for example) are included in its hiring agreement, some are charged back. Cost control is extremely important for every serviced office building, because it has large, long-term fixed costs, plus the costs of running the building and providing these extras on top. Controlling cost increases profitability.

My long-term goals were to increase occupancy or raise satisfaction: it would be almost impossible to show a tangible improvement in these measures in a few weeks.

Action: Look beyond the aggregates

I looked at the aggregate numbers for some obvious mistake but, as you would hope, all the obvious cost savings had already been made. The finance function found that costs were broadly consistent across every country as a percentage of overall revenues. In the big picture, there was literally nothing to see.

I looked at what made up the cost of doing business. They had a lease to pay on each building, as well as the running costs: utilities, maintenance, insurance, and so on.

Revenues were split in two. Recurring revenues were effectively what tenants paid for using the space, whether it was long- or short-term room hires. Additional services, when provided on behalf of a tenant rather than for their own business, were charged back. Note that every little service that should have been billed to a tenant but wasn't charged back was not just a lost opportunity to make revenue from a customer, it immediately became a cost to that office, because the office was then paying for it. And that interested me.

While the finance function was interested in the aggregates, as a data geek, I was naturally interested in the detail of those charges, and how they compared. This was especially true for charges that were so commonplace that no one even thought about them. In the plot of *Superman III*, Gus Gorman, played by Richard Pryor, steals money from his employer by 'salami slicing' – collecting a fraction of a cent from each cheque and depositing it in his personal account. Although no one in our example is committing a crime, the impact on the business is the same: a small, regular loss that no one thinks to look for (IMDb, 1983).

For those services that no one thought much about, for which did the chargebacks not offset the costs to them? And, if they didn't match, was that the same across 3,000 offices (we're systematically undercharging) or did it vary (we were not enforcing policy correctly in some places)?

The aggregates will not give up this information easily. If there was uneven enforcement on really big chargebacks, that would show up. But there is so much noise in this type of data, and so many separate chargebacks, you can't expect that.

But these numbers are telling stories of whether the business model is working as well as it could, whether the chargeback prices for each service need to be adjusted, or whether people are forgetting to do something. When you disaggregate the data, you can put a cost to the business on each of these potential problems.

Looking closely at the data across each location, I started to see that there were differences between offices on individual services. I was pretty sure that I was the first person to spot them, because who else would bother to look? Technically, this isn't hard to do – you can see it by looking at a spreadsheet. What matters is that you are looking for something, not just staring at the data.

In Singapore I could identify that the business was paying a very high photocopying cost every month. The chargebacks for photocopying in Singapore were zero. Disaggregating the data showed that the office, for some reason, was not implementing basic policy, and all its tenants were getting free photocopying. The cost of each job wasn't enough to sound an alarm for any member of staff, and anyone from head office visiting the building would probably not notice.

It could be that the staff hadn't been trained properly and thought that free photocopying was part of the service, or that they didn't want to charge customers, or that they just did not fill in the forms. The data could not tell me why it happened, but it mattered that it was happening. If we solved the Mystery of the Singaporean Photocopiers, we could save quite a lot of money, starting immediately, simply by enforcing policies that already existed. Whatever its root cause, the impact was to cut hundreds of thousands of pounds off the profitability of that office.

Outcome: Identify local slip-ups and change them

I put in place some KPIs and metrics and started comparing all services across 3,000 offices by calculating a new variable: what was the chargeback rate for each service, in each office? When I did that, there were irregular spikes for services that should have been charged back at the same rate across the entire estate. In most fields, in most offices, I discovered the chargeback rate would be 80 or 90 per cent. That is what you would expect: the policy is the same, but it would be imperfectly applied or reported, and there would be some use of the services that couldn't be applied to a customer. But in some offices, for some services, the rate was 20 or 30 per cent. In a matter of a few weeks, just by informing the offices that were not enforcing policy, the business's costs went down, income rose, and the operating margin went up.

It will not always be that neat. But the example shows that by looking at a small detail that was normally aggregated before it got to finance in a way that required very little technical skill, that it was no one's job to look at before, we could achieve an immediate quick win.

Make sure it's a quick win for everyone

Note that the *Harvard Business Review* article I introduced earlier was called 'The quick wins *paradox*'. While achieving an early success wins praise, gets the positive attention of both teams and the board, and secures budget for the next step, they found that the drive to achieve quickly generated negative behaviour in three out of five project leaders.

In other words, the desire for quick wins more often than not undermines the project – and its leaders if not carefully managed.

THE QUICK WINS PARADOX

The problem that the rush to demonstrate tangible value for a leader can often have the opposite effect if project selection or implementation is flawed.

Thinking back to Chapter 1, when we asked questions about whether the business needs a data transformation, we looked at a series of business problems for which openness to challenge, collaboration and cooperation were key attributes for anyone who wanted to be part of the solution. The paradox that the researchers identified is that, very often, the process of rushing to prove ourselves produces the opposite outcome. So, if you are driving a data transformation quick win, here are some tips based on the article to make sure that a quick win is also a positive step:

Avoid getting stuck in the weeds. The survey found that the desire to prove oneself created an exaggerated focus on detail. Whoever leads the project may want to do everything themselves to the exclusion of the people brought in to help. Too much focus on detail slows the project down.

Accept criticism. A new CDO can't win over everyone immediately. Yes, the project has a mandate. But this is a stage at which everyone is learning, and so it's fatal to ignore good advice that could help achieve results.

Don't intimidate. Trust at this point is probably low. A CDO wants to show authority, but research shows that too many of us focus so much on our own brilliance that we may become supercilious or arrogant in this situation. Even if the project succeeds on its own terms, it may well increase resistance to the data transformation, not eliminate it.

Don't jump to conclusions. There are many things we do not understand at this point. The strategy to achieve the quick win might be relying too much on prior beliefs or preconceived ideas, not on listening to others.

Try not to micromanage. To meet the short deadline, let everyone in the team get on with their work. It's why you hired them.

Quick wins are not strategic wins

Finally, it is important to note that a win is a win, but it's not a data and analytics strategy. A hundred quick wins in a row are not a data and analytics strategy. By creating value for the business, this quick win may have done something in a few weeks that predecessors could not do in several years: it has demonstrated the power of data to improve the business.

The temptation is to want to do it again. This has diminishing returns. The obvious reason is that there are a limited number of ways to win quickly in any viable business.

An addiction to quick wins can get in the way of strategy, because it will distract the data team from creating sustainable ways in which data transforms the business. The project will require many improvements to the quality of the data, the way it is generated and used, and the way the business is run. These are wins, but they are rarely quick.

So we need to continue to think strategically. The next steps are to choose projects for which the wins are repeatable, and run experiments using data.

SUMMARY

- A measurable result delivered in less than three months is the best way to demonstrate the value of data to management and your colleagues.
- Do not be too ambitious in the scale or scope of this project and don't be seduced by pet projects. Look for something manageable that can be applied in other contexts later.
- Look for an inconsistent result, or an unexplained statistic. This means the quick win can focus on one or two sources of data that have not been properly analysed or aggregated.
- Beware of the data team getting stuck in the weeds. Attention to detail is good, but delegation is essential.
- Quick wins buy kudos, attention and budget, and so can be addictive. But do not let them distract you from the data team's strategic long-term goals.

References

IMDb (1983) From the Superman III plot, https://www.imdb.com/title/tt0086393/plotsummary (archived at https://perma.cc/72UB-N3DQ)

Van Buren, M E and Safferstone, T (2009) The quick wins paradox, *Harvard Business Review*

06

Repeat and learn

A results-driven data and analytics strategy is more effective if the outcomes can be repeated over and over. The correct selection and application of projects can help this. Data experimentation also speeds up learning.

KEY CONCEPTS

- Data process

- Business change process

- A/B test

Introduction

We got a quick win. Congratulations. But if every project starts from scratch, and takes three months to find the data, analyse the data, and draw a conclusion, then the second win is a few months away. The data team might not be so lucky next time, momentum dies, and that hard-won status dissipates. This is not transformational.

But if the second quick win is a week away, because the team has already found and cleaned the data, even a negative result is not a disaster. From day zero, the project should be looking to make improvements that can be reused and repeated. This chapter focuses on how we do that.

Recall the Singaporean photocopying problem in Chapter 5. This quick win immediately saved some cash for the business. But it was more powerful than that, because the method could be applied to chargebacks for more or less anything, anywhere in the company. We found that most of the offices would do most things right, most of the time. But I had uncovered a method that could discover the rare and costly exceptions to the rule. It could be applied to any office, or to any service in that office, at any time and was therefore repeatable.

Aside from a financial benefit, applying the same process in many contexts is the first step on a rigorous journey of organizational improvement. It demonstrates that we are not just solving ad hoc problems, we're helping the entire organization to learn how it can do better.

Why build a repeat-and-learn culture?

A quick win doesn't encourage anyone to act differently. In fact, it may do precisely the opposite: by achieving better results without asking anyone to think hard about how things are done, or why they are done, the data team is positioned as an ad hoc team of fixers, rather than a catalyst for organizational change. So at an early stage, we need to build a repeat-and-learn culture, both inside the team and across the organization.

Repetition gives context

Repeating a successful process helps to explain why we are doing it. This is much more effective than making PowerPoint slides out of an abstract strategy and expecting everyone to invest in it. So, if the offices in our example above were told that we were running an analysis on their chargebacks, we could explain why, how it had helped other offices raise their margins and become more successful within the company. It didn't seem like the data police were coming to town to tell people about the mistakes they made, which is sometimes the unintended message.

Repetition helps to focus limited resources

Quick wins can help obtain budget for the transformation, but rarely a blank cheque. A series of one-off projects will drain resources. An example common to many data transformations I have been part of is that HR sends a request: 'We just need to make sure we've got the right people aligned to the right process.' Imagine that you complete the quick-win project successfully. Now what? There's no repeatable process. Even if you took the same project to other offices, you are starting with an entirely new set of data. This doesn't mean you don't do it, if it aligns with strategy, because clearly it can deliver benefits to the business. It just means that for a project like this, it's hard to achieve a large returns-to-time-spent ratio, and that's what you are targeting in the early months of any project.

Repetition means documentation

Not enough businesses capture what works, what doesn't, and the methodology. This playbook shortens the time taken to create value, and it also shifts the data team away from an artisanal approach to creating value, instead building fresh data sets and asking different questions each time. Recording what you did and how you did it is an opportunity for your team to optimize how they work, but there's a bigger prize here, too.

Repetition helps the whole business to learn

This is the beginning of sustainable improvement. Discovering missed chargebacks saved money in Singapore, and ultimately could ensure that the recharge rules for photocopying were followed consistently in 3,000 locations. But the business can also learn from this: the data showed incontrovertibly that management practices were being followed inconsistently, that there wasn't sufficient monitoring in place, and put a cost to the business of this inefficiency. This is normal – every business has these challenges. But it's evidence for a bigger conversation about organizational change that would lead to better monitoring, better training, even changing the way that services are sold and charged. It also reinforces the point that the data team are part of the business and should not operate in a silo.

HOW TO MEASURE: DOCUMENTING A SUCCESSFUL PROJECT

This can be used to communicate the steps in a project to others in the data team (and outside, if appropriate). There are many software tools to do this, but this is not a technology problem at heart. It's about being able to capture the elements of an improvement so that when someone changes roles, goes off sick, or is simply too busy, the project doesn't grind to a halt. Any good documentation will capture, at minimum:

Purpose: The reason it exists.

Scope: What is included, and not included, focusing on the data.

Input: What needs to be done to achieve results.

Flow: A description of all the steps needed to complete the project.

Output: The changes that this project produces.

Measurement: The way to evaluate and report its success.

Risks: Factors that may complicate the process, and how to mitigate them.

This need not be an exhausting red-tape burden, but it is essential for someone on the team (remember cognitive diversity: this seems like a job for an analytical team member) to complete.

The ultimate test of whether this documentation is successful is whether it is a complete enough guide for someone to replicate the project on their own (given the technical skills, of course). This is the first step towards the standardization and automation of the data function that we aspire to.

Listen to what data is telling you

There is a temptation for businesses that have a data success to jump straight into the big league and over-invest in some extravagantly resourced, aspirational but poorly defined IT project. It's too soon to do this. We don't build factories before we know which products will be made in them, yet too often we build a data warehouse or data lake before we have properly evaluated what we want to do with the data, or even whether we have the data we need to put in it.

The process of learning by working with the data in your organization gives a cautious signal of what to do next, because if you listen to what it is telling you, it will expose weaknesses in the way information is captured, communicated and used. Indeed, a reasonable conclusion at this stage might be that there are not large-scale, long-run benefits to investing in a more ambitious data project, because we need to prepare the ground first.

Another might be that a change in business processes or incentives to gather data would be the priority at this stage.

A hypothetical example: imagine a fictional office services company that discovered one of its business units was not handling the manual processes around chargebacks efficiently. The data team discovered that it could boost revenue by £100,000 each year in the North region.

Predicting similar benefits from the separate systems run by the East, South and West, the business commissioned a new accounts system that aggregated the data, automated the chargeback process, monitored service use among its customers, and cut off services to those who did not pay immediately.

But there was no financial benefit to the business at the end of the year; the customer churn rate was up, and satisfaction was down.

The reason? Management had jumped straight to the endgame, without looking carefully enough at the data, or the business processes that were generating that data.

Imagine that the chargeback processes in the East region, though also manual, had been much more efficient. Additional revenues from automation were therefore small in the East. Automation could offer a benefit in satisfaction for loyal customers or save management time – both good results, but not the benefit against which the project would be measured.

In the South, the data was recorded differently, making it seem at first like the extra charges were not being applied. But they were just being wrapped into the total cost. Before any progress could be made in the South, the accounting system had to be changed, and the data defined differently. This took several months.

In the West, the entire billing structure was different, which customers in that region preferred. They had the option to pay a higher initial cost, which included all services. The type of customers who chose this service preferred it and didn't like the new system. Some left for a rival. There was no uplift in revenue from those who remained.

The CFO was unhappy too. The cost of additional development had swallowed up the limited additional revenue. Customers and staff were unhappy and would resist further changes to the way they did business.

In this case, the initial analysis was sound. The data process was repeatable. But the business would have been well advised to let the data speak before rushing to implement an IT solution to what was a more complex problem than it seemed.

You need to move quickly in the early months to maintain momentum. But that cannot mean jumping to conclusions (or letting others jump to conclusions for you). One of the most useful ways in which you can stop this happening is to make sure that you and your team talk to people in the business, rather than just stare at the data. Ask them why they do things the way they do and find out what motivates or frustrates them about the data they generate and use. This will not only help you to do your job but will make it more likely that they will realize you are trying to help them when you attempt to create better processes.

Task: Define a data process

To create valuable repeated projects, first we need a well-defined data collection and analysis process that is explained to everyone who will be affected by it. This gives the data team the chance to explain that their idea has worked before, and what it entails. It will also give others the chance to question the assumptions or explain their context. This might not be fresh information but at least it encourages others to engage and participate.

> DATA PROCESS
>
> A defined way to achieve value from data for the business. This includes a definition of the data, where it resides and how to access it, the question it seeks to answer, and the processing and techniques required to find that answer. Defining a process can be used to communicate the value of a project to all stakeholders.

In creating a data process, the point is *not* to think: how can we generate more data? At first, you will be seeking to maximize the value of the (limited) data you can access.

Focus on data that you can reuse. This will often expose (as above) problems in the underlying data, and inefficiencies or bad decisions that happened because of these limitations. In the short run, it will be necessary to work with what you have, to do the analysis with a smaller set of consistent data, while working on ways to improve it.

Then define the consistent question that you want to answer using this data. You might want to address these questions differently in different business units. But what matters is that you have enough data, and a clear idea of which insights you would like, and their benefit to the business (and, of course, that they align with the overall data and analytics strategy).

At an early stage, seek out a key advocate or sponsor who supports the aims of the project and would benefit from it, but is senior enough to push it through, give you good guidance and ensure that you have access to data and cooperation. Then you can launch your project.

Task: Develop a business change process

Your goal is to define a consistent set of actions that are repeatable and will have a business benefit that aligns with your strategy.

BUSINESS CHANGE PROCESS

A way to realize value from data for the business. This is a complement to the data process, as it focuses on the actions that users of data can take to realize value. This can be used to communicate the value of a project to all stakeholders, but specifically to those who use the data on a regular basis.

Every business has different needs. If you are focusing on cost reduction, you will need to focus on supplier data. Customer data is the focus for revenue generation. Knowing more about employees helps to optimize productivity. Alternatively, you may want to improve competitiveness by using data on products and services.

Whatever the focus, at this point the answer to your problem is to be intentional in everything you do, linking insight to a repeatable data process that creates the case to adjust a business process.

It is not yet the time at this stage to build a data warehouse, a data lake, or any other large receptacle for data. Start small, build quality.

CASE STUDY
Reducing customer churn at an entertainment company

Challenge: Reduce churn

One of my clients, among other activities, provides online gaming to its customers. The data team had a strategic data goal to reduce customer churn across the business. We achieved a quick win solving one of the churn problems by looking at the customer data to discover customers who had reported a problem. Our customer services team could then contact them quickly to resolve it. We wanted to reuse this data to further reduce churn.

Analysis: Deliver incentives where they are justified

Using the same data, the data team realized that we could tell marketing which customers were most likely to leave. Using the same data again, we could start to calculate lifetime value for these customers. This meant that we could target incentives to use our products better.

The key to making this work was not to do incredibly complex things with the data at this stage. Most of the data work was quite straightforward. The point was to use the data to enable better business processes to evolve.

Action: Timely contact

We set up a process by which marketing sent those unhappy customers an incentive offer. Using the data, every week we were able to run out a list of customers who were most likely to churn. Or we could do it daily, so that they could be contacted. This might be a customer who (this is a gambling business) had a big loss.

Outcome: A process for customer retention

We knew from the data that any contact, and offer, would have to be made quickly – not in a few weeks when someone at the company noticed that the customer's account wasn't active. But this necessitated three steps: an evaluation of the value we were providing to that customer, the reuse of data, and then tactical changes in business processes. When this was achieved, churn fell dramatically, and safer gambling controls were improved.

Learning and innovating through experimentation

One of the other ways in which you can use repetition to your advantage is to run experiments.

Having large amounts of data means we can bring the culture of the science lab to what we do, day by day. For more than a decade Google and Amazon have been refining their web pages by running hundreds of A/B tests a day, in which half of the users would see one interface, half the other, and the more successful one was adopted.

A/B TESTS

Simple tests to establish which of two products or strategies is preferred by customers. Usually one is the 'control', representing business as usual, the other the 'innovation'. Statistically the test is valid only when group A is similar to group B in all relevant ways. If the difference in outcome is large enough, then this is attributable to the innovation.

This is not a new idea (the Pepsi challenge (Yglesias, 2013) has been running since 1975), but it becomes much more accessible when using data. Even a result that shows you didn't make a difference is valuable, because it means that either you shouldn't waste any more time on it, or perhaps (and very likely at this stage) you need better data. As long ago as 2011, Greg Linden, one of the experimenters at Amazon, argued that experiments were the key to progress. 'You need to try a lot of things,' he said, adding that 'Genius is born from a thousand failures. In each failed test, you learn something that helps you find something that will work' (Brynjolfsson and McAfee, 2011).

The process has become much more common, and our approach to standardization means that even at this stage you can begin to build a culture of experimentation. If you wanted to test whether one of the interventions would work, you could apply it to all customers and watch the uplift. But if you do that, be aware that there may be confounding factors on that day, or with that group, and what you are seeing may be the result of something else.

Or it might happen that what you are seeing is genuinely the result of your intervention, but the business attributes it to something else: the line manager will want to claim it for the staff, for example.

If you can show that each intervention is moving the needle, then not only do you learn, you create immediate value for the business. It's another quick win, but one that also helps you learn about the next steps.

What you will probably learn from this is that you will need better data if you want to sustain your success. The definition of 'better', and how you achieve it, will be our focus in Wave 2.

SUMMARY

- When looking at which projects to take on at an early stage, always consider how you can reuse the data and methods, and standardize and document your approach to make reuse possible.

- Repetition makes the most of your limited resources, and helps you learn about the business. It also helps you to explain the benefit of what you do, because you did it before.

- Take care not to jump too fast. Your quick win in one area of the business may not be easy to apply in other contexts, so talk to the people who generate and use the data before you act.

- By demonstrating the benefits of using data across the business, you can begin to break down silos, or create a consistent way of dealing with customers, or costs, or products across more than one business unit. This gives you the opportunity to create more fundamental change at a later date.

- When you are working with consistent data, A/B tests deliver quick results, and even a negative result is valuable.

References

Brynjolfsson, E and McAfee, A (2011) The big data boom is the innovation story of our time, *The Atlantic*

Yglesias, M (2013) Sweet sorrow, *Slate*, https://slate.com/business/2013/08/pepsi-paradox-why-people-prefer-coke-even-though-pepsi-wins-in-taste-tests.html (archived at https://perma.cc/2NZM-7RP5)

PART THREE

Wave 2: Mature

Through the delivery of some quick wins, and the learning we took from those, we were able to demonstrate real progress and have realized some benefits in *Aspire*. We'll have created some repeatable processes. We'll have learned a lot about the data in the business, its data strengths and weaknesses, and about the organizational blockers to progress.

The data team can now start to build consistent, high-quality sources of data that will create business value now and help transition to new ways of working. The hard work that goes into this wave will pay off many times in later stages.

This wave also demonstrates the incredible power of having a single source of truth in the organization, and of the single customer view, as we move towards *Industrialize*.

Value, Build, Improve content of this wave

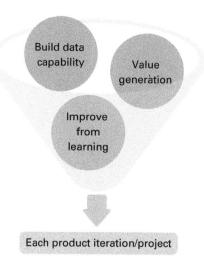

The activities for our VBI model in this wave are:

Value. The data team will be able to create high-quality data, which can be used with confidence in the business. The ability to do this, and to demonstrate value from it, will build trust in the data transformation.

Build. This wave focuses on quality and governance in every part of the data process. At this stage it is used for reporting and a single view of the customer, though this is the foundation of later work.

Improve. These innovations can inform the business of underlying problems that reporting has identified, resolve conflicts over data, help manage risk and compliance, and show what is possible in the data transformation.

07

Data governance

We are often unintentionally vague about where data is, how it is collected and used, or even what it means. And so, when we try to interpret what it is telling us, we are likely to make mistakes. Rigorous data governance is one of the foundations of an effective data and analytics strategy.

KEY CONCEPTS

- Data governance

- Data provenance

- Data accountability

- Data steward

- Data owner

- Data executive

Introduction

On 16 July 2020, the Centre for Evidence-Based Medicine at the University of Oxford published an article with a frightening title: 'Why no-one can ever recover from COVID-19 in England' (Loke and Heneghan, 2020).

The authors, Yoon Loke and Carl Heneghan, were not making a medical observation: their point was purely statistical. The researchers had spotted an important statistical anomaly in the way that Public Health England (PHE) was counting deaths from Covid-19 that, eventually, would mean that the English death toll from the virus would be counted in tens of millions.

When Covid deaths began to be counted, Scotland, Wales and Northern Ireland registered a Covid-19 fatality as a death that occurred within 28 days of a positive test. This was a statistical convention that was common, but not universally adopted (the World Health Organization, for example, has no single definition of a Covid-19 death).

In England, however, statisticians thought this might undercount fatalities, and so anyone who had tested positive, and subsequently died, was counted as a Covid-19 death. This approach had much to recommend it at first: if someone tested positive and was admitted to intensive care in Newcastle, was kept alive for a month by the heroic intervention of medical professionals, but sadly died five weeks later, this was appropriately registered as a Covid-19 fatality. If the same person had been admitted to hospital in Edinburgh – 120 miles north – with the same outcome, this would not have officially been recognized as a Covid-19 death. In this case, the English method of counting seems superior.

But, as the pandemic dragged on, a different statistical anomaly became increasingly important. As many of the people who were most affected by Covid-19 either had pre-existing medical conditions or were at an advanced age, they were statistically far more likely to die relatively soon after they recovered. So, after several months, an increasing proportion of deaths would be misattributed. And because everyone who had ever tested positive must die at some point, eventually everyone in England who had tested positive, subsequently got better, and died from a completely unrelated cause would be recorded as a Covid-19 fatality.

As Loke and Heneghan wrote:

> By this PHE definition, no one with COVID in England is allowed to ever recover from their illness. A patient who has tested positive, but successfully treated and discharged from hospital, will still be counted as a COVID death even if they had a heart attack or were run over by a bus three months later.

I wrote to the Prime Minister, Boris Johnson, explaining this because it showed the United Kingdom in a poor light compared with other countries.

And so, on 12 August 2020, PHE revised the total number of Covid-19 deaths in England down by 5,377, reporting 36,695 people had died after contracting the virus. The day before, the tally had been 42,072 (Griffin, 2020).

Note that making the adjustment had no effect on the true number of people who died in England as a result of contracting Covid-19. But, like the actual profit a company makes, the exact level of customer satisfaction, or even the precise value of sales – we don't know what that is. Like all estimates, both the figures of 36,695 and 42,072 are likely to have some measurement error.

In this case, we have good evidence that they were both large underestimates of the overall impact of Covid-19, as the Office for National Statistics was tallying excess deaths – the number of people who died in this period who statistically we would have expected still to be alive in a non-pandemic year. This statistic was several thousand higher.

So we can legitimately ask why it was the right thing to make the correction at all, if in all likelihood it shifted the official data further from 'the truth'. This is a perfect example of data governance in action. There were two good reasons to move to the 28-day standard:

- The first is that, by construction, the previous statistic would deviate further over time from the true count, and so would eventually make no intuitive sense. It would fail the test that you should be able to explain the data sensibly in a meeting.

- But, just as important, the English method made meaningful comparisons impossible, and so the Covid-19 mortality data was fatally flawed as a basis for decision-making. After it was moved to the new standard, data from all over the UK that had been captured and analysed using the same method could be used for comparison by British politicians and epidemiologists who held meetings to discuss the progress of countermeasures or the effectiveness of emergency care.

'Data governance' sounds to outsiders like a dull box-ticking exercise to please a regulator or an auditor. True, done well it will make both of them happy, or as close as they are likely to get.

But you know that it is far more important than that. Creating a common, meaningful definition of the data we use, allied with consistent ways to extract, compile or calculate that data across the organization, is one of the most important projects you can possibly undertake. This is best illustrated by the creation of a single customer view – more on this in Chapter 9. Data governance, together with the data quality programme that we will investigate next, will underpin every other piece of work you will do and make the difference between success and failure for most of them.

Data governance can be surprisingly tricky to pull off, and it also has the potential to put noses out of joint across the business. This will be your first, and one of your most important, exercises in tough love through data.

What is data governance?

First of all, we should decide what the problem of bad data governance is. We already discussed a simple tell-tale in Chapter 1: do your colleagues argue about whose version of the data is correct? But there's much more to data governance, because why they disagree and what can be done about it will vary.

For this important concept, we use the Data Governance Institute's definition (The Data Governance Institute, 2021).

DATA GOVERNANCE

A system of decision rights and accountabilities for information-related processes, executed according to agreed-upon models which describe who can take what actions with what information, and when, under what circumstances, using what methods.

In most of my jobs through the years, achieving high standards of data governance has been one of the most important problems I have been asked to solve. But it is easier to say 'we need to improve' than to work out what to do, or how to do it.

The first thing to recognize is that this is not an irritating bit of corporate box-ticking that we can let slide. Bad data governance undermines good decisions and makes bad ones more likely. It exposes the business to risk. It creates needless conflict. Left unchecked, the problem will inevitably get worse. These are high stakes, potentially existential.

One of the best, by which I mean worst, examples of bad data governance helped cause the collapse of WorldCom in 2002 (we mentioned this in Chapter 1). At that time, it was the largest corporate failure in history. WorldCom was the world's biggest telecoms carrier, and so held leases on a lot of the international cables that carry internet traffic. It held leases on rather too many of them in 2001, because there was a recession and many of the first wave of internet businesses had gone bust. It was paying $771 million in operating costs every year for this unused capacity ($1.13 billion in 2020 prices), waiting for demand to return.

The way WorldCom attempted to get through this difficulty was to redefine these leasing costs as 'construction in progress', as if it had a half-built factory and the money it was paying was investment. Under this definition, the leases magically became assets.

If you have taken a course in finance, you know this isn't even close to being a grey area, and external auditors – who later admitted they took the confusing numbers that WorldCom submitted on trust – should have spotted it. But no one queried the data. Whether it was because they didn't know or preferred not to ask, almost everyone in WorldCom thought the numbers that it reported were just fine (the whistle was eventually blown by the internal audit team).

We can assume that most of you are not going to uncover a billion-dollar fraud like this. But, when we unpack the dry definition of data governance, it suddenly becomes obvious that the problems are universal and fundamental – not just to the success of your mission but to the health of the entire business.

The WorldCom and Covid-19 examples tell us about three dimensions of data governance:

Data has a provenance. It is transparent where the data came from, and the description makes intuitive sense that fits with that provenance.

Data should be accurately described. The data is what it claims to be, and the same word is not used to describe different data in different parts of the business. The word 'revenue' is often the culprit – as an experiment, look at your internal reporting to see if different departments are describing revenue in the same way, and consistently through time. In data governance you have to elaborate on 'revenue'. It needs to be clear that this is gross revenue, needs a time period associated with it, and needs a currency unit. Without those qualifications it is open to misinterpretation, especially when people are desperate to use data and find a field called revenue and use it in a report without truly knowing its definition.

Data is consistent throughout the business. This means that if you and I are in different parts of the business and we look for data, we will retrieve the same values.

DATA PROVENANCE

Metadata that allows us to attribute an item of data to its source. This is used for financial reporting and auditing, for example, but it should be defined for all data that is used to influence business decision-making. Provenance means we can answer why, how, where, when and by which person or process the data has been produced, which means we can make informed decisions about the level of confidence we should put in it.

WorldCom failed all three tests: provenance, accuracy and consistency. The company collapsed partly because no one could work out where its numbers came from (that's why Arthur Andersen, their overstretched auditor, had ended up taking the numbers on trust). Clearly it had taken its liabilities and simply decided to describe them inaccurately as assets. And if you had spoken to different business units about revenues, they would have pulled data from different systems that didn't reconcile. This is what the internal audit team did, which eventually alerted them to the problem.

It's likely that every department in every business has some problem with data governance, but the problem is usually more 'Public Health England' than 'WorldCom'. It evolves out of people trying to get the job done, making decisions under time pressure, not updating definitions or systems, or not having the appropriate training. Reasonable people, in this context, can make bad decisions. Here are three examples based on real experience that you might relate to.

Data provenance in a decentralized business

Typically, a decentralized business has many small locations and reports its financial and other performance data every year by combining aggregated returns that were created manually in each location, using local staff. But if a regulatory issue arose, the board wouldn't know where the problem came from. Also, it struggles to compare performance between offices, because no consistent method was used to create the data. As a result, managers have little confidence in allocating resources between offices, and live with heightened regulatory and reputational risk.

Data accuracy on a complex invoice

The goods on a large supplier invoice have different depreciation rates. In accounts, someone tries to enter that in the system. But the accounting system won't allow many depreciation rates if there is one invoice number. The data entry person makes a decision: 'We can't depreciate our assets too fast, so just choose the slowest rate for all of them.'

Data accuracy and consistency conflict between departments

A company's salespeople book the deals on which their bonuses are calculated at the price each salesperson agrees with the customer. The director of sales proudly points out to the board that revenue numbers are 10 per cent up. The finance team can't understand it – according to revenue numbers, business is flat. Managers discover that what the salespeople record as revenue does not include the automatic discounts applied by marketing – understandable in this case, because bonuses are based on the price before discount.

The importance of accountability

There was a fourth implication of data governance in the Data Governance Institute's definition: someone must be accountable for data.

The governance problem, or at least its day-to-day manifestation, was probably apparent long before people started thinking about a data transformation. It's just that, in an analogue world, managers usually didn't think of it as primarily a data problem. It's possible that they just thought of it as one of those chronic problems that increases the cost of doing business, like staff sickness or a recession.

As we discussed in Chapter 1, the first manifestation of an approaching crisis of governance can be as simple as two people arguing in a meeting. It may be a nagging question about whether the reports that the business is turning out are a fit basis for decision-making that no one wants to say out loud. It might be a disconnect between apparent stellar operational performance and lacklustre financial results that gets kicked down the road once a quarter.

Most likely, someone in the business has their head in their hands, staring at a spreadsheet, thinking 'nothing seems to add up'. Equally likely, someone else in the business doesn't see what the problem is.

Someone must be accountable

Our project to improve data governance implies that a named person should be responsible for the provenance, description and consistency of every item of data in the business. Once you expose these problems, it's embarrassing and shows the inefficiencies. *We should be doing better*, people think. And there may be a widespread push to do better in future.

But someone has to be professionally responsible for data and, surprisingly often, I have discovered multinational companies in which it's no one's job. Perhaps managers make the assumption that because IT systems or other governed processes are generating the data, accountability is either not necessary or already assigned.

This is not only bad business, it flouts the General Data Protection Regulation. The UK's information commissioner states that:

> Accountability is not a box-ticking exercise. Being responsible for compliance with the UK GDPR means that you need to be proactive and organised about your approach to data protection, while demonstrating your compliance means that you must be able to evidence the steps you take to comply (Information Commissioner's Office, 2021).

DATA ACCOUNTABILITY

The principle that the governance of each item of data is someone's responsibility. This means that the person is also able to demonstrate the steps taken to ensure that the data is properly governed. Note that this is part of data regulation, as well as good business.

Lack of accountability can be accidental

A lack of accountability is often accidental, because the processes that create data can be informal, created on the fly, and constantly evolving. Look back at the problem of counting Covid-19 deaths. There was no international standard, there was no measure that was automatically 'correct'. There are methods that are more consistent with others, there are methods that are a good basis for decision-making, and there are statisticians doing their best. How highly those considerations are valued is not based only in technology or statistics, it is a management decision.

Lack of accountability can arise from conflict

Imposing governance on data may mean assigning accountability to one department over another. This can be seen as the power to 'punish' one or more business units. Consider the sales team that books revenue without a discount, and finance that considers revenue as net of discount. Neither will want to give ground. When one becomes the single source of truth, the other may feel (or be) disadvantaged. This problem is often solved by creating two fields – one gross revenue and the other net revenue (after discounts, credits and returns).

But someone has to be accountable, and it is not the CDO, or anyone in the data team. These are operational, management decisions, and it is impossible to answer questions of provenance, accuracy, or consistency asked by the executive team or a regulator without deep knowledge of the business. Accountability cannot be delegated exclusively to one business function, such as finance, as a lot of data is non-financial (employment or performance or customer data). There are multiple stakeholders who all want to impost their often-divergent views and risk perspectives, so this needs to be managed carefully.

Data stewards, data owners and the data executive

So there can be no effective accountability without either an accountability structure or a forum for resolving the conflicts that arise from it.

It's never too early to set up these structures. A lot of the early activity in a data transformation has an ad hoc nature to it: quick wins, learning by doing. You can manage much of it with the cooperation of interested individuals – some of whom are self-selecting because they come to see you – and the buy-in of senior management.

But from now on, the data team's interaction with the business needs accountability too. There has to be a way to make changes and decisions that are not based on heroism, inspiration, or personal relationships.

Two distinct roles come to mind.

Data stewards

On a day-to-day level, it is time to identify 'data stewards' in each department. Think of them as the people in each department who have been designated as fire marshals: they don't make the rules, but they have some expertise, they know more about the relevant policies than you do and will occasionally have a word with you. A data steward will be savvy enough to understand the data in that part of the organization. You can find out a lot, and resolve some simple problems, by going to the data steward, or helping data stewards to talk to each other.

DATA STEWARD

A (non-statutory, non-management) role for someone in a department who understands how it collects and uses data. The data steward acts as a two-way conduit of information between the data team and that part of the business.

Appointing a data steward will also help to build a relationship with the business because you will have someone who shares the responsibility for governance with your data team. The data stewards are often identified as the experts in a given system; they are the people who understand and end up fixing the data. The more the data governance team can do by dialogue and establishing common interests and benefits, rather than by the data team enforcing onerous rules, the better. A data steward will in all likelihood own the data in specific systems; for example, the accounting system will be managed by a data steward in the finance team. These are key roles to ensure that the data in these systems is accurate and not modified without an agreed business process.

Data owners

The data owners are the people who should be accountable for data in their area. Again, we are not talking about regulatory responsibilities here. This isn't a formal job title and there isn't one job in each department that maps to it, but it does imply that whoever is the data owner has decision-making responsibility.

DATA OWNER

A (non-statutory) role for someone in the business who has decision-making authority for each 'type' of data – people, financial, customer, and so on – and can act as an enabler for projects and process improvements in that area.

Don't think about this as delegating a representative from each business unit – think about it as having an owner for a type of data. So, you need someone responsible for all people data, and I've generally asked the director of HR to take that role. The owner for finance data is simple, and supplier data will probably be owned by procurement. Customer data's a bit more challenging, though, as it is shared between customer support, sales and marketing. But effectively someone has to 'own' the customer data.

There also needs to be a decision-making and reporting body, the data executive.

The data executive

The data owners, the CDO, and optionally the CIO will be represented on the data executive body.

This decision-making body does not need to be involved in the daily decision-making, but it is a forum that you will need every month to present your progress to, to get approval for what you do next and, in this context, to resolve disputes.

DATA EXECUTIVE

The decision-making and dispute resolution body on how to execute the data and analytics strategy, at which senior representatives of the business interact with the CDO. It should meet regularly, when the data team can update the business on the progress of the transformation. It reports to the board.

At its best, the data executive can be a way to cut through bureaucracy and drive for simplicity. For example, you need to establish a single source of truth in the organization, but this is easier said than done. While we can all agree that it's a good idea in the abstract, it implies the consolidation of many systems, and so can seem like a power grab by one department over another.

One way to get round this is to put all the systems that generate data for one of these responsibilities on a big diagram – for example, all the systems that generate people data, and how they interconnect (or, more likely, do not interconnect) – and use that as a way to encourage the other areas of responsibility to do the same.

You can then point out that there are 20 systems in that part of the business, and seven of them do the same thing. Each of the seven systems may deliver different data with the same definition, which is your priority at this point. But it also makes the case that having multiple sources of truth is very expensive as well as inefficient. They want to consolidate, so do you, and this is the place to kick off that project.

CASE STUDY
A failure of governance at Tesco

Challenge: A reporting scandal

In October 2016 I walked into an interim role for a company that one year previously had made the biggest loss in UK corporate history. Not only that, but it was facing an investigation by the Serious Fraud Office (SFO) which had been going on for two years, as well as multiple class action lawsuits from investors and potential criminal charges. One month before I arrived, three of its directors had been charged with fraud, and they risked prison sentences of up to 10 years. When the company contacted me, they said, 'We know you know about data, but do you have experience of governance and data quality?'

Analysis: Multiple governance failures

As scandals go, Tesco was a big one (Ruddick and Kollewe, 2017). And I was one of about 200 people who were simultaneously trying to fix it. There were IT people, finance people, consultants who specialized in business processes, and lots of lawyers.

Tesco was the runaway leader in the supermarket business that had grown from near-extinction in the 1980s to become arguably the UK's most successful global business a quarter of a century later. It had done this with a combination of thrift in head office, tough business decisions that squeezed every last piece of profit out of its relationships with suppliers, and carefully managed folksy charm ('every little helps').

It had also been the first supermarket in the UK to understand the value of data, using the information about its customers' shopping habits that it gleaned from the Clubcard loyalty card to drive growth and inform decisions. That alone should have made it a pleasure to be a part of Tesco's management team, if only for a year.

The adoration of management at Tesco collapsed on 22 October 2014. One month into his tenure, the CEO admitted that Tesco had artificially overstated its first-half profits by £263 million (later revised to £326 million). Shares dropped 11.5 per cent on the day, wiping £2 billion off the company's value. Investors immediately launched claims for damages, claiming that Tesco had given a false impression of its profitability, which had induced them to invest in the business.

You might ask yourself, why did a business that was responsible for £1 in every £7 spent in retail, operated 3,500 stores with 310,000 employees, need this? That was my question when I arrived.

In the time between finding that profits had been overstated and my arrival, the company had realized that its continuous rapid growth had created finance systems that were not adequate for a company of its size and complexity. And so it had been defined as a systems problem. But managers also realized that this was fundamentally a data problem: rewriting the finance applications but porting over the data risked simply moving the underlying problem from one set of computers to another.

Action: Deliver a structure for data governance

I was going to have to redesign, build, manage and cleanse profit and loss, sales revenue, and supplier costs data sets across the firm, and put in place the data governance, changes to business processes, and formal data management to make sure this could never happen again.

Outcome: A chastened recovery

This didn't make the headlines, because the dominant story was how Tesco was telling its suppliers to pay for promotions in advance, a distortion of its hard-driving management strategy that had often put noses out of joint in the industry even at the peak of its success. But the accounting systems allowed these practices to occur, and so when the accountants checked their records, the problem was hard to identify. When you looked at the data, it was much easier to spot. Under duress, the move to a governed financial system, with better lines of accountability, was completed under the cloud of potential sanctions. This was stressful for management and employees alike. In 2017 Tesco settled its case with the SFO and paid a fine. In 2020, it settled with its shareholders.

The problem at Tesco may have been, like the company itself, huge and multi-dimensional. But in many ways it was not atypical of any governance project. What can we learn about how to implement better governance?

Task: Implementing data governance

You might be thinking at this stage that this is not a short process. You're right, it isn't – and it will be a constant drumbeat in the background of all your company's transformative activities. The maturity model, Figure 7.1, shows the progress the CDO might expect to make, although the urgency and order of some of the milestones will vary, depending on the business. But there are some important steps along the way.

FIGURE 7.1 Data governance maturity model

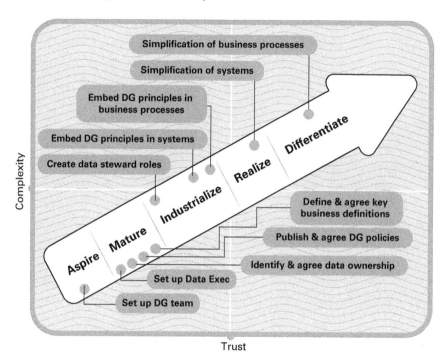

Where is the data?

This is often a surprisingly complex question to answer given the presence of shadow data resources, for example (see Chapter 1). But there are many technical tools to do this. Discovery can be automated and, at this point, we just need to know what data there is in the business.

How is the data created and stored?

Most businesses of any size are a collection of data silos. Tesco certainly was: the company had grown a number of businesses, with each headquartered in its own building. There was a very small and overstretched corporate office overseeing these processes, so very few people looked across the whole organization. When this occurs, each department creates and curates its own data.

Find provenance for data

This will be a challenge to diagnose, because we will have to untangle the processes that create aggregate numbers. There is little alternative to a thorough, item-by-item audit. This is not a task in which it is possible to cut corners, so the data team must define the most important data to investigate first.

Focus your energies

Most of what an investigation of this type discovers will be unexceptional. But focus on 10 or 15 items of data, and occasionally you will have eureka moments, and find the problem data that needs attention. This must be thorough and forensic, because your investigation must precipitate a decision on how to solve the problem.

Define the data's origination process

We can now rigorously identify who can enter the data, and how. What choices can they make? What, or who, is checking the data? Who owns that data? Identifying these processes and options can quickly reveal the manual or business process that needs to be upgraded. Often these processes are set up to fail, mostly because they present options on how to interpret and enter data to the wrong people.

Create a plan for today

This may take a few days or many months, but after this the business will be able to show provenance and transparency. At Tesco, we were constantly reminded that we were on the clock and had to deliver answers, because the investigation was proceeding and the regulators needed answers (Ruddick and Kollewe, 2017). The first step may be to be able to make a clear statement, based on transparent, consistent data. This applies whether the governance problem is hundreds of millions of pounds of overstated profits, or an argument over a pie chart between two heads of department. The plan for today effectively puts a stake in the ground: this is what we consider to be the truth. This may imply some frank discussions. After all, not everyone can be right.

Create incentives to retain governance

Work with management, or the data exec, to find ways to ensure that the governance principles put in place will persist, not just after the end of the project but after the end of your tenure. There is a reason that bad data entry and data handling habits developed. It might be that the bad habits are quicker, or easier, financially beneficial, or even just make people look better in a meeting. You may also solve many of these problems by automation, a topic that we will return to later.

Note that this last step is guaranteed to create conflict, not least because anyone attempting to develop governance may be told to mind their own business. A successful governance project is essential as a foundation for all the work we will do at later stages.

But any data team that is tasked with transforming a business cannot be investigating governance all the time. It needs to create an environment where trusted data is being created and used as part of the process of doing business, because then it is building on that trust. This goal is impossible to achieve without sponsorship from the highest levels of the business, and universal recognition of why it is necessary. I have recently heard a peer of mine refer to data governance as 'data excellence' (Monckton, 2021) on the basis that every business wants to have excellent data but may not be sure they want the data police all over the business. It's a 'little bit of spin' but if it gets the business bought in then it's surely worth it.

SUMMARY

- Data must have provenance. Everyone who uses it needs to know – or be able to find out – where the data comes from.

- Data must be accurate. That is, it must be agreed that it presents the truth, or as near to it as is possible to get. Note: in the world of data there can be only one truth.

- Governed data is consistent. It is created and reported in the same way throughout the business, and through time.

- Accountability is vital, or else improvements will be small and temporary. This also means that there must be incentives in place (or disincentives removed) to retain governance.

- The data executive is the forum to resolve the disputes that arise around governance, and to carry that message throughout the business.

References

The Data Governance Institute (2021) https://datagovernance.com (archived at https://perma.cc/Y85G-VQ2F)

Griffin, S (2020) Covid-19: England comes into line with rest of UK on recording deaths, *British Medical Journal*, **370**, p. 3220

Information Commissioner's Office (2021) Accountability and governance, www.ico.org.uk (archived at https://perma.cc/555S-3XYJ)

Loke, Y K and Heneghan, C (2020) Why no-one can ever recover from COVID-19 in England, Centre for Evidence-Based Medicine, https://www.cebm.net/covid-19/why-no-one-can-ever-recover-from-covid-19-in-england-a-statistical-anomaly/ (archived at https://perma.cc/6CDV-LMBN)

Monckton, N (2021) Head of Data Engineering & Science at Just Group plc refers to 'Data Excellence' rather than Data Governance to get the business to buy in.

Ruddick, G and Kollewe, J (2017) Tesco to pay £129m fine over accounting scandal, *Guardian*, https://www.theguardian.com/business/2017/mar/28/tesco-agrees-fine-serious-fraud-office-accounting-scandal (archived at https://perma.cc/PT3P-2347). In March 2017, halfway through my tenure, Tesco was able to reach an agreement with the SFO to pay £214 million in fines and compensation for investors. The deferred prosecution agreement committed Tesco to clean up its accounting and management processes (in effect, to do all the things that my work could help to make possible). The payment was made up of a £129 million fine, plus £85 million to compensate investors. 'We are a different business now,' said Dave Lewis, whose time as CEO had been dominated by the fraud.

Further reading

Ladley, J (2012) *Data Governance: How to design, deploy and sustain an effective data governance program*, Academic Press

08

Data quality

From day one, any data project must make data quality a priority. When data quality improves, so does its effectiveness and the trust put in it. Some improvements are swift, some extremely resource- and time-intensive.

KEY CONCEPTS

- Data quality
- Data quality leader

Introduction

Data quality is the yang to governance's yin. One of the most effective ways to raise data quality is, of course, to make sure it is governed correctly. But this is not sufficient. There are other aspects to data quality that go far beyond governance.

DATA QUALITY

A measure of how well data represents the real-world phenomena it describes for the purpose of the business. The four dimensions of quality are that it should be accurate, valid, accessible and timely.

It's not hard to find anecdotes about the problems caused by bad data quality. A decade ago, in his book *Information Quality Applied*, Larry English, an expert on the topic who is the president of a consultancy called Data Quality International, was already able to list 122 business failures due to poor-quality data that have become public (English, 2009). The combined cost to the businesses involved was $1.2 trillion.

For example, British Gas. It spent £300 million on an overhaul of its billing systems in 2006 that led to thousands of problems with overbilling; the systems might have been exemplary, but clearly the data in them was not. By 2007 the company was getting three times as many complaints as all the other gas and electricity suppliers in the UK put together. In 2007, managing director Phil Bentley described this as 'teething problems', which he said were being sorted out (*Daily Mirror*, 2007). This was far more than teething. The company wrote off £200 million in 2008 after customer complaints due to overcharging and lost a million of its 17 million customers. 'The majority of complaints over the six-month period – 15,456 – were about billing, said EnergyWatch, on subjects including incorrect meter readings and out-of-date account details' (BBC News, 2007).

These are big numbers, but this is just a tiny proportion of the loss from low data quality. The real impact of poor-quality data is a small leak of value from almost every organization that carries on over months and years. Poor-quality data means that a business will miss potential opportunities to grow, and when it finds an opportunity and tries to capitalize on it, results will be disappointing.

Producing information that is fit for purpose is not an end in itself. It is an integral part of your operational, performance, and governance mission. That's why the next step in our journey will be to begin actively managing data quality in all aspects of day-to-day business.

The risks of low-quality data

As British Gas's management would tell you, poor data quality slowly poisons a business. Without good data it cannot make good decisions (in fact, it may prevent anyone from making informed decisions at all). It means we miss opportunities – for example marketing will not know which customers are unhappy, or which customers are happy and might want to do more business. It might be possible to find the happy customers, but poor data means the marketers are unable to contact most of them.

The risks of poor-quality data go much deeper than this, though, and may even lead to prosecution, as with Tesco. It is important to know what your potential problems might be with data collection, and what can be put in place to reduce these risks.

Some examples include:

Poor GDPR compliance

Principle (d) of the General Data Protection Regulation (GDPR) states that 'you should take all reasonable steps to ensure the personal data you hold is not incorrect or misleading as to any matter of fact'. But there are other GDPR risks, even if the data is correct. Poor-quality data means that you may have multiple records, for example, of the same customer. When that customer asks to have information deleted, you delete one instance of that customer's data, or a subset of that data.

Poor statutory reporting

Regulated sectors need to report constantly on their compliance. If the data is of poor quality, these indicators of compliance may take a long time to compile, which can be a large cost to the business or a problem because when the business is not compliant, no one knows until it is too late. Worse, the indicators may be meaningless because the data is inadequate. This is a risk to the business (fines, reputation, even prosecution) or, even more important, to customers and patients.

Projects fail to deliver

Failure to achieve a return on investment is an obvious risk, both for the business and for your data project: managers blame the process of data analysis or data-driven marketing rather than the data itself. For example, it doesn't matter how sophisticated your marketing programme is: if you are targeting it at the wrong people because your data is poor, it will disappoint. Even if you achieve some progress, it can't be measured or reported, and so you don't even know when you are succeeding.

Small cohorts

If you have a limited set of customer data, then that data might be unbalanced and is unlikely to be representative of the larger population of your customers. But we still use it as a basis for decisions, or for warnings, or to measure improvements, because this is all we have. There's a real danger that the business will miss important trends or changes in parts of the business that are hard to measure, or just not measured well.

Complex or irrelevant performance indicators

The business is forced to report measures of success that are neither intuitive nor easy to compile, and so may be misunderstood or misreported.

The upside of high-quality data

The first step in a project to improve data quality is to convince the business that this is an important and useful goal. Often this is done with a scare story, which is probably a useful way to get attention (I just did that to you).

But it does not always tell you what to do. I described data quality as a 'yang', because that's the sunny side of the yin-yang duality. We can think of data quality as a creative process that uncovers the potential of data. But the British Gas example is a negative way to motivate a discussion about data quality.

The most important point we can make is that data quality is right in the middle of everything that will be achieved in the data transformation. Poor quality creates a constraint to the effectiveness of every business process, and improving the quality almost always eases that constraint. It's in the middle of every interaction with customers, suppliers and the general public. It informs every discussion about strategy and business planning.

It is not hard to show how these processes are failing. It may be that your colleagues are accustomed to underperforming: reports that don't reconcile, direct marketing with low impact. An example: in a recent job, I found that the CRM team was using its email database to try to acquire new customers, with low returns for any of its propositions.

An analysis of customer data quality showed one reason for what seemed like low response rates: the database contained email, post or SMS details for only 32 per cent of those customers – the marketing wasn't reaching the rest of them. We also discovered that by cleaning up the data we could contact an additional 35 per cent of our customers. Based on the experience that 4 per cent of customers contacted would take up our offer, the additional revenue generated by improving data quality alone would be £4 million per annum.

So, there is a good news story here, as long as we tackle the problem. Often, no one has recognized that this is an option. You may find that business units are playing the cards they have been dealt, assuming quite reasonably that this is the best their employer can do. You will probably find repeatedly that poor-quality data is lamented by the people who use it every day, but rarely challenged. There needs to be a cultural shift here to get people to want to change it and to create the business case for that.

So we can also flip the message from a warning of doom to an appeal to the potential of the project: discuss what we can do when we have high-quality data, that we cannot do today. There's a lot to talk about that can be mapped to your data and analytics strategy:

- **Create efficiency.** High-quality data supports continuous improvement, and more effective use of resources.

- **Eliminate errors.** Bad data causes bad performance, but also fraud and misallocation of resources. Who doesn't want to eliminate at least some of these persistent problems?

- **Improve your decisions.** Good data quality is the foundation of effective decision-making – not just performance management, but also helping business planning.

- **Better security.** High-quality data is less likely to lead to inappropriate or wrongful disclosure.

- **Quality of reporting.** The information you give to management, auditors, and regulators is of higher quality too.

- **Link and share.** Profitable insight from data relies on making connections between data sources, and easy sharing of data. This could be between departments, across different subsidiaries, or with your partners.

- **Honest appraisal.** How well are we doing? High-quality data means better, and more consistent benchmarking, either across the business or through time.

- **Meet legal obligations.** With high-quality data, compliance with the Data Protection Act 2018, the Freedom of Information Act 2000, the Computer Misuse Act 1990 and all other regulations is quicker, more likely to be automated, and less expensive.

- **Measure performance.** Vital indicators of performance are more likely to be accurate, meaning that interventions to get the business back on track can be early, quick, and effective.
- **Control budgets.** No nasty surprises, and more effective investigations of over-runs.

A limited data quality audit and fix is a useful quick win, as we discussed. Recall, however, the warning that quick wins may distract from strategic goals. Data quality projects are not usually in this category: they have the advantage that they can be quick wins that naturally expand into more strategic initiatives, for example by applying the same process to another department, another application, or another data field.

One example of a quick data quality win: I once worked for an organization that had a business unit dedicated to a product that was used almost universally by seniors. And, of course, the marketing department had a mailing list whose quality had never been investigated. When we did a simple test of the data that took a matter of minutes, we found that 20 per cent of the customers were, in fact, dead. Deceased customers have a very low response rate, and we were wasting £35,000 a year marketing products to them, in addition to the potential upset to their families.

Showing this as an example of how a little work has an immediate benefit opens the door to more strategic, ambitious projects. But our methodology will be the same.

You don't need to stare at data for long to realize that, at first sight, most data looks equally good.

There are some obvious tell-tales that your data is poor (big gaps in it, for example). But the most obvious test is to try to do something basic and useful with all the data. Poor quality means that either you can't get started, or you fail when you try. This is a useful way to start a conversation about quality, which will lead to an invitation to state clearly what 'success' would be instead.

There is no unified process or standard procedure that can easily be applied to ensure data quality. Each business unit will have different information requirements, which implies subtly different standards of quality. But although the information requirements vary, the need to receive good-quality data does not. So let's first consider the four principles of data quality.

The four principles of data quality

I like to focus on four data quality dimensions because they are the most relevant to a business. These are illustrated in Figure 8.1.

Availability of data

- **What this means.** Data users need data to make decisions, so make sure they have all the relevant data they need made available.
- **How you do it.** Relevant data and information should be accessible to users via online information systems, as soon as it becomes available. It should be presented using simple definitions that don't need an expert to understand them.
- **Practical considerations.** Your managers may be happier to broadcast good news and bury bad news. This is understandable, but bad for the business. In this case, a mark of data quality is that is shows both negatives and positives with equal visibility.
- **Example:** Having a data catalogue so anyone can find out what data is available and where to find it, perhaps in a data warehouse.

FIGURE 8.1 Data quality dimensions

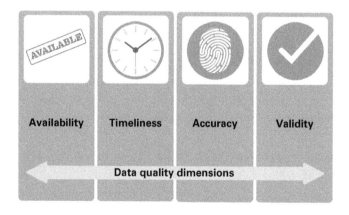

Timeliness of data

- **What this means.** Data should be captured as quickly as possible and be available quickly and frequently enough to support effective performance management.
- **How you do it.** You do this by streamlining processes, eliminating rekeying, integrating the processes that capture the data and those that report on it.
- **Practical considerations.** Timeliness does not mean the same thing as speed. Some data – for example for emergency response – needs to be captured quickly. But other processes are slower, and for them it might be more important to be accurate than to be speedy, because decisions require either more precision or more confidence in the numbers.
- **Example:** When a customer is browsing holidays on a website and it looks like they're about to leave and go elsewhere then that's the time to incentivize them to book now with a discount or offer. If you take too long to calculate the offer they will have left your site and be buying from your competitor. Timeliness is key; more on this when we discuss data architecture in Chapter 9.

Accuracy of data

- **What this means.** Data needs to be correct, appropriately precise for its intended purposes, and presented clearly in the appropriate level of detail. Ideally, to achieve this, it should respect the discipline of COUNT, which stands for 'Collect Once, Use Numerous Times'. Use numerous times also means you need to consider that it will need to be used downstream, not just for the task in hand.
- **How you do it.** Accuracy is most likely to be achieved if you capture data as close to the point of service delivery as possible. The result: data that is consistent is more likely to reflect the real-world process that generates it, and so can be used with higher confidence when you make decisions.
- **Practical considerations.** This must be balanced with the importance of the uses for the data, and the costs and effort of collecting it. For example, if you need to collect data quickly, the methods you use mean there's a trade-off in how accurate you can be. It's important that the people who will use this data internally know about these compromises, so they don't assume that accuracy is greater than it is.

- **Example:** Customer age is critical for some businesses (ie age 18 or over) and so this data needs to be stored with a date of birth and then calculated to be accurate.

Validity of data

- **What this means.** Some data may need to be recorded and reported in ways that comply with compliance requirements, or to match internal standards or definitions.
- **How you do it.** Much of this will come directly from your data governance policies. As we have seen, quality and governance co-exist. What matters is that you know why you are collecting data and can account for what you are collecting against a fixed set of obligations.
- **Practical considerations.** Different departments or offices may have different ideas of how to collect or capture the same data. When you capture data or information, it is important to also capture the way in which it was acquired, for example the method, document, report, website or system.
- **Example:** Postcode needs to be in a valid format XXYY YXX and yet sometimes forms for capturing address are a little confusing and you'd be surprised how often country and town appear in the postcode field. Which is why many firms use smart lookup fields to capture valid data.

A data quality strategy

The last part in the process of planning what to do about data quality in your business is to create a strategy. This is important because decisions on which data to capture or to prioritize will change in different contexts. There will also be different opinions depending on the geographical location, or the business unit inside your company. So it may be important to create systems that ensure data quality (checks, validation of fields, automation, redesign of surveys) when a group performs data capture in every location, even when that is considered over the top by the people who are tasked to capture or enter that data. It may be important at another time in a downstream process.

For example, the sales team might see a need to capture only the data that they need to make the sale, at that moment. However, marketing, post-sales support, compliance or analytics have more requirements than just those at the time of sale, and the sales process itself is by far the most convenient time for the sales team to get that data.

There are limits to what any process can achieve. One constraint is that we resist the temptation (at least for us data people) to capture as much data as possible every time we meet the customer, especially when there are pressures to just 'get the deal done'. This data collection ordeal quickly becomes tedious for everyone involved, leading to skipped fields, generic responses, and low-quality data.

Regulation may also limit what we can capture. Put simply, GDPR principles dictate that data can only be collected and stored if it is relevant at that time. In some parts of the world, regulation might permit the collection of data, but the local culture would consider it inappropriate. A strategy will take account of these limits and make it clear what is achievable. All this, and more, needs to be decided in advance, with consensus, and communicated. If not, you will set yourself impossible goals that cost too much, take too long, or make enemies.

Data quality is everyone's business. Your data quality team should work with everyone in the business. The team can help them, educate them and occasionally even police them, but it cannot do the job of creating data to a standard of quality for them. Unless the entire business understands the importance of (for example) a correctly spelled name, you will miss your targets, and the business will continue to underperform.

Your strategy has to create a baseline and a target: where you are now, where you want to be. We need not only to aspire to improve but also to measure quality.

Task: Setting a baseline and a target

It is extremely important to measure data quality before you try to improve it using practical measures. There's no need to focus on every item of data, because it is likely that you have plenty to do to increase the quality of the data that is used every day. Focus on the critical data items. Once it is at your target level of quality, you can work on improving the quality of other customer-related data that attaches to it.

If you're talking about customer data, for example, that would be the name, address, email address, and telephone number. That data will uniquely identify any customer. Customer data makes it easy to tell the difference between good- and bad-quality data, for example by examining the format, checking it for consistency, looking for holes in the data, or comparing it to easily available external sources such as commercial address databases. Figure 8.2 shows some examples of the challenges here.

FIGURE 8.2 Customer data quality examples

Title
Prin
Prof
Professor
Q
Miss
,Mr
mrs

Forename
Smith
K.T.
M.Atrta
John Paul
J
James & Julie

Surname
Pickford999
6cmp
Mo0rrissey
Vmbgopst2
Test224

Titles mistyped, forename not standard and sometimes surname used instead, surnames incorrect. All of these prevent automation of letters and emails and lead to duplication of name 'not found' because it's misspelt.

Address postcode
NN1 4QT,5
NN1 4PW, 46
NN1 4LU,25
NN1 4LQ,9
NN1 4LJ,51
NN1 4JS,106
NN1 2HS,218
NN1 2HL,

Postcodes unusable due to incorrect formatting and invalid characters.

Home phone no
(02392) 646046
(01241) 411132
(01902) 561 605
0181 998 7454
+447466771054
0151-4244331
01922-443-598

Phone numbers unusable due to incorrect formatting and invalid characters.

These examples are anonymized, but from real databases. This is what is stopping you getting more value from your data.

Mobile phone no
N/A
Unknown
07985242290
07716 863335
0790 583 0635
07968-767008
+447833457070
7825577622

Populated mobile phones UK standard 11/10-digit formats including spaces, hyphens, brackets and +44 prefixes. These errors prevent use in auto dialling tools.

Email
master44.msn.com
4mshan@hotmial.co.uk
+reva25b@icloud.com
JWBROWN45@GMAIL.COM

Inconsistencies in emails, containing special characters outside the valid range eg (underscores, hyphens, +, no @ symbol, switched order of characters). These issues render emails unusable.

Dat of birth	Years
2006-07-06	16
1901-25-01	121
2006-01-25	Error!

Months and days switched, ages out of viable range, or customer still on database after death.

Fixing the fundamental data first is usually the best route. Until this critical data is at the right level of quality, you would be effectively building on sand by creating fresh data about people when you don't know who or where they are, or how to contact them to find out.

HOW TO MEASURE: DATA QUALITY IMPROVEMENT

Once you have a baseline, think of data quality as a ladder, and your improvement process as a way to climb that ladder: in the table below I have graded it from 3 to 1, in each of our four dimensions. If the score is 3, the data is of high quality. If it is 1, then it is of low quality. The table helps to express what that means in terms that you can observe throughout the business and communicate easily. It also helps to make comparisons, for example to identify parts of the business that have the worst problems.

As an exercise, you can try to replicate this table but to map it specifically to your business goals and challenges (for example, increase response rates on marketing campaigns). Be precise and use concrete tests of quality wherever you can. For example, 'rapid reporting' is not a standard you can either pass or fail. But an aspiration of one week for financial reporting rather than the current one month, for example, is a useful measurement and a tangible target.

This will expose where the improvements need to be focused, and also give you an insight into what is going wrong in the way that the business captures this data.

There's nothing sacred about this three-point scale. Use whatever scale works for you. The test of what is meaningful would be that the definition made sense, and was recognizable, to someone who worked regularly with the data. What matters is that everyone in the business knows:

- what the current score is, and how to spot it;
- how that score negatively affects how they do their job;
- the impact of this score for their colleagues and the business;
- what actions they must take to get to the next level;
- how achieving that goal will improve how they do their work, and benefit those around them.

So, let's look at some examples of projects that your data quality team can use to achieve these improvements, and how you might measure them.

Quality score	Accuracy	Validity	Timeliness	Accessibility
3	• Your data is of sufficient accuracy to meet the needs of all users. • Any reported changes are within statistical confidence intervals for the data set being reported.	• Data is recorded and reported consistently and accurately under specific calculation rules or definitions. • Data source metadata captured where available. • The data is recognized by users as a measure of success.	• Data is available quickly and frequently enough to allow rapid intervention or corrective action by frontline staff/ management.	• Data is accessible to users online in near-real time. • Data is presented using easy-to-understand definitions or descriptions. • Data is available and accessible if stakeholders want to find new ways to leverage it.
2	• The data is sufficient to meet the needs of key users. • There are still data gaps or statistical viability areas that need to be addressed.	• Data is reported under a specific theme, but there is no formal guidance on definition or calculation.	• The data is produced promptly to allow management to respond to problems. • Delays sometimes reduce the usefulness of the data.	• Data is accessible to some stakeholders straightaway but many others experience delays. • Data is often presented in a format that requires analysis to understand improvement. • Definitions are understandable to most people in the company, with support from the data team.
1	• It is widely known that the data is inaccurate. • The data is not trusted by the company or its partners as a basis for decision-making. • The data is ignored, or not used, in meetings.	• There is no formal guidance on the definition or calculation of data. • Comparative information is not used or sources are rarely referenced. • Data is not valued by stakeholders.	• Data is released so late that it is not useful for anything other than looking back at what actually happened.	• Data is difficult/impossible to get hold of outside formal reporting periods. • Data has complex definitions. • Stakeholders cannot understand how data relates to improvement or delivery targets.

Task: Build a data quality team

Who will do all of this? The CDO's role is to lead the conversation that sets the goals, first with the data team in general, so they are signed off by leaders in the business, then with the company as a whole, so they know that change is coming.

This is a joint responsibility, and the data quality team needs to help people in the business understand their role, their importance to the success of the project, and what they should be doing differently. Also, you need that team to measure and report success. (It would be a strange data quality programme that didn't report with accuracy, validity, timeliness and accessibility how successful it was.)

Select a data quality leader

This will be someone who understands thoroughly how to get the best out of the data that the business holds, whether that means improving it, extending it, or augmenting it. This is a detail-oriented role, but it isn't about software or systems, it's solely about looking at the data we can extract from those systems. The data quality leader will need to understand your business processes, how to drill into the data problems you uncover, and how to communicate with the business – both up and down – about that. The data quality leader will be responsible for reporting on which projects are running and how well they are doing; with the help of the data team, the rest of the business can improve quality and timeliness. The data quality leader should be a direct report of the CDO.

Create a data quality improvement team

The data quality improvement team's job is to identify the specific challenges that are damaging data quality, and to extract and analyse the statistics on data quality. The word 'improvement' is key here. You rarely see the underlying problems until you dive deep into the databases. For people who enjoy this work, it is an interesting detective story, and there are plenty of clues. We can learn a lot by running ad hoc queries that simulate the things the business might want to do to see what does – and doesn't – come back. For example, try investigating any data that stores phone numbers that the contact centre could use. You will probably learn that there are far more numbers stored in the data than can be used, but the formatting is inconsistent. The team needs to standardize the phone numbers so that they have the same use of spaces, consistent dialling codes, and no letters or full stops that would stop the systems from recognizing them. This is often not difficult work, but it is extremely productive.

DATA QUALITY LEADER

The person within the data team tasked with analysing the data in the business, evaluating its quality, and making recommendations on how to create improvements. The role straddles technical improvements (for example, removing duplicates) and process improvements (for example, improving the ways in which data is acquired and entered). The leader also reports on improvements in quality.

Your data quality team needs to balance the writing of a lot of SQL queries and reports, with reporting to the data exec every month or every quarter about the precise improvements in the quality of your data, based on what the team members have discovered.

Task: Improving data quality in the short term

FIGURE 8.3 Data quality maturity model

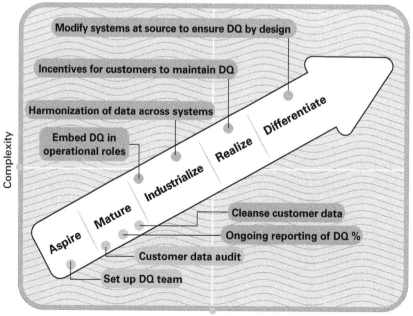

As with data governance, solving quality problems will be an ongoing process, and one that will pay off at every stage of the data transformation. We can think of performing different data quality activities at different stages of that process. In Figure 8.3, I have mapped out what I think is a realistic maturity model to measure your progress.

This isn't a rule: in some cases, your business will need faster action on data quality (for example when regulation, criminal liability or safety is important). Think of this maturity model as a baseline. If you are behind the maturity curve, it will limit your ability to achieve the improvements that you want to make in each wave.

Now that you have a team, the first task is to assign a score to measure its quality.

An internal data quality audit

Think of your stock of data as an asset. You are improving its quality using the specific metrics that you have defined in either the three-point scale above, or through your own method.

This data is also important because it is a driver of profitability. Improving it can quickly lead to better returns on existing business processes, a simple measure of success that can help drive attention to the project and stop it becoming a chore. It also means you have evidence to argue for the resources you need. It may be helpful in uncovering good ideas that will help boost quality or motivate data quality initiatives.

Reporting on quality improvement can be done using a simple dashboard, because the difference between success and failure is easy to understand. See the examples in Figure 8.2 above. A dashboard, which we will deal with in Chapter 10, is a useful device because it communicates success.

For the dashboard, pick a few of the most important measures: the percentage of incomplete records, for example. As the process proceeds, this measure will consistently improve. Sharing that data with the data exec, and with the people who use the data, is a way to demonstrate that you are making progress. A simple traffic-light measure for data fields would be appropriate, for example red for fields with less than 40 per cent correct data, amber for 40 to 70 per cent, and green for greater than 70 per cent. When setting the targets it's important to make them a stretch but achievable.

An external data quality audit

You can also get a data audit from an external supplier. This is a larger investment, but it can be extremely powerful. If customers don't respond to you, does this mean that they are no longer at the same address, not replying, or that they have passed away? External data will help answer this question.

Data cleansing

This, as previously noted in this chapter, is a quick fix, but in my experience a surprisingly powerful one. Taking out obvious typing or cut-and-paste errors (there's a comma at the end of this phone number) is swift and creates instant value. It's basic data hygiene, but the data is all the better for it. A couple of days' work can have a noticeable impact.

With the ability to contact customers, there's huge potential for improving data. Using that permission and a correct address or a phone number, we can capture an email, and perhaps some preferences on how the customer wants to be contacted, or any relevant details. This is dogged, tactical work. But imagine that a loyal customer has been contacted by you over a period of years, offering inappropriate products, with a name spelled incorrectly. They might be relieved to find that you're actually engaging.

Task: Improving data quality in the long term

The short term will fix the data that you have, but your business is constantly creating new data. There is an overriding reason that your data is of poor quality: the processes that create it are of poor quality too.

There are two broad categories here that describe the right-hand side of the maturity model. Note that this assumes trust – that is, we are empowering employees and staff to be custodians of data quality. To do this, it is important that we help them to help themselves.

Employees (or customers) are not incentivized or trained adequately

If either group creates or captures the data in the first place, for example in a retail location, maybe they don't know how it's going to be used downstream and so they don't know why they are filling in forms. The data they are asked to capture or provide might be considered an inconvenience. No one explains to them that in six months from today, someone that they will never meet is going to use that data to improve delivery routes or change pricing, which not only helps the customers and improves profits, but makes employees' jobs easier too.

Ensuring data quality is rarely formalized as part of someone's job description, or something that is recognized as an achievement. If someone captures a customer's phone number or (much more complicated) an email address over the phone, the accuracy of what they type will not be tested until later, and there's no direct incentive for them to get it right.

As organizations go through their data transformations, I have found that employees are often given more data capture tasks without explanation. These may involve complex processes that are easy to get wrong if not done with care. The lack of communication or appreciation means that the business just captures more poor-quality data. Managers congratulate themselves, thinking they are doing a good thing for the business. If the data is of poor quality, the opposite is likely to be true.

This isn't just about the task. Communication about the big picture – why high-quality data is the foundation of every future activity – is also important. For example, machine learning and artificial intelligence need to be trained on existing data and their success is based on the quality of the data it rests on. But as well as creating better processes to reduce rekeying and similar errors, it may also be important to incentivize more of the company to benefit from the outcome of good data. You can't do this directly, but you can demonstrate why there is a net benefit.

Higher-quality acquisition processes will outlive you and be a permanent engine of improvement for the business. We will be looking at how to achieve some of these growth goals later in the book, particularly when we discuss automation.

Data is created manually, with errors

The data you hold is often degraded by being retyped from forms, or from phone calls. You might not suffer a data error like that of Deutsche Bank, which accidentally transferred $35 billion to an outside account in 2018 (Canny, 2018), but the problem with rekeying errors is that you *don't notice them* at the time.

There are simple fixes that you can put in place: more data validation when it is entered, or address lookups using postcodes. You can also push more of this to the customer: if they have an incentive to enter their own data, then they are likely to do it with care (of course, if you simply give them the job, with no reward, the opposite may occur).

SUMMARY

- Poor data quality can arise from bad governance, but improving governance is not sufficient to improve the quality of your data. It needs its own project.

- The costs of poor-quality data may not be apparent, but they are real. They combine underperformance and elevated risk. You can demonstrate the former with cheap, quick projects, especially through marketing.

- When looking for attention and budget, it is often more effective to sell the positive benefits of data quality internally: what can be achieved with high-quality data that is currently not possible.

- Data quality has four dimensions: accuracy, validity, timeliness, and accessibility. You should measure your baseline in all four and use concrete milestones and dashboards to measure improvement.

- There are short-term fixes to clean up existing data, but long-term improvement will require changes to data acquisition processes and incentives.

References

BBC News (2007) Surge in British Gas complaints, http://news.bbc.co.uk/1/hi/business/6573929.stm (archived at https://perma.cc/ZCG5-EG24)

Canny, W (2018) Deutsche Bank's bad news gets worse with $35 billion flub, *Bloomberg*, 19 April, https://www.bloomberg.com/news/articles/2018-04-19/deutsche-bank-flub-said-to-send-35-billion-briefly-out-the-door (archived at https://perma.cc/69VL-V7TP)

Daily Mirror (2007) HOT AIR. Gas boss: Bill fiasco is 'teething problem', 21 April

English, L (2009) *Information Quality Applied: Best practices for improving business information, processes and systems*, Wiley

Further reading

Parkinson, J (2016) *The Data Quality Blueprint: A comprehensive step by step guide*, Holifast

09

A single customer view

Good quality data allows you to know more about each customer, or about your customers' behaviour in general. Creating a single view of your customers takes that a stage further. It is a powerful initiative with transformative revenue generating, risk reduction, and customer satisfaction potential. It repositions the data team to the front and centre of the business, and is a key foundation of your data science capabilities.

KEY CONCEPTS

- Single customer view (SCV)
- Data model
- Single supplier view
- Single employee view
- Single product view
- Data architecture
- Golden ID

Introduction

In any business the customer is king. They are the primary reason your business exists. Having the correct information is important but the challenge for most businesses is that information on their customers resides in different systems. Each system has its own unique view of the customer. Bring those views together and you'll find inconsistencies in data and discover broken business processes. These result in a plethora of missed opportunities and poor customer experiences. It's also worth mentioning that different parts of the organization see an SCV in different ways. Marketing will see it as a way of providing consistent messages to the customer across all channels; data science will see it as a key enabler for building accurate models; risk and compliance will see it as a way of reducing and managing risk. The danger is that all stakeholders have a view of it, but they are just that: stakeholders. The SCV needs to meet the needs of the whole organization, but more importantly the needs of the customer.

During 2019/20, accelerated by the disruption of Covid-19, companies were forced to rethink how they deal with their customers. Many were delighted to find that customers quickly learned how to use technology like chatbots or self-service, and switched from coming into stores to buying online. But, having created omnichannel ways to communicate, a common failing is not to tie them together so that all customer communications have a 360-degree view of the customer. Organizations that attempt to migrate customers to digital channels before they are fully ready can trigger the 'boomerang effect', in which customers (with a complaint) can keep coming back to a company multiple times in an effort to resolve a problem. For those customers, the cost of each customer query has actually gone up.

The problem is often, unsurprisingly, a lack of integration between the channels. Customers find that different parts of the business have different information on them. Some of that is because the services are new, or experimental. But much of it is due to the inconsistencies of data capture in different systems at different times.

A survey on the correlation between customer experience (CX) and business growth (Businesswire, 2020) made the following findings:

- Eighty-five percent of companies surveyed have more data on their customers than two years ago; however, less than one-third (29 per cent) have high confidence in data quality.

- Only half (51 per cent) of companies surveyed can use this data to personalize and customize interactions and less than half (46 per cent) can orchestrate actions in real time.

- Decision-makers surveyed indicated that the top challenges of delivering a good CX include the existence of internal silos (38 per cent).

- Only 57 per cent of executives agree that the CX budget has been spread across various departments to create a more integrated CX plan.

All of these points argue for the development of an SCV, delivered to service the needs of the whole organization, not run in silos. We all experience the irritation of an organization's spotty knowledge about us, whether a retailer, a utility, a bank, or the government; being passed to operators on the phone who ask the same questions over and over again or being told that another office is dealing with that particular matter. But, in business, we also do this to our own customers. There's really no excuse. Creating a unified record for each person who deals with our business is one of the greatest gifts we can give to both the customer and the CEO.

What is a single customer view?

Because it is the focus of this chapter, let's repeat the definition of the SCV from Chapter 1.

SINGLE CUSTOMER VIEW (SCV)

The process of collecting data from disparate data sources, then matching and merging it to form a single, accurate, up-to-date record for each customer. It is also known as a 'golden ID' or '360-degree customer view'.

An SCV is not one thing, it is a combination of several components. Figure 9.1 gives a good overview of the SCV, showing the components described below.

Customer data sources

There will be many sources of customer data. It's not uncommon for each product, service, region and brand to have its own system. Acquisitions are a problem because the number of systems grows exponentially as they are rarely rationalized. On top of that you will have another layer of finance systems, sales systems, customer service systems, and multiple marketing systems. All of these will contain a slice of your customer data. We need to think about customer contact details, customer characteristics, preferences, purchase history, invoices, complaints, visits to our website/shops, access times, favourite products, brands used, channels used, our contacts with

FIGURE 9.1 Overview of single customer view

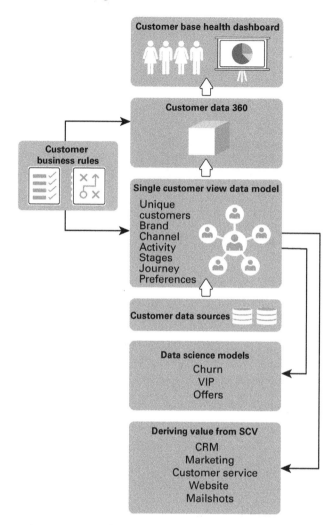

them, and their take-up of our offers. If you think this sounds complicated then I'd agree. It's one of the toughest challenges we'll face.

SCV data model

We need to develop a data model (see definition below) to enable us to capture the data needs of all stakeholders to see what their view of a customer looks like. Initially we might run this as a workshop with all stakeholders present. We'll need to explain what the model is and why it's so important; they may never have seen one before. Try not to limit the discussions to their current requirements, and also try to capture their future requirements. Don't worry too much, as we'll be using business language; the technical translation is done later. Try to capture as much information as you can but don't worry about capturing everything; models are designed so you can extend them later. Part of the value of this workshop is that we identify all the differences of opinions between departments and start to resolve them. If we don't deal with this here then they will not trust the data when it's delivered. This process helps us generate trust and understanding and helps the business take more ownership of its data challenges.

We also need to consider things from the perspective of our customer. We are creating a powerful view of them and we need someone who represents their views, normally the Data Privacy Officer and someone from the compliance team, plus someone from our data ethics team, to ensure that we are not using their data unethically. Where necessary we get their permission to store data this way, or where we have two sets of data about them we verify which one is correct. We touched on this in Chapter 4.

DATA MODEL

A data model is a visual representation and design of [the] data [in your organization], showing business components and the data elements within them, the relationships among these data elements, and the data's formats and attributes.

Customer data 360

This is the data repository that stores the data captured from the data sources in the same structure as the data model, from which data will be extracted to feed reports, dashboards, data science, etc. Typically this will be a combination of real-time data, snapshot data (such as end of day, end of month) and data that is relatively static (such as customer name and address), but it becomes increasingly valuable when you backload historical data so you can see changes over time. Beware at this point: we have created something extremely valuable to our business, but also potentially to someone who wants to steal our customers. We'll touch on the risk management issues later on in Chapter 11. When we created our data model it is likely that we will have identified data that we want but don't currently have. This is good news, but we need to act on it. The model remains as we want the data to be, but we also need to focus on sourcing the missing data.

One of the 'problems' of creating an SCV is that when you combine customer records it looks like your total number of customers has reduced. That's because previously we might have counted the number of customers in system A and added them to the number of customers in system B to give us a total number of customers. However, an SCV gives us one ID per customer, known as the Golden ID, and this rationalizes the total number of 'unique' customers. But this is good news. 'Many companies have expected to save more than 40% through reducing live contacts. Yet companies that take this approach often see their customer interactions increase rather than decline,' says a research article published by McKinsey (Amar et al, 2019).

GOLDEN ID

The field in an SCV that identifies the customer. It is created by stitching the customer records together. The customer can have other identifiers in the data that has been carried over from other databases, but those IDs must be uniquely linked to the Golden ID. A Golden ID avoids creating duplicate records.

Customer business rules

Customer organization and hierarchies are generally more complex than we'd wish them to be. Imagine a business customer who has multiple brands, branches, and people with different responsibilities we interact with. From a pricing perspective they'll want to negotiate group discounts across their whole business, but perhaps each region has its own billing system in different currencies and perhaps our sales contacts speak to people based on products. Part of this is the customer hierarchy: showing the structure of our customers, in itself a valuable piece of information. All of this needs to be linked to business rules so that it makes sense not only to us but more importantly to the customer. This is where we start to create that good customer experience we mentioned in the survey at the start of the chapter.

Customer base health dashboard

An SCV is invisible. It is a set of data that resides in a repository, and although we have a data model to show us the design, we need to see the reality. That's why I'd advise a dashboard that does nothing more than give you a view of your customers so you can see them in any prescribed way – by product, history, region, brand, gender, segments, etc. Once you create this you'll be surprised how useful it is. All of a sudden you can ask that infamous question – 'how many customers do we have?' In fact you'll find that when you do your annual report, website or requests for information from prospective customers, you get lots of valuable information. But those are instances in time – what makes it incredibly valuable is when you add history and can see trends over time. Please refer to Figure 10.1 in Chapter 10, the example SCV dashboard, which illustrates some of what I've discussed here.

Data science models

The most valuable and common data science models are customer focused. They include models to predict when customers might churn, and opportunities for cross-sell and upsell, which are wholly dependent on the data we will build in the SCV. These models should all be based on the output of an SCV. That's not to say they cannot be built without one, but the data engineering required to build the models will duplicate and be less reliable than an SCV. If you already have these models you'll need to plan to migrate them to the SCV so they are using the same customer data as the rest of the organization. The SCV will also provide them with richer, more accurate data sets.

Deriving value from an SCV

Most value from an SCV will come from day-to-day operational activities with the customer. These include marketing, sales (using the CRM system), customer service and your website. Ensuring that these solutions all have access to the latest version of customer data is critical. For example, as a customer of a bank we now expect to go to one website to access the information from all our accounts in one place. This is a great example of an SCV in action, but in reality not all banks can do it yet, and few companies can do it well, if at all. One way that we get value from the SCV, having collected and rationalized key customer data, is to ensure it is propagated back to the source systems so that the operational activities are using the better-quality, consistent data. One example might be that we check the dates of the customer address field and ensure that the latest version, as long as it's a validated data source, is then fed to all the other systems so that the customer only needs to change their address in one place.

The SCV is, in short, an engine for success and something that no customer-facing business can do without.

CASE STUDY
The SCV at a gambling company

Challenge: Multiple brands, overlapping customer bases

In 2016, a gambling company had grown and diversified across multiple brands – some online, some not. So customers had many touchpoints: email, direct mail, live chat, telephone, online forms, in-person conversations. Customers expected the company to know about their entire experience with them. But they didn't: different channels were run by different teams, with different priorities. A valuable customer in one channel was not valuable in another. As a business that involved gambling, this also presented the challenge of how they could manage problem gamblers whose activity on each channel did not raise a red flag – but aggregated it would.

Analysis: Gains from data quality

During the drive for an SCV, a data quality improvement plan was submitted. In some of the company's businesses almost 9 per cent of the customer records were duplicates. Around a third of the records in the digital businesses had incomplete customer data. Fixing a significant number of these helped the SCV outperform its targets.

Action: A Golden ID with incremental effectiveness

The company's SCV would store a Golden ID, contact details, brand activity, customer activity, customer preferences, customer journey stages, segmentation, and responsible gambling data. It was built in stages:

Version 0: Cleaning and de-duping of accounts.

Version 1: CRM automation, multi-channel customer service, and crucial metrics.

Version 2: Wider metrics, customer journey mapping and customer preferences.

Outcome: A powerful driver of all customer-facing activity

SCVs provide the data for customer dashboards. For the data scientists, this provides the high-quality data needed to analyse customer churn, to recognize VIP customers or potential problem gamblers. And for the rest of the business, it is the engine behind customer relationship management, marketing and customer service.

Benefits of the SCV

We've touched on some of the benefits of the SCV but there are so many, and as this is an area that requires investment these benefits need to be included in your business case. They fall broadly into two categories: benefits for the customer and benefits for your business. These are illustrated in Figure 9.2.

Benefits to our business

I'd start with more effective and personalized communications; because we know more about the customer, the more our communications are relevant, and the more loyal they will be. Based on the data we can now see what products they buy and how often so we can recommend products that are complementary; we can spot from their buying behaviour any changes that indicate they might churn (leave us) and then try to retain them. Bearing in mind that it costs five times as much to acquire new customers as to keep existing ones (Wertz, 2018). These are some of the key benefits. I'd summarize by saying that in Chapter 3, I mentioned the periodic table and identified 36 ways that data can help you generate more revenue, as well as ways to decrease costs. Many of these are underpinned by the SCV.

Benefits to the customer

Some of the benefits to the customer are the same as benefits to our business – that makes them a win win! The primary one is a better experience. In addition to that I'd suggest that when we protect customers' interests

FIGURE 9.2 Single customer view benefits

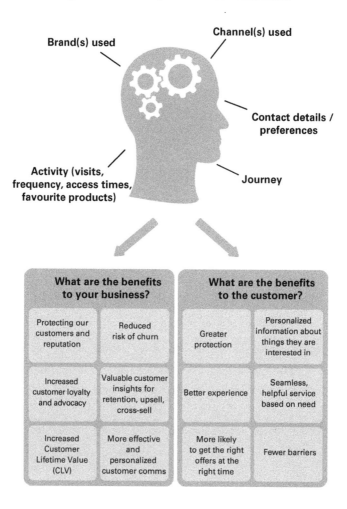

(and data) they will trust us more. The fewer barriers there are to doing business with us because everything is one place and consistent, the better. Again, I'll refer you to the periodic table in Chapter 3.

Other single views

Whilst the single customer view is critical I would suggest that when you've built that you can use the skills, architecture and capabilities to build a single supplier view, a single employee view, and a single product view. The principle is the same. The benefits are also significant. In Chapter 13 we discuss scaling and this is another great example of how you can build one thing, SCV, and then scale across other parts of your business.

Single supplier view

Often many parts of an organization will contract with a supplier, but in different ways. A single supplier view will enable you to review where you spend your money across products, identifying opportunities for reductions in cost through the rationalization of suppliers. It will enable you to look at the contracts for those suppliers and the invoices, so you can ensure that you only have invoices from approved suppliers. You can spot buying trends, which helps with budget management, and fraud – for example when you are invoiced for services or products from a supplier with whom you have no contract. The consolidation of spend with one supplier will enable you to spot supply risks, etc. Procurement and finance will significantly benefit from the single supplier view – again, I'll refer you to the periodic table in Chapter 3.

SINGLE SUPPLIER VIEW (SSV)

The process of collecting data from disparate data sources, then matching and merging it to form a single, accurate, up-to-date record for each supplier. It is also known as a '360-degree supplier view'.

Single employee view

This will give you a 360-degree view of an employee, combining data across the different systems, such as pay, benefits, expenses, training needs, performance, sickness and holidays, and skills. Linking these together is, in my experience, rarely done because HR is at the bottom of the prioritization, but it does give a much more rounded view of employees when making decisions on major events such as promotions, transfers, redundancies, etc. Human Resources will benefit significantly from the single employee view.

> **SINGLE EMPLOYEE VIEW**
>
> The process of collecting data from disparate data sources, then matching and merging it to form a single, accurate, up-to-date record for each employee.

Single product view

This will give you a view of products, which would include sales, product development, pricing, support costs, customer feedback, competition, etc. If you are a product-based company then it's an incredibly valuable data set. Product development, operations and marketing will all benefit directly from the single product view.

> **SINGLE PRODUCT VIEW**
>
> The process of collecting data from disparate data sources, then matching and merging it to form a single, accurate, up-to-date record for each product.

How do you build an SCV?

The creation of a single customer view is underpinned by data governance, data quality (see the first finding in the Businesswire survey towards the start of this chapter) as well as the data architecture required to bring the disparate data sets together. Bringing together all the information about each customer into a single repository interaction is no small technical task.

Data governance

The SCV needs to be underpinned by the key principles of data governance we described in Chapter 7: data provenance (we know where the data came from), data should be accurately described, and should be consistent across the business. When you design an SCV the first challenge you will have is inconsistent naming conventions, definitions and formats across different systems and different parts of the business. A typical problem could be that you want to look at the revenue for a customer across two systems, each supporting different products in your business. Both have fields called 'revenue', but when you look at the data you realize that one system may have revenue as the full invoice amount and the other the revenue less credits and discount. They are used for different purposes, but ensuring you are comparing like with like matters.

Data quality

The SCV must have data that meets the four data quality principles we defined in Chapter 8: availability, timeliness, accuracy and validity. For example, if the data is available in a system one week late because of some technology feed delay or business process, this might cause significant issues; or if an email address is not valid we may have the best offer for a customer but not be able to send it to them.

Data architecture

The architecture of an SCV consists of the components outlined at the start of this chapter and in Figure 9.1. It is the role of the data architect to ensure that all these components work together and deliver the expected outcomes. Data architecture (see definition below) is a whole subject in its own right, but this should be a sufficient level of detail at this stage, as well as to know that the lead data architect is a key role in any data organization.

DATA ARCHITECTURE

The design of the logical and physical elements of a company's data assets that includes the data model, rules, storage, integration, access, visualization, performance and security as well as the tools required for data management, which includes data governance, privacy and quality.

Integration

This will be one of the most complex integration projects the data team will have undertaken. The challenge of doing this should not be underestimated. It will require working very closely with the IT department, with technical challenges such as scheduling work on production systems, different team agendas and prioritizations, testing processes and ways of working – all of which need to be overcome for success.

Shadow data is the enemy of the SCV

We mentioned the problem of shadow data resources in Chapter 1. They occur when departments or individuals start collecting and storing their own data, unknown to management or the data team.

In one of my recent jobs I was delighted for six months with our progress on the SCV project that had, as one of its primary goals, the strategy of persuading our retail customers to become digital customers. One day, a director told me that he thought (quite rightly) that a particular report that we were relying on to manage the move of customers across channels contained errors. Investigating, I discovered that a team in the digital business had been writing its own reports, with numbers that were not drawn from our source of truth. I investigated further and uncovered a whole shadow industry of report writing.

FIGURE 9.3 Shadow data resource

**Shadow data resources
(up 10× data team)**

Core data and analytics team

This defeated the whole purpose of having one team that coordinated activity to implement the SCV. After further investigation, using the HR systems to look at people with data and analytics roles and activities across the entire organization, we discovered that there were between 40 and 50 people across the organization who had shadow data roles.

A large part, if not the whole, of their role involved the creation, management and analysis of data. This was a very long shadow: it was twice the size of the central data team. It was not governed, and while they were superficially following our data and analytics strategy, they had missed the point: one truth.

I hadn't counted on so many people taking the strategy, thinking it was a good idea, and then feeling inspired to do their own thing with it. It's like running the kitchen in a restaurant, then finding that table 12 had decided to cook their own meal in the bar and were just about to set fire to the curtains.

Those teams across the businesses which were delivering their own private initiatives were building their own data sets requiring further investment in capabilities far more than just the staff costs. We could have completed the work much faster, and much cheaper, without the distraction of other teams.

Once shadow data resources have been created, they are very hard to eliminate. The decision in this case was to try to coordinate activity across the business, but this has huge disadvantages.

The moral: the most important word in the phrase 'single customer view' is the first one.

Ownership of the SCV

We discussed at the beginning of this chapter that the SCV was needed to service the needs of the whole organization. This is a critical point. Many parts of the business will have a need for an SCV, and as discussed they may decide to build aspects of it themselves – this is the worst example of shadow data resources. It's important early on to establish ownership, and the difference between ownership and sponsorship. The owner of customer data, as discussed in Chapter 7, should sponsor the work, and the data team should own it. It is after all a data product.

SUMMARY

- The SCV underpins your multi-channel offering, it helps to create new digital services, and means problems can be spotted more quickly, resulting in a better, seamless experience for customers. It also means the business can communicate with accuracy and give unambiguous advice to customers, and is a foundation for more accurate customer segmentation and personalization strategies.

- The SCV is the basis for upselling and cross-selling, both of which are large revenue-generating opportunities.

- Integration of all your customer systems data to give you an SCV is a tough challenge, but all organizations should consider rationalization of their systems at the earliest opportunity.

- A project to implement an SCV can focus on core activities at first and be expanded to embrace deeper insights, for example by providing better data for data scientists.

- Trust in, and commitment to, an SCV project are fundamental to its success. Shadow data resources will undermine this, and make gains harder to achieve and more expensive, even if they are integrated.

References

Amar, J, Raabe, J and Roggenhofer, S (2019) How to capture what the customer wants, *McKinsey*, 1 February, https://www.mckinsey.com/business-functions/operations/our-insights/how-to-capture-what-the-customer-wants (archived at https://perma.cc/6ZQ7-RZ55)

Businesswire (2020) CSG Survey: Internal silos, data overload hampering great customer experience delivery, https://www.businesswire.com/news/home/20200513005072/en/CSG-Survey-Internal-Silos-Data-Overload-Hampering-Great-Customer-Experience-Delivery (archived at https://perma.cc/5GLD-XK7T)

Wertz, J (2018) Don't spend 5 times more attracting new customers, nurture the existing ones, *Forbes*, https://www.forbes.com/sites/jiawertz/2018/09/12/dont-spend-5-times-more-attracting-new-customers-nurture-the-existing-ones/?sh=10f1ed4d5a8e (archived at https://perma.cc/42YA-82AK)

10

Reports and dashboards

Decision-making needs to become data-driven. Improving the quality of reporting and implementing dashboards focuses the entire organization on a single source of truth. This requires both data skills and the ability to drive cultural change.

KEY CONCEPTS

- Business report
- Role-based reporting
- Business dashboard
- Certified report (or dashboard)
- Drill down

Introduction

'The problem is,' my CEO was telling me, 'that no one trusts the data. Can you fix this for me?'

Management meetings, he told me, were not happy or productive occasions. They were dominated by conflict. Not over strategy, but over whose business reports were correct. Nevertheless, decisions had to be made.

In business we can assume that the information we have to make decisions is incomplete: we can't know everything. Given that, the risk that the board will make a bad decision is always higher than zero. But, if the available information itself is in doubt, that risk is much higher.

BUSINESS REPORT

An analysis of data to evaluate an issue, set of circumstances, or operational goal that relates to the performance of a business. The report may be regular, or a one-off that has been commissioned to aid decision-making.

This is a pervasive problem. Most businesses have a cottage industry of bad report creation. The vast majority add no value. They are primarily used to create excuses for what didn't happen, rather than to suggest what we should do to create better outcomes.

It is likely that, when kicking off your projects on data governance and quality, the poor quality of reporting was one of the problems that you diagnosed and improving this was one of your key objectives. Inconsistent reporting is a waste of resources. There are reasons why managers may be tempted to tolerate bad or inconsistent reporting.

Self-interested managers, and all are self-interested to some degree, will instinctively favour reporting that shows them in the best light. It's a secondary consideration if the numbers in the report are of low quality, not transparent, or just incorrect. I'm not suggesting that managers lie on purpose – often the data they use is the result of 100 small decisions on what data to capture, or what not to include.

But if the report is designed to inform decision-making, then without consistent data quality and data governance, the CEO – my CEO mentioned at the start of this chapter – is nowhere.

One of the most important potential benefits of improving data quality and governance is that we can use reports and their real-time, drill-down counterpart, dashboards, to confidently share the data to inform everyday decisions. So now that our work on data quality and governance is under way, it's time to make good on that objective.

Task: A report audit

The first task is to discover the size and scope of the challenge, which means a thorough investigation of how reports are compiled and used.

How are they made?

To fulfil my CEO's request, the first task was to understand how the most important reports were created. I interviewed all the key stakeholders, both the C-suite and below. It is likely that, often, the most senior people who use the data do not know how the sausage was made, so it is important to ask some hard questions of the people who are responsible for departments, functions, regions, countries.

How big is the cottage industry?

Independently, I researched all the reports that were being produced from systems and distributed around the organization. This is a huge audit task, but not one that you can rush: it is extraordinarily valuable, and quite surprising. In this case, I was surprised to find that more than 500 reports were being used across the organization. It reported on quite literally everything. Ambitious managers had begun to create dashboards too.

Estimate the quality of the reports

There are five levels of value in any report (see below). If levels 1 and 2 are inadequate, then forget measuring 3 to 5. But this will provide a scorecard. You can put concrete milestones and goals to each of these five levels, and I encourage you to do so. They will help to health-check existing or emerging reports as you work through the process.

HOW TO MEASURE: REPORT QUALITY

1 **Quality and source of data.** Recall this: is the data accurate, valid and timely, and was all relevant data available to the person making the report?

2 **Clarity of definition.** Are the naming conventions consistent, is the data compiled from systems that treat it in the same way, and is this the same for all reports?

3 **Transparency of data presentation.** Does the report make it obvious how statistics were compiled, from which source, and the timeliness of the data?

4 **Insights and story the data tells.** Do the reports ask the best questions that map to the business strategy or the needs of that meeting, and does the data used help to answer those questions, and not create noise to distract from them?

5 **Actions that these insights suggest.** Is it clear what options are possible, which decisions are implied by this analysis, and what the consequences of these decisions might be?

ROLE-BASED REPORTING

A discipline that states that internal reporting is to be done only when it makes a difference to a task or role in the organization. Reports are primarily forward-looking, aligned to the specific challenge, contain only data that is relevant to the KPIs and clearly state progress or decision options.

CASE STUDY
Role-based reporting

Challenge: 'No one trusts the data'

The business was drowning in reports that were created but not used. Managers disputed the veracity of inconsistent reports. Senior executives did not know how to use reports to make decisions because the level of trust in them was low. An audit discovered more than 500 regular reports in the business.

Analysis: Lack of shared understanding

What was discovered in this case was also common, and fundamental. *The people using data did not understand what it was.* This is problematic both because they thought they understood more than they did and also because any data point looks equally convincing when it's on a PowerPoint slide. This is an example of the Dunning-Kruger effect, which states that we are often ignorant of our own level of ignorance. The psychologist David Dunning has found that the effect is universal. Dunning-Kruger (Dunning, 2011) applies particularly to managers (and, by implication, CDOs) because we instinctively assume that our specific domain knowledge is broader than it is, and so fail to investigate important potential problems. So managers often think they understand the quality and origin of data in a report because it comes from their department. In reality, they usually know very little about the governance and quality of their own department's data.

In the case that kicked off the project, there were two competing reports. Sales had decided to take the headline revenue numbers from the customer relationship management system that their department used. A rival used numbers extracted from the finance system, for which the definition of revenue was completely different (see point 3 of the report quality list above).

Sales numbers did not use credit notes, discounts, currency conversions and failed payments (points 1 and 2 above). Because these varied deal by deal, you couldn't just discount the sales numbers by a percentage to reconcile the two. Sales also clung to their numbers: their bonus literally depended on it.

The audit of all 500 reports showed that many were duplicated. Business decisions were driven by reports but more than 98 per cent of the items in the reports were looking at what had happened, not forecasting what might happen. There was a vast amount of data, so it was difficult to know what to focus on in any meeting (point 4).

As a result, only a small number of the hundreds of reports were being used in any sort of business process (point 5, which is an inevitable consequence of the other failings), and these were typically operational reports such as a list of customers with outstanding debts, for which the data was clear and the actions obvious. Not surprisingly, these reports were very successful. Few others were.

I told my CEO: this was not news to him. This is not surprising in itself, but it should be.

Action: Fewer reports that drive decisions

We set up a project to address reporting across the business. The goal was to identify every area that needed to report because it would help them make a difference to their role. We called this 'role-based' reporting:

- Every report that was to be produced would have clear KPIs and metrics that would drive change and behaviours across the business and be aligned to the business goals.

- Each report should be embedded into a clear business process such as a salesperson's monthly review.

- Data sources and definitions had to be consistent through every level in the organization, for example from salesperson, to territory manager, to country manager, to regional manager, to CEO. Every line item (KPI or metric) had to be clearly defined, with the source of the data displayed.

- Reports focused attention using a traffic-light system, with an overall objective to take actions to turn everything green: this 'turn it green' message became a cultural activity.

Outcome: Single sources of truth increase margin

Data quality enhancements meant that managers who were taking actions had confidence in what they were able to do. Reports that were used as a basis for compensation used consistent numbers from the finance system, with incentive scales adjusted.

Within one year we had moved from more than 500 reports to 60. The difference this made to the organization was not just in the reporting but in the effort and thinking that went into how the reports were used across the business. It let managers align KPIs and metrics to the goals of the business.

Role-based reporting was a key tool that led to an increase in margin for the organization of 64 per cent.

From static to dynamic decision support

One of the problems with reporting, no matter how well it is done, is that it is a data snapshot. It is out of date as soon as it is created. Some indicators do not move quickly or need to be evaluated over a period of weeks or months. For example, sustainability reports make sense if they are compiled quarterly, which will highlight trends and prioritize signal over noise. Strategy decisions for this type of activity are multi-year and require careful thought.

Other types of data – for example response times in customer service, or occupancy rates for serviced office space – may need to be compiled more often. The decisions that these statistics imply need to be reached quickly, and the resources or prices can be adjusted weekly or daily in response.

For these activities, reporting is second-best, especially if it requires manual intervention. Reporting is often too slow, aggregates data and so often cannot be used to investigate the source of problems or successes, and any actions taken can't be evaluated until the next reporting cycle.

Your report audit may uncover many of these reports, which become monuments to opportunities missed or problems that are never solved. Instead, we have the opportunity to create data-driven, dynamic decision-making using data dashboards. Even a simple dashboard can create engagement with a business goal, because it is a persistent reminder of success or failure. It is also a great way to engage the business with data-driven decision-making, because the data is always present, and perhaps to use data to investigate problems by drilling down to increasing levels of detail, or evaluating the impact of operational decisions in near-real time.

BUSINESS DASHBOARD

An information management tool used to present the data points relevant to the performance of a business at a glance. Complex data is simplified and summarized using graphics and visualizations, and users may be able to drill down or filter information to help understanding.

There are many vendors, publications and books that will tell you how to design a dashboard, and which data visualizations and software to use. This is not our focus. I argue that there are too many dashboards using low-quality, ungoverned data. They may look good, but they are not a useful basis for decision-making as a result, and so are potentially just as dangerous as a bad report. Or even more so, as one of the intentions of many dashboards is to devolve decision-making. This is admirable, but a source of risk if the data is poor. Our focus is to have dashboards with high-quality data that enable the business to trust them.

You probably will not need to evangelize dashboards – which, after the work you might have had to do in persuading your colleagues to invest time and money in governance and data quality, will be a relief.

The inspiration to embrace dashboards might be the work you do in improving reporting. But the business might be using dashboards already, perhaps provided by the IT department helpfully putting a user-friendly front end on existing reporting systems.

This has some value, but it is not the correct starting point. Dashboards are about telling the right people the things they need to know. This informal approach makes the easiest-to-access data more visible, introducing a bias in what is reported, and possibly in decision-making too.

Task: Designing your dashboard

When deciding what to put into a dashboard, it is important to reconcile your data and analytics strategy with the stated preferences of users – but aligning strategy and competing internal interests will require skill and perhaps the intervention of the CEO.

Stick to the data and analytics strategy

You can't just throw a whole load of information on a dashboard. It has to tell the user where to focus today, and this needs to be aligned to the business strategy. That means if cost-cutting is the priority, a dashboard showing sales growth based on the sales tracking software may look great and be encouraging, but it is a distraction from the priorities of the business.

Ask users how to measure success

When implementing a dashboard in a department, the staff might be familiar with how they are judged at the end of the year but not have given much consideration to how they measure their progress day to day. So if you gather them in a room and ask them what they want to know, what would help them, you can be a catalyst to get people talking to one another and finding agreement on what success looks like on a dashboard.

Manage conflict

Be warned: this might cause conflict and take more than one visit to resolve. It also might create differences of opinion between business units that want important metrics to be measured in ways that place them in a favourable light, or just ways to which they are accustomed. Breaking this tie may even require intervention from a CFO or CEO. But, on the positive side, this may uncover implicit incentives that explain why the business is failing to realize strategic objectives. For example, the wider strategy might be focused on raising margin, but your workshop could uncover that the sales operation is focusing exclusively on measuring revenue.

Start with what needs attention most

There will be pressure to focus only on the good news. But that doesn't demand the business's attention as urgently as what needs to be fixed. On day one a dashboard with mostly red traffic lights isn't the best news, but on day 100, when some are green and the rest amber, it has been a much better agent of change than a cheery and encouraging report on what you're already doing well. See the example SCV dashboard, Figure 10.1.

Visualizations give context

Dashboards use simple devices (rev counters, bar charts, coloured arrows) to send the message at a glance. Distinguish between indicators that are on target and those that need attention. As with reports, the dashboard must always send a signal prompting action. Colours usually do this best: for example, if the plan is to get £100,000 of revenue a year from a customer, and you have that £100,000 revenue, a traffic light on the dashboard would be green. But if you're getting £90,000 it is amber, and at £70,000 it is red.

Add drill-down functionality

Depending on the needs of the person looking at the dashboard, the data will be aggregated to some extent. But drill-down capability allows the user

FIGURE 10.1 Example dashboard – single customer view

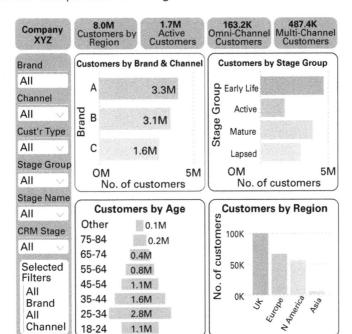

of the dashboard to investigate and create the story. For someone with group responsibility, is one country doing worse and dragging down the aggregate? For someone tasked with improving margin, which customers are profitable and which are a drag on the business? In some cases, and for some users, the drill-down might even be able to expose individual customers, clients or transactions that are out of line, providing an even more direct link from dashboard to action.

DRILL DOWN

Access successively deeper levels of hierarchically ordered data, for example to see the contribution of individual customers, products or regions to a headline statistic.

Task: Dashboard implementation

As ever, this innovation cannot be done *to* a business, it must be implemented in cooperation *with* the people who will use it. This is both to find out what they think is useful and to ensure that it is recognized as an asset in their jobs, not as a creepy show of corporate surveillance.

There is not just one dashboard

It's obvious from the above that the dashboard in HR will have different indicators and different access to drill-down data than the one on the CEO's laptop. In a large organization this might mean 20 separate dashboards. But recall, with a single customer view and a consistent source of truth in your data, the administrative overhead to create it isn't as large as it may seem. Plan your dashboard as a set of modules so that you're not repeating work. That means everyone who needs finance indicators, for example, gets them alongside their departmental data, but they will be delivered as part of the finance dashboard too, ensuring that they all reconcile and reducing development effort.

Quick-win dashboards

You might want to deliver early results, and so, for example, a procurement dashboard is a visible and easy-to-implement source of improvement, showing for the first time how much the business is spending, and with whom.

Simply making data more salient can change behaviour. Similarly, a dashboard that tracks the time taken for debtors to pay can focus effort without the need for formal decision-making or meetings.

Discovering data challenges

Given probable widespread demand, where do you start? We need to reconcile what is possible – some areas of the business may still be struggling with data quality and what is a priority to drive decision-making.

So far, we have focused on the work that the business does when specifying the elements of a dashboard, but it will help direct your data quality and governance programmes too. Having agreed on a set of KPIs and metrics to capture on the dashboard, it creates two sets of decisions:

- **Precise definitions.** What are the precise definitions that we will use? We're modularizing our dashboard, so there is even less justification for reporting revenue in one way in one part of the business and another way in the department next door, because both will share the same module on the dashboard. There will be some discussion about this, which may not always be polite.

- **Appropriate performance indicators.** You may discover that some of the important KPIs are not quite measured in the way you need them or are measured at a quality that is far below what you need: for example, not split by office location, or infrequently measured. This again is a creative moment. The data you can provide for the business is beginning to match the priorities of the people who want to use it. Note that in the workshop discussions you should not be hypothetical: 'If we could measure this, would you like it?' Instead, present known sources of data for the business to make use of, that may need more attention as part of the project.

When you have a mock-up of the dashboard as you will implement it, with some working data, it's important to take it back to the business. If this is a new concept, then they will struggle to imagine what would help them in the abstract. But, faced with your mock-up, you are likely to get some more useful feedback.

Determining levels of data access

There are regulatory concerns here, though of course the data is usually aggregated, so these are few. But the feeling of being monitored creates tension. It's a good-news story that more people have more detailed and timely information to do a job. Do not forget that those who are generating this information, for example working in the contact centre, may feel that 'big brother' is monitoring their work if their performance is captured on a widely shared dashboard. It is important to explain (and demonstrate) how the dashboard can help them as well.

Negotiate common thresholds

We mentioned the idea of traffic-light thresholds before, but that rather assumes we all share a common view on what the dividing line between good and bad performance should be. This is emphatically not true. Be warned that typically no one will have thought hard about what the threshold is between amber or red, so this is a conversation that you will need to have, because you are effectively creating a company-wide policy that defines failure using data. This is enormously powerful and useful, but threatening for those who worry that they will fall foul of it. That group may include entire departments or business units. It's likely we'll need some people with high EQ during this process and this may be more than one good reason to involve HR in this work.

The discussions that you will guide to resolve these matters may be taxing, but they are an essential part of your value, and what separates your role from that of the IT department. In IT, there are many extremely competent people who can build a dashboard and implement it. But it is not their task to decide what is on the dashboard, how it will augment the business, or the definitions of important concepts like underperformance. You are also not the ultimate arbiter of this, but it is important that you make this discussion happen. You can use this debate to create a better understanding of the data transition as a whole.

From reporting to insight

It's also important that we don't think of the dashboard as simply an animated version of a report. The evolution to dashboard-driven management also means a change in emphasis from reporting past performance to beginning to think about what this means for the future.

At this stage, the way data is used in the business for this purpose will probably be weak, or at best uneven. But dashboards also provide a bedrock for and a way to think of future-facing disciplines like analytics and data science, which we will cover in more detail in Chapter 16.

Even if the analytical skills of the business are not good at this point, we can still use historical data to compare progress against targets at a more detailed level. This can mitigate the informal use of misleading indicators. For example, the sales team of a retailer might employ a basic dashboard, implemented by shadow resource from outside the data team. It implicitly assumes four identical quarters and constant market conditions. The data team's intervention can upgrade it to use a year-on-year comparison adjusted for market conditions, or a share-of-wallet analysis against competitors, creating insight into where the business will be at year end.

This seems trivial, but cutting out simplistic reporting or dashboarding, in my experience, avoids a month of frantic discounting at the end of each business year as the sales team attempts to make a target that it had no idea it was going to miss.

Task: Information architecture

With reports, we can stop the proliferation and pare back the number of statistics and indicators that are reported, but the document or presentation has to withstand detailed scrutiny. A dashboard, on the other hand, should avoid too much information on first glance if it is to be used effectively as a tool. There is no hard-and-fast rule but, in my experience:

- **Fewer than eight items.** Our brains tend to be selective, and too many pieces of data on a dashboard will confuse, not inform.

- **Group by headlines.** If you have three main sections for reporting, group the indicators for each under that title. Again, it helps people to selectively focus their attention.

- **Standardize presentation.** User experience shows that we are calmer and work faster when information is presented in a consistent way. Allow dashboard users to recognize information instinctively, don't make them work too hard.

- **Allow what-ifs.** The dashboard should be the focus of a progress meeting, but remember we got into this because we wanted to make better decisions. One way to do this is to build a what-if capability into the dashboard. Imagine: all indicators are amber and are stubbornly sticking that way. But drilling down has shown that one service is underperforming. What happens if we kill that service? If it turns the indicators green, that's a forward-looking piece of information. It suggests the consequences of an action.

- **Certification and provenance.** You build out the dashboards, carefully testing at each stage that the data satisfies governance and quality standards. But to others they seem no more accurate than any other report in the organization – and remember where we started: 'no one trusts the data'. So when you have a reliable source of truth that updates every day, and that is confirmed by the relevant department in the business, create a label that certifies the data and display that certification on the dashboard. This is called a certified report (or dashboard). It doesn't mean that the quality is perfect, but it means the data team knows that the data will be updated, and where it came from when it is. Lack of certification undermines many IT-built or homebrew dashboard initiatives. Users trust the dashboard only when it delivers good news. The data team can go further and display a box that explains when the data was last updated, or a pop-up box that lists the provenance of the data when you mouse over it. Even a warning next to data items that might have quality problems is useful. All these devices are created to communicate to users the appropriate level of confidence in data, and especially in bad news.

CERTIFIED REPORT (OR DASHBOARD)

A business report that has been 'certified' in terms of its data quality, governance, sources of data, timeliness and knowledge of any transformations, aggregations or calculations in its creation.

You'll start to appreciate by now that there is a lot to reporting and dashboards. That so often a report is asked for and the consequences of that request not fully understood. It is worth reflecting at this stage that reports and dashboards start to expose some underlying business problems, potential flaws in business processes, and data collection issues. Also, as soon as people see reports and dashboards they will ask for more data. It always happens. I've put together a reports and dashboards maturity model (see Figure 10.2) that adds some context to the whole journey, from building basic reports to sharing data with customers (something we cover more in Chapter 17).

FIGURE 10.2 Reports and dashboards maturity model

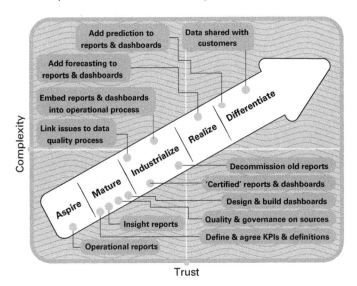

Avoiding short-termism

Finally, a warning. In 1975 the economist Charles Goodhart coined the law that bears his name, which is now generally summarized as: 'When a measure becomes a target, it ceases to be a good measure' (Goodhart, 1975).

This is why it's very important to create realistic measures of performance in a dashboard, because when there is a red light, everyone will want to make it turn green. And that means many people will try to change the indicator by any means necessary, which may or may not be good for the business.

This is why it is vital to agree on measurements that reflect the long-term health of the business, not just the numbers that are easiest to move. Or you can build in a history to the reports by (for example) estimating the lifetime value of a sale. For example:

- Product A is hard to sell, but carries a high margin, and customers buy a third-party maintenance contract.

- Product B has the same sticker price and margin and is quicker to sell because it uses an interest-free credit deal. It has a free lifetime warranty provided by the company itself.

If your dashboard prioritizes revenue, then of course the short-term way to move the needle is to sell lots of B. If you are prioritizing short-term margins, again B would be more attractive to the sales team.

In the medium term, the cost of providing the finance, plus delinquent customers who stop making payments, will lower margins for B.

In the long term, product B becomes even less profitable because of the cost of servicing the lifetime warranty. As defects rise, so do the repair bills. Your most loyal and committed customers may become the ones you earn least from, and the more Bs you have in the market, the bigger hit the margins will take.

This is not just a dashboard issue; it goes to the heart of the strategy decisions that created the products in the first place. But having a dashboard that can capture these trends and allows decision-makers to drill down into why service or credit finance charges have risen faster than expected gives early warning of bad news. It also encourages different parts of the business to communicate and work together, driven by data.

This applies equally to reporting and dashboards: used properly, they are profound and creative engines for growth. But, if you neglect data quality, or the design process, the success of your project may accidentally destroy the business by degrees.

SUMMARY

- Reporting is how data is used to make decisions. Your first priority is to ensure that those reports are of the highest possible quality and are trusted.

- Most businesses have too many reports with inconsistent data. An audit will help you discover how many, and where the inconsistencies come from.

- Dashboards fulfil a similar function, but use dynamic, regularly updated information.

- To create both, ask the people who will use them what information has highest value, taking care to align it with the priorities of the data and analytics strategy. Clear communication on the changes you are making is essential.

- Do not overcomplicate the data that users see, but it may be appropriate to give them the opportunity to drill down into the details.

- The decision to use single, high-quality, governed sources of data may cause conflict and drive changes in both business practice and compensation. This is tough, but essential.

References

Dunning, D (2011) *Advances in Experimental Social Psychology*, Elsevier
Goodhart, C (1975) Problems of monetary management: The UK experience, in *Monetary Theory and Practice*, ed C Goodhart, Macmillan. The generalization was coined two years later by Marilyn Strathern, an anthropologist. Goodhart's Law actually states: 'Any observed statistical regularity will tend to collapse once pressure is placed upon it for control purposes.'

Further reading

Wexler, S, Shaffer, J and Cotgreave, A (2017) *The Big Book of Dashboards: Visualizing your data using real-world business scenarios*, Wiley

11

Data risk management and ethics

Most of an organization's time is spent working out how to do more business. But recent history tells us that one of the most important things you can do with data is to use it to stop people doing bad things at work and protect your profit. This can create not just a safer business but a better one too.

KEY CONCEPTS IN THIS CHAPTER

- Data privacy
- Data security
- Data ethics
- Data compliance
- Data fraud

Introduction

We cannot simply talk about the value we get from data without considering, at this point, the risks to the business of the actions we take. As well as the risks of underperformance or failure that are the focus of much of the work the data team does at this point, there are the ever-present risks of data misuse or even data fraud.

We can think of these problems in terms of motive, means and opportunity. The motive is the reason for committing a transgression. We have already concluded that data has high value, but that much of that value can be undermined by keeping it in silos, not paying attention to its quality, or not keeping it up to date. Unfortunately, we have just raised the value of the data asset enormously by improving its quality. We have increased the motivation to steal or misuse this data.

The means are the tools or methods to commit a crime. The data transformation process gives more people access to more data, often massively more. So, we can conclude that many people have the means.

The opportunity is the occasion. Your company presumably spends a lot of money on security. But that's never perfect. Indeed, with many of us working from home for an extended period, the opportunity to breach security, or to appropriate or misuse company data, has never been better.

In that case, what can we do? Not everything but – in my experience – using data creatively in these circumstances can be transformative for some potentially problematic business processes.

Five pillars

There are five separate elements to managing risk and ethical compliance. They are data privacy, data security, data ethics, data compliance, and data fraud prevention. Although privacy and security are large, important subjects, I will have little to say about them. This isn't because they have no value; they are hugely important. It's just that they are topics on which many books have been written, and which deserve the in-depth treatment that they get in those.

Data ethics, data compliance and data fraud prevention are areas in which data can play an important role, and where focus is often undervalued. This is particularly true in the financial sector, sadly the location of much unethical and fraudulent activity over the years.

Data privacy and data security

DATA PRIVACY

Determines whether, or how, data is used internally, shared with third parties, how data is legally collected or stored, and the regulatory restrictions in which the business operates.

DATA SECURITY

The practice of protecting data from unauthorized access, corruption, or theft throughout its entire life cycle.

One of the consequences of making data useful and accessible in the business is that the data we are granted by customers can create a larger, more insightful picture of individuals. This represents the trust they place in us.

Part of the way in which we repay that trust is by taking care with their data. We have improved its quality by ensuring that if we have been given a phone number, we store it in a way that means we can use it to contact the customer. And when the customer doesn't want to be bothered by marketing or sales, we store those preferences too.

And when we create new and powerful tools – for example, the single customer view of that customer – we take care that we determine the specific privacy requirement for each and every field. By definition the data in the SCV is valuable and sensitive. We ensure that the data is carefully protected from hackers, internal and external, from malicious employees, and from accidental and inappropriate access.

It is important that these fundamentals are built into our projects from the start, and not added later. For example, controlling access to data feeds is built by design, as part of governance. Requests to access data must go through a formal process. While your data team should enjoy creating new insights or applications, those experiments must not inadvertently give them access to sensitive data (this encompasses both formal and informal definitions of 'sensitivity') or compromise the security or privacy of that data.

When creating self-service applications for consumers to modify their own data, for example, access to that data should be as closely controlled as when a member of staff is accessing it. And, if there is a privacy or security breach, then it must be communicated and handled with the seriousness the situation demands.

The trust that makes our innovations possible takes seconds to lose but years to win back, if that ever happens.

Ethics

DATA ETHICS

The responsible use of data, doing the right thing for people and society even when no one is looking or checking.

How can we be ethical in the way we handle data? In most cases by ensuring transparency in the use of data in any business activity.

In the 1980s the emerging research topic of business ethics was seen, at best, as problematic. Phillip V Lewis, an academic who specialized in the subject, wrote a research paper, which concluded that defining ethics in business was 'like nailing Jello to a wall' (Lewis, 1985).

Since then we may not have completely solved the problem of definition, but we have all seen examples of behaviour in business for which we don't need an academic to conclude it's unethical. It's clear that there are still grey areas, but our job is not to solve the universe of ethical questions. Instead, we can take potential ethical problems and try to use data to limit the space in which employees can behave unethically.

The most appropriate way to do this is to take the stated principles of the business – for example, non-discriminatory behaviour – and monitor them. This can be applied, for example, in HR and recruitment. Data isn't going to resolve all questions, but it can raise some important flags.

The second area is to remove an employee's discretion when it creates either the appearance or substance of unethical behaviour. The more decisions are made on gut feel, the more potential there is for ethics to take a back seat to ego or a closed mind. Basing decisions on business rules is not only more efficient, it's exactly as fair as those rules, and those rules can be examined and communicated.

As we'll see when we investigate the potential, and pitfalls, of machine learning and artificial intelligence, this is not a small problem. On the other hand, it is a problem that data can inform, if not resolve.

Compliance

DATA COMPLIANCE

Ensuring that data is organized and managed so that organizations meet enterprise business rules and legal and governmental regulations.

One criticism of internal and external compliance regimes is that they give a map to people, who want to break them, of what they can do and not get caught. The case of Jérôme Kerviel, rogue trader at Société Générale, is one that I investigated (Tidey, 2014).

Kerviel had joined the middle office of SocGen in 2000, ironically working in its compliance department – though, of course, what better location? In 2005 he was promoted to junior trader. By 2007 and 2008 it was revealed that he had taken massive fraudulent directional positions, far beyond his limited authority. His employers accused him of unauthorized trades totalling €49.9 billion – more than the bank's total market capitalization.

After the positions were revealed, SocGen closed them out for losses of around €4.9 billion. Kerviel was arrested, found guilty of abuse of confidence and illegal access to computers, and went to prison.

My job was to help find out what had happened, and how, through the lens of data. It was clear that Kerviel's trades were being captured by SocGen's systems, but they were being captured in a different place to where they could be analysed and the risk measured. Different systems with different databases weren't joined up, and someone like Kerviel, with a background in compliance, knew how to get around it; for example, he would close his trades just before they would trigger a notification in the bank's internal control system.

The reason that Kerviel and other rogue traders survive for so long is that there's no holistic view of their data. There are two things we can say about this: first, ethics is about what you do when no one is looking, so whatever the state of the systems, he had an ethical problem that in a perfect world would have disqualified him from doing the job. But the financial sector is not a perfectly ethical world, so the second point is that when you work towards a single source of truth you can use your data toolbox to automate the ways in which the data tells a story, making it harder for anyone to cheat. In this case, it would have been relatively straightforward to eliminate the ways in which Kerviel could game the system.

But the siloed nature of the underlying data made that impossible. Silos and compliance don't mix.

Fraud

DATA FRAUD

The deliberate fabrication or falsification of data for financial gain.

Fraud will happen in the weakest data links in the business. If you want to find them, ask a fraudster.

While most opportunities for fraud can be closed off using automated checks and reconciliations, you can't spot every opportunity, in the same way that security flaws in software can never be exhaustively patched. And as business processes evolve, new opportunities for fraud arise. If you assume that you're constantly being probed by people who want to find that opportunity, then you also have to assume that sooner or later, someone will succeed. At that point, you have to stop them.

But just as security software now looks for patterns of suspicious behaviour rather than trying to identify every piece of malware, so we can build fraud detection into data processes: anomalous invoicing patterns, spikes in activity, or figures that won't reconcile.

At the beginning of the data transformation, the spikes aren't apparent, and the figures never match up, so fraud can pass unnoticed. Improving the quality of data can make a serious dent in low-level fraud. At a gambling company, when they were removing duplicates in customer data for an online casino, they discovered a very enthusiastic customer. He had 3,000 open accounts, each opened to claim the £10 free bet.

CASE STUDY
An accusation of fraud at an investment bank

Challenge: Rein in the analysts

I joined a large investment bank as a managing director in 2000, with a brief to investigate and improve the process of creating investment research. This was created by sell-side analysts, who were all experts in their own specific fields. Analysts would look at a stock using their proprietary methods and recommend that investors should buy, sell or hold.

Analysis: We have a problem

There was a mystery: many analysts were recommending stocks as a 'buy', but the underlying research didn't seem to imply that recommendation. The bank had as clients many of the companies that analysts were rating, so the bank earned money if those stocks went up.

Action: Reconcile the data

My job was to improve the recommendations process all the way from the underlying data to the analyst models, through to the final recommendations.

I rebuilt the underlying models containing financial and forecast data and added sentiment from unstructured data including news alerts and financial results.

Outcome: A new way of doing business

There was one parameter that, at first, I couldn't get to: the proprietary models the analysts use to come up with their recommendations. These were their property, fiercely guarded. But, as the regulators were investigating, the analysts were happy to hand over their models – because my data could show they acted in good faith.

Our work changed the process of using data in research reports for the entire industry. We created and shared an open standard called RIXML that allowed clients to see how the models were constructed and how the data influenced the conclusions. This project revolutionized the way ratings were awarded and created more transparency in the process of rating – which had seemed an unattainable goal when I took the job. There is more detail on RIXML in Chapter 17.

Task: Working with a regulator

Some businesses discourage their employees from working with a regulator. I've never really understood this. Not many people like an unscheduled call from the regulator, that's true. But regulators are not going anywhere, and I believe there is unexploited potential for mutual gain if we can speak a common language: data.

I have found that discussing data – within the limits of privacy obligations – is an extremely useful way to create a positive environment with regulators. This is because the regulators have to uncover and mitigate the same ethics and fraud problems as the executives of the firms they regulate. But they have a smaller budget, and no direct access to the customer or transaction data that regulated businesses can use. Any joint work may also become a template to share with other business partners when there is a mutual benefit, and when regulation allows.

Different cultures can prevent ethical gains through sharing

On the surface, opening a line of communication with a regulator to share data insights should not be complicated. Regulators broadly want the same thing as most market participants: no one should profit by breaking the rules.

I first dealt with a regulator in the 1990s, at that time the Financial Services Authority (FSA). I was working for another investment bank at the time. The conversations were about our regulatory reporting to the FSA, ensuring that that reporting was aligned to their goals.

But neither our compliance department nor the supervisor at the regulator really understood how the data was created and managed, which meant that the process was breaking down. Our side didn't know what data it could share, and their side didn't know what to ask for.

Align goals

But this was about compliance, not an investigation. Compliance is about processes and models, not individuals. Therefore, I worked out that we could easily share those models with the regulator. We weren't sharing the underlying data, but we were sharing the processes of how we managed and stored that data. The ways in which we analysed the data to detect insider dealing were of real interest to the regulator, and there was no conflict of interest or disadvantage in sharing these ideas.

What this information sharing did do, however, was break down the barriers to create a lot more understanding during times when there were serious investigations. These events became far more collaborative and productive, with a lot less suspicion on both sides.

SUMMARY

- Data is valuable, and so needs to be protected from misuse. That protection needs to be built in from the time the data is captured, not added as an afterthought.

- When creating projects, methods of data protection, security, ethics and fraud protection must be part of the proposal and agreed to by all stakeholders.

- Ethical behaviour is expected but, for many reasons, does not always happen. Data can help create systems to protect the business, customers or even the employee by removing conflicts of interest or subjective decision-making.

- Visibility of employee behaviour is the key to compliance – this doesn't just mean sounding an alarm when rules are breached but also monitoring patterns of behaviour.

- Regulators are often kept at arm's length. But limited data sharing can be a useful way to achieve results and boost the trust between your employer and a regulator.

References

Lewis, P (1985) Defining 'business ethics': Like nailing Jello to a wall, *Journal of Business Ethics*, **4** (5), pp 377–83

Tidey, A (2014) SocGen 'rogue trader' Kerviel heading for jail, *CNBC*, https://www.cnbc.com/2014/03/19/soc-gen-rogue-trader-kerviel-heading-for-jail.html (archived at https://perma.cc/F8YR-4GUU)

PART FOUR

Wave 3: Industrialize

With the well-defined, high-quality sources of data we gained in *Mature* we can now begin to optimize how that data is used in the organization using the principles of scale and automation.

This means embracing automation where possible to acquire the data, which eliminates inefficiencies and errors introduced in manual processes and automation of the reports and dashboards so we're not wasting time running everything manually. This automation gives us the capacity to scale without having to significantly increase our data resources. It also means scaling up the generation of value in one part of the business or scaling out those processes to other parts of the business.

To achieve the maximum benefit from the transformation, it also means that the executive team must begin to reorganize processes and capabilities based on the flow and use of data. This is the first step to becoming truly driven by data and on towards the next stage of *Realize*.

Value, Build, Improve content of this wave

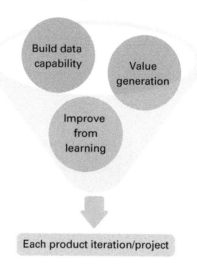

The activities for our VBI model in this wave are:

Value. The data team will automate data acquisition and reporting and dashboards and standardize processes, capitalizing on the achievements in data governance and quality.

Build. This means that similar methods and business processes can be used across the business, creating significant value from scale.

Improve. This creates insight into new avenues for optimization and simplification of business processes, but also informs the organizational change required to make them happen.

12

Automation, automation, automation

Reducing the number and scope of manual processes in the generation and use of data will be a powerful way to improve business performance. You are likely to discover many undocumented processes that are suitable, and this will improve their quality while reducing cost. Employees worried about their roles may resist.

Introduction

William Lee, a British technology entrepreneur, created an automated knitting machine and applied for a patent, but the patent office refused his application. The bad news was delivered to him by the person who had decided that his machine was a bad idea: the Queen.

That is, Queen Elizabeth the First. This was in 1589.

The problem with the machine, everyone agreed, was that if there was a machine to do tedious repetitive jobs like knitting stockings, what would we all do instead? The idea that we're all about to be made obsolete by a machine and that the robots are coming for our jobs is a powerful one. Many people hold this view, privately or in public, and they are not Luddites. In 1930, John Maynard Keynes, at the time probably the world's most famous economist, was worrying about how society would cope with the 15-hour working week based on imminent technological change and productivity improvements (Keynes, 1930).

The resistance to automation within organizations is a powerful force. We all like to think that what we do is special, that each working day is unique, and that any job that requires a learned skill can't be done by a machine.

The truth is that for many tasks, automation isn't just possible, it's the only sensible thing to do.

The work we've done on data governance and quality has created a huge opportunity to industrialize administrative and analytical processes that are wasting literally years of your company's time and dragging down the data quality that we worked so hard to create.

There's another reason to embrace automation. If you don't, your competitors will, and to their competitive advantage. In 17th-century England, Lee died in poverty. His boss's attempt to hold back change didn't help Elizabethan hand-knitters hold onto their jobs either, because his knitting machine technology was soon widely adopted all over the world.

BUSINESS PROCESS AUTOMATION

Using data and technology to automate processes in a business that have more than one step. This improves quality and timeliness, simplifies administration and governance, and saves cost.

What can we automate?

Any data activity begins with a temptation to dive in and start 'hand crafting' things. This is natural, and it is also not bad because you can understand reports and dashboards better if you understand the steps to get to a result (often many more than anyone assumes, including the people who have been building them for the past five years by hand). In Figure 12.1 I've identified the types of data activities that can and should be automated. One example, which we'll look at in more detail later in this chapter, is the use of a tool to automate the creation of your data repository.

For any stable, repeatable process, the point at which the artisan approach becomes sub-optimal is the moment that someone does it twice. At this point, whoever is completing the task is acquiring a habit, a mental shortcut that internalizes where the data is and what to do with it. This has two negative effects: it becomes an unacknowledged part of the job, and no one is

FIGURE 12.1   Automation maturity model

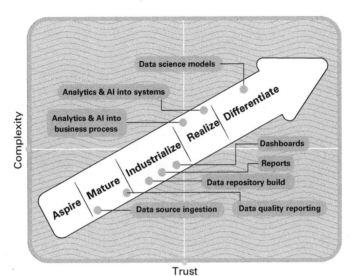

documenting how it is done. This is partly how we arrive at the 'irreconcilable reports' problem discussed in the previous chapter – each output is lovingly handcrafted as an artisanal product by someone in the department who creates it. Sally in sales will defend the figures to the death in an argument with Graham in finance but, in reality, the only person who knows how these monthly reports are put together is Eric, her PA, and he's on annual leave right now. These artisanal products are, at best, unmanaged. At worst they put the business in peril (if marketing hasn't filled in its expenses data, we can use last month's number instead, the meeting is tomorrow… does the total include the figures from the Belfast office?).

It's easy to understand how this happens. Imagine a start-up with two staff who know each other well. Information is shared. Reports for investors or prospects are a joint effort. Data is either external (research, markets) or comparatively recent. Often systems are haphazard or inconsistent.

The start-up grows: it acquires a small sales team, working on commission, and a couple of people to handle finance. It starts to look for investors and gets a bank loan. It thinks about opening another office. Everyone is working 80 hours a week, and building structures is either an afterthought, or something that the entrepreneurial management resists.

Suddenly, reporting becomes vital for the business. For the first time people begin to specialize, and not always in jobs they are trained for, so trust is not automatically given. Cashflow is tight, so the finance team needs to know what's being sold, what will be sold, and who sold it. Investors need to know that their investment is solid. What's happening in the other office?

Whether your business started a year ago or 100 years ago, this creates a cottage industry of data preparation. When I was working at a serviced office business, I discovered that the business created 500 regular reports, all by hand. That meant that lots of people were staying late or at weekends, cutting and pasting data from spreadsheets. They all had their habits, often inconsistent with one another, maybe varying a bit from month to month. The problem was, we didn't really know what the people involved were doing. I'm sure not all of them could explain it themselves.

HOW TO MEASURE: POTENTIAL FOR AUTOMATION

Successful data engineering. Your data quality work has no doubt shown everyone that quality data is valuable and made them realize what an enormous pain manual data acquisition is for the business. Paper-based processes, retyping, cut-and-paste, all create ways to acquire data that are labour intensive and prone to error.

A stable, repeated process. What we do with the data can also be automated. We will see that it's not just a case of standardizing the raw material, but of treating it in a consistent way through time, and across the organization. As soon as someone touches that data, the process breaks down (or, you don't know if it has broken down or not).

Decisions that don't require judgement. So far we have considered data mostly as an input for decisions that are made by people. From now on, we begin a transition that will take unnecessary decision-making out of their hands.

How much can we automate?

There are two answers that, in my experience, are universally true about how much you can automate:

1 More than you are automating today.

2 More than you think.

The second answer interests us at this point. When I described the process of creating reports as artisanal, this was not a criticism of a lack of qualification or intelligence. The smartest, most highly trained data people in your organization – your data scientists – often tend to work this way too. We will return to this later, but one of the weaknesses of data science as it is practised is that it is too local. A one-off insight can be valuable (recall our quick wins), but the ones that really generate returns are those that are repeatable. Automation and documentation of how data is used in those models make them better.

At present there are some wild figures thrown about as part of the 'the robots are coming' reporting, but there is also some very careful research. The first point is that there are very few jobs that can be automated in their entirety today, no matter how good your data quality and IT systems are.

McKinsey's research (McKinsey Global Institute, 2018) suggests that 6 per cent of all occupations have at least 30 per cent of tasks that are suitable for automation. Fewer than one in 20 is 100 per cent automatable, and that's hardly a surprise: employing someone to do only robotic jobs means that person is unlikely to be able to use judgement or skill when there is a non-routine task to deal with. Tasks with the highest potential to be automated are predictable physical activities (81 per cent) (that's why robots build cars), and that doesn't concern us. But McKinsey argues that 69 per cent of data processing and 64 per cent of data collection can be automated. In the United States, the calculation is that this is just over half of all work activity, and globally it accounts for \$15 trillion in wages.

The research into precisely which jobs are most likely to be automated is more complex. We know that, in the last 30 years, the labour market has 'hollowed out'. Some low-skilled jobs have been automated away, such as the people who used to build cars, elbowed aside by the precise mechanical arm of a robot. Other low-skilled jobs are too badly paid to make automation feasible: for example, you can buy a robot vacuum cleaner for a few hundred pounds, but most of us either do it ourselves or hire a cleaner who will clean the bath as well.

Businesses have also responded by outsourcing some jobs to emerging economies. This has driven growth on both sides of the contract, but two developments mean this can't last forever. The first is that, as those economies develop, wages rise. The second is that Covid-19 has shown us that there is risk in outsourcing.

Carl Benedikt Frey, an economist, used artificial intelligence to classify every task by how automatable it is (Frey and Osborne, 2016). The conclusion is a list that orders automation by likelihood.

Dr Frey and his colleague, Dr Michael Osborne, analysed 700 professions, finding that social workers and carers were among the least vulnerable at the time. Accountants and telemarketers, however, were much more likely to be replaced. Frey says that the jobs that are not automatable are 'likely to be intensive in creativity, in complex social interactions... things that computers are still relatively bad at'.

This is a conversation for a different book, but it makes a final, important point: what you decide to automate is not primarily a technical decision. McKinsey and Frey agree that automation is not an immediate process of replacing entire roles. It's a process of improving what you do by selecting tasks that are ready for automation and for which there is a business case, improving the way in which those tasks are done, and using that success to inform the next step.

A gradual approach moves us from the bottom left to the top right of the maturity model. It also means that the business case is constantly changing, depending on your data and analytics strategy and the underlying business, but also on what you have been able to automate.

Task: The business case for automation

Is your company ready for automation? The short answer as of yesterday is yes, because automation is one of those projects that is much more likely to succeed if you start early, before bad habits and shadow data resources have become embedded. You are likely to encounter some resistance at all levels, though, and so it is important to be able to make a coherent case for change. Counter-intuitively, some of the reasons to automate might seem at first like objections to the process.

Frequent changes

One of the reasons why data handling is so manual is that requirements for reports change regularly, as systems are upgraded, as projects come and go, as products and services evolve. This is often cited as a reason why reporting has to be manual, when in fact it is the opposite. The point of these frequent changes is that you need to be agile enough to respond to them, and to pass information around the organization in a consistent way. The only way to do this is to automate all the data feeds, and then you can apply them as requirements change. You can think of the overlap of information systems in different parts of the organization as the core, and the other parts that are not so widely shared as the periphery. So moving from department to department, or location to location, is similar to the process of change: you use automation so that data is not a constraint on decision-making in the new environment.

Manage risk

Looking at the maturity model, the second task is data quality reporting. This is a straightforward application of automation (how many fields are empty? How complete are our customer records?) that can often be satisfied simply by counting. Yet its impact on risk is huge.

Automation means that risk-based decisions are always using the latest data, and that we can be sure that it is not data that has been massaged or slanted. This can change risk appetite: there's no need to kick the can down the road in case the reporting is out of date, or inaccurate.

This is also hugely important for financial reporting, in two dimensions. The first, as before, is that it creates financial reports in a timely manner, without conflict over reconciliation. Recall WorldCom, which went bust because none of its financial reporting systems had been reconciled. The second is that it aids governance and compliance: the CFO can explain to an auditor where the number came from with complete confidence.

Undocumented processes

This relates to a third important dimension: how was the sausage made? Manual data wrangling aggregates many, sometimes hundreds, of small decisions and tasks that may exist only in the minds of whoever does them. If you asked that person to write the process down, chances are they would miss some of it out. As your automation maturity develops, you may encounter the same problem with analysts and data scientists, or anyone who decided to write code to extract data: they have not documented what they did. When that person moves jobs, goes on holiday or simply forgets, you need to know how to extract that data.

Reporting backlogs

If one of the objections to automation is that 'we'll do it, just as soon as we get through all this reporting we have to do', then it's the signal to speed things up, not slow them down. There are a limited number of people that the business can enlist to do this data curation job, but the requirements keep on coming (often on top of processes that are routine, not needed and carry little value).

This is occasionally a huge bottleneck in the functioning of the organization – and again, it's not confined to interns and admins. In one role, the administrator of the data warehouse had come to act more like its gatekeeper. If we wanted to extract data, we had to go through him, and do it his way. Automation was almost a loss of sovereignty. It is not uncommon in my experience for someone who runs the reports without documentation to 'hold the company to ransom' over pay rises and job security.

Technological change

We are going through a digital transformation, but what does that mean? Often it means that data will move around as applications are shifted to the cloud. Manual processes need to be updated every time the technology changes, often in a state of panic when someone repeats last month's manual process and finds that apparently the business suddenly has no staff or zero turnover. A script that extracts data is almost entirely focused on how to extract it, in which format, and which fields to combine. If there are 100 lines in the script, 99 of them will be about this, and one will tell the application where the data lives. If you've automated, this is all you need to update.

CASE STUDY
Spinach that sends email

Challenge: What's in the soil?

At the beginning of 2021, we were briefly amused by the news that 'Scientists have created spinach that can send emails' (Thred Media, 2012), which was actually a five-year-old MIT research report that suddenly went viral. 'Spam's new frontier' quipped the *Guardian* (2021). Not so much the robots coming for us, but the plants. This, of course, missed the point of what spinach would be trying to tell us. What is in soil matters to billions of people, and we have very poor, manual techniques for finding out.

Analysis: Teach plants to talk

The original research work (Trafton, 2016) was based on the insight that plants are extremely well suited to detecting the composition of soil, but they just can't tell us what they find (other than by flowering or wilting). If plants could communicate automatically when the soil was too dry, or contained dangerous chemicals, then we could report soil conditions continuously and automatically.

Action: Automated alerts

'The goal of plant nanobionics is to introduce nanoparticles into the plant to give it non-native functions,' said Michael Strano, a professor of chemical engineering at MIT and the leader of the research. They embedded carbon nanotubes in the plant leaves that emit a fluorescent signal when they encounter a particular chemical. These signals can be read with an infrared camera connected to a smartphone, which automatically emails the alert. There's nothing particularly important about the email process. Spinach could just as easily update a dashboard or trigger an alarm, and thanks to MIT one day it undoubtedly will.

Outcome: 'Maybe runner beans could even jump on a video call every now and then too?'

This was the response in the press (*Guardian*, 2021). But this is a good – though undeniably weird – explanation of the benefits of automation. It can adapt to detect many substances in the soil (frequent changes), it manages risk and reports precise information. It solves the problem that the information takes a lot of repeated effort to acquire, and the way it reports the data means that it can be communicated in a number of ways.

Task: Manageable automation projects

You can do a lot of automation work for very little reward if you do not manage the scope of the project. Returning to the 500 reports at the serviced office business, it clearly would have been self-contradictory to create automated processes for all of them, one by one, and then spend the rest of my career trying to keep them running. Automation is another process that you will embark on in which the scope expands in proportion with management's enthusiasm. So how do we make automation manageable?

Limit the workload

The most important step is to manage expectation by focusing on what the business needs, not the activity that is driving it. This is a process of negotiation. At the serviced office business, we examined all 500 reports and found (not surprisingly) that there was considerable overlap in what was being reported. This is a similar process to the one we encountered for dashboards – most managers think they have a unique need. There is much less variation in what needs to be reported than the report compilers assume.

Part of the problem will be that staff feel defensive. If the person creating the report can convince themselves and others that the report is special and requires unusual skill, then they are making a case for being given special responsibility. It might also help them to explain why, once a month, they voluntarily stay late making pie charts after their managers have gone home.

At the serviced office business we settled on 40 reports, one for each major function in the business. This was still a lot of automation (and could not be done all in one bite), but it was 8 per cent of the 500-plus reports we started with. A rationalization like this will create fewer, more comprehensive pieces of information. If that means there are meetings that intentionally skip some of it because the business now knows too much, provided the presentation is easy to understand, this is not a bad problem to have.

Discover and simplify the process

As above, the process by which data gets into a report is also likely to be a nasty shock. You will be familiar with this because it forms part of your work on data governance and quality, but the informal, home-made techniques used to create the output might be undermining your attempts to provide a single, high-quality source of data.

Standardize data sources

Rather than focusing on the actions (we open this spreadsheet, copy these numbers, add them to this, divide by the number of days in a month, and so on), it's important to match what is trying to be communicated to the data source mandated by the organization's governance structures. Note that this will change the report's contents: sales reports and finance reports will, for the first time, use consistent data without any opportunity for someone to helpfully frame it to their advantage, and you have to negotiate that.

Be ready to scale

The second-stage benefit of this approach is that it is more scalable. This isn't a practical consideration at this stage – you have enough on your plate – but it will pay off later, as you replicate the work for different offices, different parts of the business, different products. Automation should aim to reduce the amount of configuration (or, if you have to go there, coding) needed to achieve this.

Will I use a tool?

This is clearly important and there are many tools you could use. One that I have used, for example, is WhereScape. It 'solves a significant challenge for data infrastructure projects by automating tasks like building data pipelines while consolidating multiple tools and disparate skills into a cohesive solution'. The company says, 'WhereScape's tools reduce timelines, generate significant ROI, and deliver immediate business value' (Businesswire, 2019). My experience of this tool is that it works well to automate the discovery of data in your systems and creates the data set automatically from a data model, no matter what the underlying cloud data environment is. Examples are Azure, Amazon Redshift, Microsoft SQL Server, Microsoft Azure, Oracle, Snowflake, Teradata, etc.

The focus of this book is not to define the data architecture, but it's important that you know there are solutions that work well today, and that this ability to automate and be independent of technology environments is key. My argument is that automation tools should be intuitive and ideally used by business-savvy people in the data team. So instead of having to create code manually, you create a diagram of the flow of data and the processes that it goes through, and it self-documents. My experience suggests that you can automate 70–80 per cent of the data warehouse work and get productivity improvements of 500 per cent.

This works in that you can experiment, iterating based on what works best and most universally. It also automatically documents what you do. Clearly, we're skipping over some technical detail here, but there are plenty of manuals that will teach you how to do this. What matters is that this does not become the focus of what you are doing with automation.

There is clearly a sunken cost to using these tools: apply them to one report and it's cheaper to hire someone to do the job manually; apply them to 50 reports and your finance director will be supportive not only because you made reporting quicker but also because you're saving money by automating the activity of collecting and communicating information, as well as the result.

In 2017 David Wright, a director in the consulting business at Deloitte, told the Institute of Chartered Accountants that the automation projects his firm had undertaken with clients had been extremely effective. Among them, 92 per cent found that the project met or exceeded expectations of delivering compliance, and 86 per cent that it improved productivity.

Wright also reported that only 31 per cent found that the IT function had been supportive with automation because the process often bypassed the IT department.

You might need friends in IT, because our next stage is using all the good work we've done so far to massively scale up and optimize the data function.

SUMMARY

- There are many repeated, stable projects – reporting especially – that involve unnecessary manual labour as people extract data and hand-craft solutions through habit.

- Understanding how to create the report or insight might become an unofficial part of that person's job that is never documented. This is bad for governance and creates a problem when that person is not available.

- Automating these processes improves quality, can absorb process changes and cure reporting backlogs. These advantages are often cited, ironically, as reasons not to automate.

- Do not try to discover every existing data process across the organization and then automate. Rationalize first.

- Be sure to keep the business onside, which will be worrying about what happens when jobs are automated, and the IT department, which may need to help you implement the tools you require.

References

Businesswire (2019) Idera, Inc. acquires WhereScape, advancing portfolio of cross-platform database tools with data infrastructure automation, September, https://www.businesswire.com/news/home/20190919005152/en/Idera-Inc.-Acquires-WhereScape-Advancing-Portfolio-of-Cross-Platform-Database-Tools-with-Data-Infrastructure-Automation (archived at https://perma.cc/VA3N-4WH9)

Frey, C B and Osborne, M (2016) The future of employment: How susceptible are jobs to computerisation? *Technological Forecasting & Social Change*, **114**, pp 254–80

Guardian (2021) Spam's new frontier? Now even spinach can send emails, 3 February, https://www.theguardian.com/food/2021/feb/03/spams-new-frontier-now-even-spinach-can-send-emails (archived at https://perma.cc/ES8G-YKJQ)

Keynes, J M (1930) Economic possibilities for our grandchildren, in *Essays in Persuasion*, Harcourt Brace

McKinsey Global Institute (2018) A future that works, McKinsey

Thred Media (2012) Scientists have created spinach that can send emails. Here's how it could fight the climate crisis, 2 February, https://thred.com/culture/scientists-have-developed-spinach-that-can-send-emails/ (archived at https://perma.cc/AXA5-AJC9)

Trafton, A (2016) Nanobionic spinach plants can detect explosives, *MIT News,* https://news.mit.edu/2016/nanobionic-spinach-plants-detect-explosives-1031 (archived at https://perma.cc/3G25-2UPB)

13

Scaling up and scaling out

Consolidating and deploying your innovations across the whole business brings a range of new challenges if you want to preserve the business benefits. The data team's experience in replicating gains across the business offers potentially huge return on investment. But be careful not to become overwhelmed.

KEY CONCEPTS

- Scale up
- Scale out
- Resource multiplier
- Hackathon

Introduction

One of the most inspirational people I have met from outside my world is Kenton Cool. Aside from having an excellent name, he climbed Mount Everest 15 times, including twice in a week in 2007, and was the first person to send a tweet from the summit. He has been described as 'the most formidable mountaineer of his generation' by Sir Ranulph Fiennes, who he guided to the summit of Everest in 2009, a trip that raised £3 million for Marie Curie Cancer Care. He did all of this while living with the pain from two shattered heels sustained in a climbing accident in 1996 that, at first, convinced doctors he would never walk unaided again.

Of course, as a data geek, I'm most interested in the process by which he becomes more adept at summiting as he goes along. The point is that, if you are going to climb your personal Everest, you want someone to guide you who has been to the summit before, who knows every step of the route, and can let you know if you wander off the track.

In this way, the scaling up in this chapter is similar to Cool's amazing physical accomplishments of scaling the world's toughest peaks. We don't want the people we work with to report their data transformation as a once-in-a-lifetime ordeal, something to tell the grandchildren about. If we want to scale this effectively, we have to identify opportunities, spot the regularities (and differences) and guide the organization along the way.

Also, when Kenton Cool guides climbers on an expedition, he cannot climb the mountain for them. Scaling up isn't about a heroic data team swooping down on a department, a subsidiary or an office, magically solving a problem, and leaving in a blaze of glory. Scaling up requires cooperation with the organization. This isn't just about delivering more; the data team's capability is also scaled up through automation, by leveraging the emerging data skills throughout your organization, by the investment you earned from your early success, and by using all the data sources at your disposal.

From quick wins to big wins

Recall where we started: a quick win. And recall also the advantage of a quick win from our definition: 'The best quick wins can be built on or repeated at a later date.'

That later date has arrived.

So far we have focused on projects as if they were monolithic: a single type of data problem, requiring a set of tools or processes, with a defined goal. What you will know by now is that large-scale changes like data quality at the outset, or dashboarding, are always incremental. The process of transformation is never sudden. If you achieve something and it works, we can parlay that into widespread board support and funding for a more ambitious project based on the same principles. We climbed the mountain once, we can do it again.

It's counterintuitive to think that by starting small you can achieve scale quicker, but this is indeed the case because when you limit your early scope, you learn quickly and show tangible results.

If you have been the leader of a data transformation project, you will have no shortage of people who will want to return to the summit with you, because you are successful. This may present us with a problem: you have limited time in your day and too many things to do already. This means that scaling up isn't about suddenly doing everything, everywhere, all the time, for everyone who sends you an email. Scaling is about putting in place ways to achieve a maximum return on the data team's investment.

Tony Robbins, an influential author, motivational speaker and philanthropist, says:

> In business, the definition of 'scale' is to increase revenue at a faster rate
> than costs. Businesses achieve this in a number of ways, from adopting new
> technologies to finding 'gaps' in their operations that can be streamlined.
> Businesses that are able to add revenue and increase operational demands while
> maintaining the same costs – or even lowering costs – will be able to scale
> successfully. (Robbins Research International, 2021)

In Chapter 5 I discussed the Singaporean photocopying problem. This is a great example of scale: find something you can fix in one location and then apply it in all locations, in this case 3,000. Then find other similar problems and repeat.

Be dull and repetitive

This is not general advice, but it is an important aspect of scaling up. From the outside, everyone can see the similarities between what you have just done and what they want for their bit of the business. Look closer, and they often overestimate the regularities. If something is a bit like something else, if there are a few aspects of that project that can be carried over into the next one, it's not scaling up, it's an entirely new piece of work.

Scaling up works when the fundamental purpose of what you are doing can be replicated exactly.

HOW TO MEASURE: SUITABILITY TO SCALE

Let's take the fundamental project of data transformation, the single customer view that we introduced in Chapter 9, as an example. What work did it require?

Data governance. An accurately described single source of truth.

Data quality. A complete record of previous interactions and knowledge of all aspects of the customer.

Golden ID. A single record that uniquely identifies the customer to everyone in the organization.

No shadow IT. No data is being collected that isn't governed and validated by the data team.

Buy-in from the business. Even though many may not be data experts, or even particularly data literate, they do not put up barriers.

If you have completed the first stage of this project – for example, using the SCV to identify which customers are profitable for one area of the business – you are aware that it involves some pretty heavy lifting. But if your data is trusted as a basis for decision-making, and the acquisition and validation of that data are increasingly automated, with care we can replicate the capability throughout the business.

Task: Choosing how and when to scale

There are, effectively, two ways to scale. But you don't have to scale if you are worried it won't work out. Your choice of project at this point can either unlock multiples of the value the data transformation has already demonstrated, or it can derail the project completely.

If you're going through this, you probably have requests to replicate projects on your desk already. It is important that you evaluate the need, the prospect of success, and the constraints on delivery that you will encounter.

Scale up: Replicate a defined project in other places

Some projects make this the natural choice. At an energy company I worked with that ran petrol stations and oil supplies in 23 countries in Africa our goal was to use data to make the retail offer more efficient. Although Mali is not Burkina Faso, the principle is the same: we planned to capture customer data and use it to find what else the customer might want in their basket based on what most people buy or perhaps seasonal demand. That's scale: you do one thing and then do it across all 23 countries.

The success of this relies not only on the ability to create quality and trusted data but also on the management task to get all parts of the business to follow the same processes and apply the same standards.

The potential for failure is the absence of those qualities. Certain variations may occur between the different places in the business where the project is implemented; data acquisition may vary, as might management ability. This may create governance challenges. Also, there may be variation in laws governing the acquisition, sharing and use of data, and in the habits and norms in the two places. The first of these is something to be aware of; the second needs to be resolved when the case for scaling up is made to you, not at an angry post-mortem on why the project didn't deliver value when scaled up.

SCALE UP

Increasing the value of data by replicating a successful process across the business.

Scale out: Find an adjacent activity

This may be more challenging. The data capability grants an opportunity to innovate across the business. So the SCV is useful to deepen the existing relationship – what economists would call the intensive margin, and what we might think of as buying the same thing more often – but also to develop the extensive margin, as your business offers new products and services.

The potential of this project is that, in data terms, you can use the same SCV in an entirely new way. The new activity might have had access to only a fraction of the data before, so this may be a big upgrade in the capability of that team.

There are two caveats. The first is that this may require new, or more, data, for example some external data that tells us more about the customer's habits when they are not transacting with our business. The second is that it may require new ways of working. That means cooperation between two business units that until now worked separately, or discipline in how to execute a marketing plan based on knowledge rather than activity. For this, you rely on the willingness of the managers in those parts of the business to evangelize data and to change ingrained habits. So it's not entirely straight-forward, but this is a huge step towards establishing a data-driven culture, which is our ultimate goal.

SCALE OUT

Increasing the value of data by discovering new applications for a process.

Know when to say no

If you have demonstrated success, you will have more requests to scale than you can handle which, at first glance, fit into either the scale up or scale out category. This does not mean they are good ideas. At this point you are constrained by the size of the data team, the knowledge of data in the busi-ness, perhaps even the amount and quality of the data you have (always a work in progress), and the ability of the business to execute.

This means that you should carefully evaluate how you allocate effort, and have the confidence to say, let's not solve this problem today.

The red flags are likely to be the inverse of the attributes we set out above. If the data you can access is not of the required quality, or you are not sure it tells the truth, it would be irresponsible to use that as a broader basis for decision-making. And if there is hidden data activity, or management resist-ance to what you are doing, then your best work will not be good enough. It will also suck up all your resources and derail the data transformation process.

A strong (polite) refusal might be the trigger to solve some of these prob-lems. Whether it is or not, don't be pressured into scaling up too soon, because it means you will take longer to achieve your goal.

Use your resource multipliers

Scaling up does not mean adding new bodies to the data team. This is every-thing you don't want: it increases the management and reporting overhead. It sucks up the budget. It means a pause for recruitment. It means that a new group of people have to learn the job and the role, just at the time you want to press ahead.

The problem remains, though, that there is more work to be done than the data team can handle at this point. Automation is your friend, but automation is not implementation. By far the most important non-technical resource you can tap into is the willingness of people elsewhere in the business to work with the data team. In Chapter 4 we discussed the need for diversity of thought and experience in the data team, and the need for problem-solvers to be practical and adaptable.

When you scale, you need to locate and develop similar skills throughout the business. You don't need the same level and intensity as in the data team, but it pays to recognize and encourage the same attitude. These will be your resource multipliers. I usually find the most useful links to cultivate are with the operations side of the business. In ops, the teams understand blockers, culture and frustrations. They know what works and what doesn't. And they are accustomed to balancing priorities. Their goals are usually aligned to ours; it's a natural partnership.

RESOURCE MULTIPLIER

A person in the business (often in operations) who understand the needs and values of the data team, but also has strong knowledge of a particular department or function. This person can work alongside it to achieve its goals and accelerate deployment.

There will also be data enthusiasts in the business who are not part of the data team. While I don't encourage unmanaged shadow data, the attitude and motivation that make people recognize that data can solve their problems in new ways are exactly what you need at this point because the first step of scaling up is to define and solve the problem of how you will deliver the capability they need.

The question remains: how can you inspire these groups to work together to solve problems in ways that will break their ingrained habits and deliver value for the business? This isn't something that can easily be done top-down, by writing a long report that is discussed, approved, never read by most people, and ignored. But this tends to be the way that many of these projects are structured. This is not the way to go about it because, just at the time you most need the cooperation and emotional investment of the business to make a success, the data transformation is presented as something that will be done to them, whether they like it or not.

The focus here is to leverage the whole data community. Everyone who touches data – creating, fixing or using it.

We should discuss by far the most effective way of leveraging that data community that I know: the hackathon.

HACKATHON

An event at which a lot of people come together to write or improve computer programs, usually for one very specific purpose or challenge. It could be people within one organization or a company with its suppliers. It's seen as a way of rapidly solving a problem by knocking down the usual barriers to success.

CASE STUDY
Facebook hackathons (Angelica, 2020)

Challenge: Accelerate innovation

Facebook had to scale innovation. Building structures and imposing tiers of management were essential to deliver a stable, consistent product. But it could potentially get in the way of the engineering culture that the organization valued. The problem was how to create big ideas and fast-track them.

Analysis: Focus enthusiasm to solve problems

One thing Facebook was not short of was talented software engineers. The often-cited problem is that they are resistant to authority. Whether that is true or not, creating a space in which they did pure problem-solving without a closely defined goal had potential to create powerful new ideas.

Action: Hackathons are go

The first Facebook all-night hackathon took place in 2007 and was repeated regularly afterwards. The organization of the events reflects Facebook's culture: a 7 pm start, a 6 am finish, takeaway food and many snacks. The events were, and are, open to all levels of expertise, including non-coders who can work with the group to provide expertise. The idea is that people from different areas of the business work together, whereas in the normal run of things they would never meet. Afterwards, a 'prototype forum' is held so that groups can present their ideas.

Outcome: A massive upgrade in innovation

Many of the ideas could be scaled in a matter of days. Things that Facebook users take for granted such as the timeline, the 'like' button, and the ability to tag people in comments (apparently the brainchild of an intern) were created at these events.

Task: Implementing your hackathon

Your organization is unlikely to have the coding or data abilities that Facebook possesses. It might also not be full of people who want to camp out in the office overnight. But it's the structure of the event, not the narrow rules of the game, that makes a hackathon so effective. I have used hackathons many times over the years, in many contexts, and they rarely fail to deliver ways in which we can innovate. They are fun and enjoyable to participate in, not the common attributes of a meeting where you say, 'Can you tell me what your requirements are for this project?'

How can you structure a hackathon that works?

It's not all about scaling

Ultimately, we're trying to find ways to make data more useful. But scale is the data team's problem. What matters in a hackathon is to create ideas that are worthy of scale. One of the things to note about Facebook's attitude was that its engineers just had to have ideas and run with them. Delivery was for another day.

Join business units and functions

When planning a hackathon, you want to break out of silos. So the attendees should mix: marketing, operations, finance, HR, all the people who work with data every day. They all have the same frustrations, so use that to your advantage. That means you purposely don't put people together with the colleagues they see every day, or with people who are only at their level of seniority, or who all do the same thing.

Value their time

We have to respect the idea that people are taking time out from their day-to-day jobs to help solve problems. Working with the operational and data-facing people also means that when you deliver the outcome, they are the people who understand the value of what they contributed. Facebook's hackers took all night, but for your hackathon an afternoon or an evening is enough. And reward their contribution at the time: provide food, maybe some beer and wine at the end. They are offering valuable help, so use it to build camaraderie.

All ideas considered

At the outset, be clear that you will consider anything that works and adds value. Do not assign teams or strict deliverables. Let teams discover what they have in common or how they can help one another. It's not uncommon, for example, to discover that one department has the data that another group needs. How they share it and use it, whether this is practical and legal, are problems to solve later.

Set an ambitious goal

There is a reason for the hackathon, but be broad. An example: how can we use our SCV to increase revenue? The overall goal needs to align with data and analytics strategy, but you want everyone there to think big.

It's not about the coding

Many people from outside the data world think of 'hacking' as technology and focus on its negative connotations. Make sure that everyone knows that the original meaning of the word was to describe innovative problem-solving. Facebook's hackathons are heavily centred around coding because that's how Facebook delivers its product. But the real value is in the idea: when a Facebook hackathon delivered the idea that engineers would be rewarded with a Pokémon each time they found a bug in the code, the implementation was trivial – but this successful innovation captured the insight that engineers were motivated by humour and respect that they could show off. A management meeting would never have considered this idea.

But don't stop them

If you mix some coding and data skills into the hackathon teams, then this can really exceed expectations, because part of the stimulation of the hackathon is that it encourages someone to say, 'hang on, let's see if we can build it', and to start to create something new to show to the group. Many of the innovations take little time to prototype and if you can see a new view on data, or that if you combine these two sources it creates much greater value for the business, that's an amazing result.

Evaluate afterwards

For sure, let participants present their ideas and get feedback. Your evaluation (and that of the people who allocate budget and measure things like compliance) will follow but do it quickly and publicize the results. It's a wonderful feeling for the people who hacked to know that they created something. It's a pretty good feeling for you that they understand how you helped them do it.

The dividend from scaling

The hackathon is humbling, because it's a demonstration that you make progress by giving away your power. But it's also a lesson that from this point on, this will increasingly be the secret of your success. Building out the data community is a massive step towards a data culture. The people in the hackathon are your data culture warriors.

Your constraint is hours in the day, and number of people in the data team. You want sufficient resources, but a data team the size of an army will perversely make the data transition less effective, because it becomes something that is imposed by them on the business. As the data transition's influence on the business increases, this may increase resistance. The people on the frontline of the business may feel less motivation to buy into what you are doing or may resist developing the data skills that will help both you and them to flourish.

While you are scaling up the impact of your innovations, you are scaling up your influence by delegating as much as you can to people outside the data team: your resource multipliers. This is successful if they feel connected to the impact of what they do, if they are trusted and valued, and if the ideas you implement are often their ideas. A data transition is, as we saw in Chapter 4, a team game.

SUMMARY

- Having created success in one part of the business, the ability to replicate this in other areas or processes offers a potentially enormous return on investment.

- The knowledge that the data team has of these processes is an important factor in applying them quickly and effectively.

- You can crowdsource ideas for scaling using techniques like hackathons, bringing together your whole data community.

- These also help to establish the importance of the data transformation, because scaling will make your work more visible.

- Implementation requires the cooperation of the business, and especially of allies inside it, if it is to happen at speed.

References

Angelica, L (2020) What exactly is Facebook hackathon? *Mockitt*, https://mockitt. wondershare.com/hackathon/facebook-hackathons.html (archived at https:// perma.cc/2VKJ-XZ7B)

Robbins Research International (2021) Scaling a business, https://www. tonyrobbins.com/business/scaling-a-business/ (archived at https://perma.cc/ A5QN-YBSM)

14

Optimizing

A data-driven culture creates organizational change. This is powerful but may cause conflict. While there are huge opportunities to exploit, this will change the nature of many people's roles in the business. But it is also a tipping point: the organization begins to be driven by data.

KEY CONCEPTS

- Disintermediation
- Straight-through processing (STP)

Introduction

When American Express outsourced some of its business processes to India in the 1990s, it chose a chartered accountant called Raman Roy to lead the effort. Decades later, Roy is credited with being the pioneer of Business Process Outsourcing (BPO) in the country. Today he is the managing director of Quatrro Global Services, which specializes in using Indian graduates and professionals to conduct increasingly high-value, data-driven processes for his global clients.

Many of us have a jaded view of BPO, perhaps through a bad business experience, perhaps just because we dealt with an inefficient call centre. But for many years, the growth of BPO in India in particular has not been driven by semi-skilled occupations. In 2005, PwC reported that 'the objective of offshoring has progressed from being a mere cost-saving initiative to one that is adopted for realizing process improvements and enhancing efficiencies' (PricewaterhouseCoopers India, 2005).

Around that time, Roy had moved on from American Express and was implementing a methodology called 'Pragati' at his company, Wipro Spectramind. Pragati is a Hindi term for continuous improvement, for his US and European clients. On winning a contract, his executives made sure that they documented the client's processes in minute detail, and then replicated them precisely at the hub dedicated to that company in India. In one case, staff who had passed exams set 5,000 miles away were acting as insurance underwriters for a UK firm. In another, PhDs were creating a genomics database.

The idea that BPO copies what you do while paying people in poor countries lower salaries to do it is known disparagingly as 'your mess for less'. The gains from this type of outsourcing are often small and, as the cost of salaries in other locations rises, eventually disappear completely. Meanwhile your inefficiencies are written into a contract that has to be executed.

Pragati took a different approach. Roy's clients found that Wipro would not deviate from the process and quality standard it inherited for three months. During this time, it could learn where the inefficiencies were, which processes could be done better and which ones could be discarded completely, and what changes in data collection and processing would be required. After the three-month period, Wipro would implement those improvements one by one, with the client's approval. The client could measure the improvement that flowed from this optimization process because it had a baseline.

The process of BPO encourages organizations to discover what data they manage and map their processes. It may also kick-start a process of data quality improvement and governance. But the big prize is to be able to use the data team's newfound capability to redesign and optimize the processes that depend on data. You don't need to outsource the process to do this, but you do need Roy's clear-eyed analysis of what can be improved, and how to do it. This is our next step.

Best intentions are not optimal

The data team's successes so far may inspire more requests to get involved in discrete areas of the business. There are usually so many things to do, and the quality of the data being used is so much poorer than anyone realizes, that just about any improvement pushes out the efficiency frontier. And this is what quick wins and single-issue campaigns target: defined tasks, done better.

If the data team has already organized a hackathon, or created a powerful tool like a single customer view, or begun to automate data collection, it will have triggered the part of the brain in many other people that asks, 'what if?':

- What if we redesigned our marketing based on a new segmentation?
- What if the information from sales calls automatically triggered follow-up responses?
- What if we could recognize unusual customer behaviour that might be fraud – could we react faster?

These are all data problems to some extent. But, more than that, they are process problems.

One of the challenges in trying to optimize a process is that, at the beginning, there may not be a process. There is a way that things are done. This has been created by the solution to thousands of small challenges, and these solutions become habits. They become locked in because people are recruited to perform them, and they learn from one another. IT systems are put in place and configured, not because it's the best way to do things but because we've always done it this way.

Even if there is a process, it may have been set in stone and needs to be revisited. The need for optimization does not imply that something is obviously going wrong in the business. Clayton Christensen, the academic who coined the term 'disruptive innovation', investigated why good companies sometimes fail. One of his insights was that 'smart companies fail because they do everything right' (Christensen, 1997).

Well-intentioned people each take care of their part of the process, and metaphorically chuck the completed task over the fence to another part of the business. Years later, with hindsight, they will be able to see what they did wrong. But when we are wrapped up in doing the day-to-day work that gets the job done, this is not at all obvious. Even worse, if someone comes along and suggests that we disrupt the 'successful' process for a completely new one, we may instinctively reject the idea.

This is the fallacy of composition. Doing a lot of small components of a task really well does not mean we are optimizing the overall task.

Task: Plot a path to optimization

Optimization requires a clear business case that documents the actions you will take.

Document the informal process

As we have seen, many processes exist only in habit and custom. Until you uncover who creates data, who captures it, who processes it and who benefits from it today, you literally will not know where to start. The good news is that a lot of your previous activity – most obviously, governance – will have uncovered most of these steps.

Be prepared to measure outcomes

If there is a process to optimize, then you need to be clear (and agree with all stakeholders) exactly what the measure of improvement will be. There is likely to be more than one measure. On the one hand, there is the technical goal: something that took three days can now take 15 minutes. On the other hand, there are business outcomes tied to this that can be measured: if the improvement is a success, we expect your company to expand market share, have more satisfied customers, cut cost, cut waste, and be able to measure these outcomes. This must align with the priorities of the data and analytics strategy. We first discussed this in Chapter 6 when we looked at documenting a successful project.

Identify silos

Optimization requires the ability to combine data or expose data to new audiences. One of the reasons that processes are sub-optimal is that the data exists somewhere in the business, just not where it is needed. Solving this will require the buy-in of more managers before you do any work on making that data available. This also requires understanding from the data team of the constraints on how data can be combined – the GDPR may decide this – and what is ethical or wise in the long run. But just because a revenue-generating optimization can be done doesn't mean that it should be.

Don't ignore data acquisition

This optimization analysis may reveal that you simply are not capturing the data in the first place. For example, a better segmentation may not be possible if you don't know enough about customers. A better way of prioritizing and allocating prospects is not practical if the sales team guards its data jealously or doesn't enter it into the system at all. The reason for this may be the (quite rational) fear of disintermediation – see below.

DISINTERMEDIATION

A reduction in the use of intermediaries between the origination and execution of a job by automating and reorganizing the data process. This improves efficiency but reduces the need for an employee to complete or monitor the job.

Task: Overcoming resistance

If you are to use data to lead an optimization process, it will be neither quick nor easy. But it will be transformational.

Use appropriate skills from the data team

The skills to optimize are not primarily about doing. The people who can redesign a process are those best suited to standing back and asking, 'What if we did it this way?' That requires understanding of the business at a deep level, and an ability to communicate effectively with people who work with the data. Too many 'doing' skills may get in the way of lateral thinking.

Get buy-in from managers

It is possible that to achieve the benefits of optimization, the data team will need help to completely redesign a workflow. At the very least, the data team will need access to how a process works, and to investigate the details. This means that whoever manages the process needs to be on board. This also applies to HR: your intervention might lead to a reduction in the need for staff, and therefore you become part of a process that may result in changes in job descriptions, or possibly redundancy. This needs to be handled appropriately.

Be clear that this may change the nature of a job

Optimization can easily lead to unforeseen consequences for the people who ask you to intervene. Imagine a scenario in which a group of people take data and compile insight documents for the sales team. But they are frustrated because the sales team is slow to input data, and so their output has low value. They ask that you automate data acquisition, which you do. Although this has a small but significant effect, the problem remains: the information in the documents is often ignored. But if you have the data, why would you not give the sales team an automatically generated dashboard with the data in near-real time? If this also has updates on commission or leads, then it becomes the centre of the sales team's job, and drives their activity. This is a great improvement, cutting delay and reducing management overhead. But it has perhaps cut out the employees who requested your help, and therefore you will need to work with management and HR to make sure this process is recognized and managed.

Be prepared to handle conflict

Given all of the above, it is obvious that resistance may come your way at every level. These are challenges that you cannot solve yourself, and for which you need the support of the board. One of the failures in my career came from a project that had identified a huge opportunity for growth, with a clear path to realize value and a strong business case. But it required changing the habits of the sales team. And, ultimately, they were not going to change for me. Management, who had been supportive, preferred to keep the sales team onside. The outcome was that we could not execute our grand plan, but it was worse: it meant that the entire data transformation lost momentum because its most aspirational goals had been taken away.

It is important to be clear that the data team's work will be compromised if it refuses an opportunity to make the data transition because optimization may mean someone loses a job. That is a judgement for someone else – the CEO, you hope – to make. You could interpret the CEO's response as an indication of whether the board really does share your vision.

You may find yourself asking, 'Why do I want to be involved in this?' The reason is that at this stage, you can take the important step towards creating an organization that will flourish, that has its future assured.

The limits of automation

Optimizing can also mean focusing on what data cannot do. A good example of this is straight-through processing. Used in financial processes – for example, in the decision of whether to grant a loan – it is extremely efficient and effective. But it is not efficient or effective to do this for all loans.

> ### STRAIGHT-THROUGH PROCESSING (STP)
>
> A business process in which data is acquired and used to trigger actions without human intervention. It is most often applied to financial services, and requires complete and accurate data.

If, for example, 80 per cent of mortgage applications can be granted using STP, and the other 20 per cent need to be reviewed by humans, then designing a process that attempts to automate 100 per cent of loans may be problematic and vulnerable to manipulation or fraud, or simply create suboptimal outcomes. Sometimes it's a lack of data or overcomplicated data that can be improved in a future iteration, but there is always the potential result that it will be too difficult, or too expensive, to optimize a business outcome through automation alone.

In this case, the optimal process is to take away the drudge work by automating what can be automated and providing the best-quality data to the people who have to make judgements that are not automated, and continually measure business outcomes to decide whether the process can be further improved.

This is a tipping point

We have reached the end of the process of industrialization. It will be apparent now that we're at a point that the transformation generates its own momentum. Automation, scaling up and optimization raise the stakes on the role of the data team.

The payoffs for success are higher

This is pushing out the efficiency frontier. Increasing the efficiency of discrete elements of a process by 10 per cent means that, at best, you will get a 10 per cent increase in efficiency for the outcome. But re-engineering the process as well means that this new level of efficiency becomes even greater.

Your intervention is more visible

If you improve the quality of the data used as inputs for a process, the day-to-day work may be better, but it isn't obviously different. Better reporting is a quality improvement that everyone can get behind, but it soon becomes business as usual. Changing the way in which a company functions, though, is a different order of intervention, both as an opportunity for the board, a threat for your competitors, and a mixture of both interventions for your fellow employees whose jobs might get much better or disappear completely.

Successful CDOs have many friends

This is the point at which the CEO, the COO and the CFO can all clearly see the value of your work. This makes it easier to fund future projects, but it also makes it easier to carry your vision for a truly data-driven organization. You might appreciate this, because at this point you might have fought many battles and put in many late nights.

Enjoy the feeling. You have done something remarkable. Still, there's a long way to go yet.

SUMMARY

- Success in many areas of the business can create a patchwork of improvements that are not optimized. At some point it becomes necessary to reorganize entire processes.

- Identifying and documenting processes or silos of data are likely to uncover huge potential to optimize the structure of the business to capitalize on the power of the data transition.

- This is not a technology problem, and it is not only a data challenge. It requires the commitment and help of the executive team and HR.

- Optimization can disintermediate, but it can also create space for skilled employees to focus on the jobs for which their judgement is necessary.

- This is a tipping point, at which data begins to drive irreversible change.

References

Christensen, C (1997) *The Innovator's Dilemma*, Harvard Business Review Press
PricewaterhouseCoopers India (2005) The evolution of BPO in India, https://www.pwc.in/assets/pdfs/evolution-of-bpo-in-india.pdf (archived at https://perma.cc/VD4S-NZ88)

PART FIVE

Wave 4: Realize

The work to this point has created a different organization in which data can create a culture of continuous improvement based on constant feedback from the *Industrialize* wave. We have reached a stage where much has been automated and we are starting to realize significant value from our investments.

We can focus now on how to capitalize on those gains by augmenting data, sharing it, and creating powerful analytical capabilities.

But at this point we must also embrace the risk of innovation, using the trust in data processes that the data team has earned, because projects are now more transformational, but inevitably experimental too, leading us towards *Differentiate*.

Value, Build, Improve content of this wave

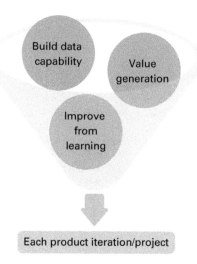

Each product iteration/project

The activities for our VBI model in this wave are:

Value. To significantly improve value, the data transformation needs to integrate internal activities with those of its customers and partners and create analytical capability. A lot of groundwork has been done ready to help us realize the value at this stage.

Build. We will build more ambitious data science, AI, and ML capabilities with links to customers and business partners. This in turn will increase risk and increase the scrutiny of our data.

Improve. We need to capture the feedback we get from our customers and business partners at this stage as it's likely to be transformational for our business, and this needs to be built into our business processes.

15

The voice of the customer

External data, social data and market research can provide important insights that enhance our understanding of the customer. But these sources must be integrated with existing data first.

KEY CONCEPTS

- Customer relationship management (CRM)
- Voice of the customer (VoC)
- Tracking survey
- Disruption
- Application programming interface (API)
- Social listening
- Firehose API
- Sentiment analysis
- Net promoter score (NPS)

Introduction

Consumers, we know, like to shop around. But many businesses would be surprised to find out just how disloyal their customers are.

For example, a test of shopping habits in the United States (Zhang et al, 2017) found that most grocery shoppers were far more motivated by the search for the best dessert topping or their preferred antifreeze than they were driven by brand loyalty. They discovered that 83 per cent of shoppers in the St Louis area regularly visited between four and nine stores to purchase groceries. Less than 1 per cent of households stayed loyal to just one store, while six in 100 went to 10 stores or more.

'We found that people aren't as store loyal as we thought' was the understated reaction of P B Seetharaman, who was one of the authors and also director of the Center of Customer Analytics and Big Data at Olin Business School at Washington University in St Louis. 'Clearly, people are polygamous.'

The study also found that this wasn't just transactional, because this polygamy was driven by different forces. Some consumers were driven by convenience and shopped only close to where they were, either at home or at work. At the other end of the scale were cherry-pickers, who clipped coupons and liked to expend a lot of effort on finding the best deals.

Don't think this is just about groceries. Many organizations instinctively overestimate loyalty because they meet most of their customers only during the later stages of consideration, at the points of transaction or consumption – all processes focused around their brand. This applies whether the activity it is buying a car, renting a film, choosing a designer brand, committing to a phone contract, or ordering a beer.

A smart business listens to feedback when it comes through the customer service department. This might flow into a mature customer relationship management solution, which uses the single customer view and inbound communication, plus observed behaviour, to segment and market more effectively.

CUSTOMER RELATIONSHIP MANAGEMENT (CRM)

A process by which a business monitors and improves interactions with customers, typically using data collected during interactions.

But now your data transformation can take this further and focus on what customers are telling the business when they are not transacting with it. Integrating this data is a prerequisite for better data analysis and strategic thinking.

Hearing their voice

The 'voice of the customer' (VoC) is another discipline that is newer than you might think. It dates from a 1993 paper published in *Marketing Science* by Abbie Griffin of the University of Chicago and John Hauser of MIT (Griffin and Hauser, 1993). They argued that the data used by marketing departments captured broad-brush customer needs, but not with enough precision to help companies improve their products. What was required was much more detail to inform interactive improvements.

VOICE OF THE CUSTOMER

A company-wide effort to capture a customer's expectations, preferences and dislikes, used as a continuous process to create better products and services.

A large part of the problem is that organizations often don't know much about what people do when those people are not buying from them or communicating with them. This raises questions like: Who else do they do business with? Why did they choose those other companies? What do they say about the product or service to other people? What outside events would cause them to leave, or cause them to do more business here?

When we present the problem like this, it seems obvious. But it's surprisingly common that we assume the data we generate internally is all there is to know, and it's extremely important that we do not make this assumption.

It's right to get excited about the sensors in our cars that generate data about wear and tear, fuel efficiency or how we drive, and communicate those insights to the manufacturer to help either support drivers or make better cars. But a report on car use in the UK, researched by the RAC Foundation (RAC Foundation, 2012) and based on survey data, found that there are 25 billion car trips every year: an average of 18 trips per car per week. This means the average British car is on the road for six hours every week. Which means that 96.5 per cent of the time there's nothing for the sensors to report. They can't describe what we do when we are not driving, or why we decided not to take the car today, or how likely we would be to use the car to do a task.

This information is just as important as the data that the manufacturer did acquire. This is why a project to combine high-quality internal data with external sources, or create new ways to acquire data, is valuable at this point. But which sources, how, and to what end?

Reasons to use other sources of data

There are many other sources of data, but for the purpose of this chapter we will group them into three categories. This is not an exhaustive list and we will look at some other external sources of data in later chapters.

What are competitors doing?

Data on competitors – their pricing, their business and what people think of them – informs any competitive advantage. But it is often captured only for a one-off project, with a bespoke brief, for a single meeting, and the research is never repeated. Automating this data collection process, and repeating, is known as a competitive tracking survey (or 'tracker'). Relevant trackers might capture pricing data, or a comparison of the features of their product range.

TRACKING SURVEY

A project to collect consistent information about the market in which a company operates at regular intervals (daily, monthly, quarterly, yearly). The information can cover competitor behaviour, customer feedback or market trends. It allows organizations to spot trends, make comparisons with competitors, and detect threats.

What are customers doing when they are not being customers?

This question is especially important if the transaction occurs infrequently. Supermarkets transact with their customers every week and so, for example, may be able to spot changes in taste or emerging trends based on these inter-actions. But customers may not interact with the retailer that sold them a fridge or a washing machine until that customer decides to replace it. This means that the retailer doesn't know how the products are being used unless there is a problem. It also means that it knows less than it could about the trends in customer behaviour. A sudden decline in sales might be the result of a competitor, it might be a problem with pricing or quality, or it might simply be that customer tastes have changed while the manufacturer was focusing on its internal systems.

Some data sources might also contain important information that helps the business function sustainably or ethically. An important example when I worked at a gambling company was to expand the SCV to identify potential problem gamblers.

What do people think of a brand?

This might be the most important missing piece of the data jigsaw. If there is no compelling reason for the customer to be in touch after the transaction, internal data misses whether the customer is excited and pleased or regretful, whether customers wish the product was larger, quieter, or a different colour.

If we are mildly disappointed with a product or service, we usually don't make the effort to tell the company we bought it from. Instead we just buy from another company next time. We might dissuade someone else from purchasing. The product or service could be a bit too expensive, it could be not quite reliable enough, or the instructions could be slightly hard to follow in places – only a fraction of this information gets back to the retailer through customer complaints, but through word of mouth it may have a huge effect on sales.

Each of these problems has at least one solution.

Understanding competitors

If your business has a strategy for growth, and thanks to the data team is executing that strategy well, and doesn't have direct competitors – well, happy days. This is unlikely to be the case, though, and if it is, it's unlikely to last.

So the ability to benchmark the competitive position of a business against a set of rivals should be a part of the data and analytics strategy, because it is undoubtedly part of the overall strategy of the business. This can mean comparing efficiency, or quality of comparable products. Pricing, obviously, but also perhaps process efficiency – how many people are there in the back office compared to the people in the back office of a competitor; how long does logistics take to deliver compared to those competitors?

It can also imply looking at the state of the data transformation: How much business is transacted online? Have competitors identified a niche or segment that your business has not? How do they discount? Market research can uncover these trends, but the potential of that research is much better when it becomes automated data that integrates with reporting and business processes and is delivered at regular intervals.

One potential weakness of market research is that it just becomes part of the wallpaper, data paid for and acquired, but poorly integrated with existing CRM and so never used as an input for decision-making. It's important to use it to create alerts and thresholds that act as a call to action. And, if it is not fit for that purpose, re-evaluate whether there is a return on this data at all.

This does not mean that all market research data has to be closely aligned to operational data. Some of the most valuable data that it can provide is specifically to allow us to lift our heads from the day to day, for example to discover new competitive trends quickly. In the previous chapter I mentioned Clayton Christensen, who did much of the original work on the concept of disruption. Protecting your company from disruptive trends is one example of why it may be time to put more focus on external information.

DISRUPTION

A process in which market entrants with novel business models challenge and replace industry incumbents. Because the product or service does not have traditional attributes, the incumbents assume that the entrant's product or service is not a threat until it is too late.

This description of 'disruptive' is used loosely in business to apply to any competitive pressure. Christensen's conception of a competitive challenge from an inferior but innovative product or new service is much more threatening. A disruptor's impact doesn't show up at all in internal data, and if the incumbent captures feedback from existing customers at the time of the sale, it is unlikely to be part of the conversation at that time. But a regular survey, showing the cumulative changes, may capture this information as it's easy to miss small incremental changes.

Web scraping is the process of collecting structured web data in an automated fashion. It's also called web data extraction. Some of the main use cases of web scraping include price monitoring, price intelligence, news monitoring, lead generation, and market research among many others (Kenny, nd). This can be done manually, but we know at this point that this is inefficient and prone to error. To automate it we can instead use software tools called web scrapers that are set up to find the data and copy it into a structured format.

Another way to automate the process of finding competitive data is through the use of application programming interfaces (APIs), which are now widely used for companies to extract data from their business partners automatically, with or without explicit permission. While the API economy has been booming, so too have API data breaches. Equifax's breach cost $1.14 billion in 2019 alone (*Forbes*, 2020). This means external organizations are extracting data from companies using tools that automate the process in ways that the company would not approve of if they knew about it. This sounds like unauthorized intruders and, yes, some of the traffic is that. But much of it, according to *Forbes*, is simply automation in action.

An example: hotel websites attract a lot of informal bot activity, designed to extract the prices of rooms using APIs. This information could be used by rival hotels to set pricing below that of the competition, or by aggregators to offer information about pricing.

APPLICATION PROGRAMMING INTERFACE (API)

A set of procedures and communication protocols that provides access to the data of an application, or to other services. Organizations may choose to offer an API to allow business partners, suppliers or customers to access their data.

Customer behaviour

There are clear privacy concerns when finding out more about customers, and the GDPR means that (rightly) if you want to gather data and use it, you have to obtain explicit permission about what data you are gathering, how, and why. This isn't just about regulation: if customers feel that data acquisition is intrusive (for example, too many surveys popping up) or even creepy, then the process of acquiring data about the relationship is detrimental to the relationship itself.

But, properly explained, your data team (or a third party working on its behalf) can acquire important insights for the business. An obvious example is to discover when customers choose to do other things: shop in different stores, take other modes of travel, eat different food. Knowing quickly when this occurs can be part of a program to offer a discount or incentive, or simply to ask why.

But not all customer behaviour needs to be tracked individually. For example, in the United States, supermarket chain Kroger tracks near-real-time data (IBM Services, 2019) on its products compared to competitors and tracked customer behaviour, anonymized and delivered by segment. The value is not simply about the sales they had made (it could find that out from its own systems) but about trends for the entire shopping experience, including what other products were bought in the basket, time of day, and information about the profile of the customer.

Social listening

The other example of using external data is social listening: discovering on social media what customers say about the business, its competitors, and the topics that are relevant to the performance of that business. This has immense promise, but also many methodological tripwires.

SOCIAL LISTENING

The process of monitoring social media channels for mentions of your brand, its competitors, your products, or topics in which your brand has a stake.

The concept is simple: Facebook, Instagram, Twitter, bulletin boards and other social media are a massive ongoing conversation, bounded only by the rules of the platform. Anyone can take part. Often users will volunteer opinions on the products, services and brands they use. This can inspire agreement or disagreement from others in the network.

If we are alive to this, it has value in two dimensions. At a basic level, customer service can monitor these platforms for individual problems and respond as part of an enhanced CRM function. This has value, but there is another source of value in social listening.

At an aggregate level, it is an important barometer of what the public experiences and believes. It's not a fully representative or a completely reliable one (we will get to that), but you can listen in real time to people without the biases that occur in other forms of market research.

There is no objective market research data, no matter how carefully it is acquired. Everything is tainted by the process. For example, there is observer bias, in which respondents change their behaviour because they are being watched. We don't remember correctly what we did or why we did it, even though we think we do. And if a researcher asks us a question about which we don't have a strong opinion, our brains often step in and create one. This is one reason that having reliable data based on what customers actually do is so vital, because it often doesn't quite match what they say they do or will do.

All the social media networks make firehose API of their data available for analysis. There are many specialist research firms which work with this data for their clients, which cuts down the process of extracting meaning from it, and means you can integrate the results in your dashboard or user experience reporting. But, if you want to take the raw data, it's there for you.

FIREHOSE API

A stream of data from a source in real time delivered to its subscribers. The volume of data will come in peaks and troughs, but the data continues to flow through the firehose until it is consumed.

Task: Applying insights from social listening

Is your brand in the conversation?

You might take Oscar Wilde's view that there is only one thing worse than being talked about, and that is not being talked about. If there is a conversation about your business sector, how big a share of that conversation is about your brand? This is important for advertising and marketing.

What do people talk about when they discuss the topic?

This is an important source of competitive information. If your logistics operation does not offer next-day delivery, your customers might hardly ever complain about this, because your customers are drawn from the group that doesn't want it. But the conversation online might demonstrate that there is a group for whom this is important (or a group of your customers for whom this will be important next time they do business with you).

What will happen next?

Consumers do not have static preferences. Trends emerge quickly online and are amplified by social media. Social listening can feed into product development and strategy.

What is working?

When consumers do or say something, social media will give you feedback in minutes, not weeks. This is especially important for new campaigns or innovations and can be useful as a way to tweak the offering.

What do people really think?

This is the big one. Sentiment analysis uses advanced techniques to extract meaning from what people write. This has turned out to be a surprisingly complex problem to solve, but it can give a reasonable steer on whether a product or brand is associated with positive or negative feelings, and the attributes most often discussed in relation to it. Sentiment analysis need not be restricted to social media. It can also be used to automate the analysis of free text answers to survey questions. Examples that can be interpreted include: I don't like product X; Product X is ok if there's no alternative; I'm not sure about product X; Product X is clunky; I love product X. They can be scored and then the data used.

SENTIMENT ANALYSIS

The use of natural language processing and text analysis to systematically extract and quantify subjective emotions in data, most often free text.

However, there are problems with social listening that mean it is not always a reliable source of insight.

Skewed samples

Social media is not a representative sample of the population. Its users are younger and more digitally engaged than the general population. Different platforms have different skews: 42 per cent of US Twitter users are between the ages of 18 and 29, 27 per cent are 30–49, leaving only 31 per cent aged 50 and over. Only 4.8 per cent of Facebook users globally are aged 65+. On LinkedIn, 60.1 per cent of users are between the ages of 25 and 34 (Omnicore, 2021). You'd be foolish to use Twitter conversations to research your reputation among seniors; some opinions may simply not be captured at all.

Exaggerated emotions

Social media users tweet and post instinctively. If you use Twitter, look back at your posts from a few months ago. It's often hard to remember why you felt an emotion, and equally surprising to find that you apparently had a strong sentiment about something at 3.26 pm on a Tuesday in October, when you are completely indifferent to it today. This heightened emotion also affects the this-or-that nature of many conversations on social media. People may say they hate Coca-Cola because they prefer Pepsi, but in real life they would not be unhappy to be offered Coca-Cola in a restaurant. It's just because they're Pepsi fans in this context, and the polarization that is part of a social media spat overstates negative emotion. Social media is playful and ephemeral, and we should not take every opinion as a serious statement of intent.

Who's speaking?

Many social media users are listening, just like your data team is. There is a reason why a small number of social media users are called 'influencers' and are targeted by marketers. They set the tone of the conversation and may distort it temporarily. Beware, as some of these influencers may be driven by commercial or destructive motives.

As an example, an investigation from *Which? Travel* has shown that some of the highest-ranked hotels on TripAdvisor reached the top by using fake reviews (Baker, 2019). They analysed almost 250,000 hotel reviews on the site, comparing the profile of five-star reviewers with those who left only three stars. The 15 that looked most blatantly suspicious included some of the best-rated hotels in the Middle East, four of the best-rated hotels in Las Vegas, and one of the hotels in Britain's second-biggest hotel chain, Travelodge. When *Which? Travel* reported them to TripAdvisor, it admitted that 14 of them – 93 per cent – had been caught with dodgy reviews in the past year.

Do we really need to act?

Social listening is a constant source of data, but the above concerns show that many of the spikes in sentiment you will see may be false positives. The correct response is often to get on with our jobs and focus on the hundreds of other transformational projects that data makes possible. It may be important to establish why, and to what extent, a data transformation benefits from social listening: short-term, for responses to particular events; medium-term, as an observatory to uncover new trends; or long-term, to track shifts in opinion. A great example would be feedback from a product that enables you to address concerns about product safety, for example. A speedy response to safety concerns with facts, such as test results and safety certifications such as CE (UK Government, 2012), can prevent reputational damage.

Task: Creating a reliable Net Promoter Score

One of the most powerful tools for hearing the voice of the customer is the Net Promoter Score (NPS). NPS is used by more than two-thirds of Fortune 1000 companies, and is also one of the most misused tools.

NET PROMOTER SCORE (NPS)

The score that you get from subtracting the percentage of detractors from the percentage of promoters when you ask whether a customer would recommend your company to others.

The NPS was created in 2003 by management consultants Bain & Company, following research into what captured the aspects of a business that generated growth in Intuit, an accountancy software company.

It subtracts the number of customers defined as detractors from the number who are promoters and reports this number. Used with care, it is a strong predictor of future growth. This is a comparatively simple data project to implement. When I was in charge of data, analytics and business intelligence at a cloud hosting provider between 2012 and 2014, my job was to use data and analytics to help manage the transition from being a hosted service provider to a full-service cloud provider. In this environment, where people knew little about which company to choose, recommendation was clearly a powerful tool. We chose to align sales commissions to customer satisfaction as well as revenue, when previously they had been based on revenue only.

This meant we had to decide how we defined satisfaction. NPS was a wonderful tool, because many of our customers would interact online. When they had interacted with us, we could send a survey immediately. We did NPS surveys based on individual transactions as well as a half-yearly relationship NPS to test the overall relationship.

HOW TO MEASURE: NPS

NPS surveys have the advantage that they are precisely two questions long:

How likely are you to recommend us to friends or family? (0–10)

Why? (Free text)

Scores of 9 or 10 are classified as promoters, and 6 and below as detractors.

Insights from this research at the cloud hosting provider helped to drive the growth of our business from less than £5 million turnover to more than £100 million. Everyone was trained across the whole business. And it worked well. How do you do this?

Measure the number

This is the easy part. NPS will generate a single number between –100 and 100. As it gets larger, you have a larger proportion of promoters. This is unambiguously good. But it is not the whole story.

Communicate the number

This is a statistic that can be on everyone's dashboard, with a target. Will people try to manipulate the target? Yes, but overwhelmingly through positive behaviour that benefits you. This is what being data-driven is all about.

Compare the number

This is more problematic. Comparison with recent history is fine: this is like-for-like. There are, however, industry averages and this needs more care. It is important to only compare with organizations that are asking the question in the same way, to a similar audience. The average NPS is wildly different in different contexts.

It's whether you are winning against competitors that counts

Cross-industry comparisons are instructive. Research shows that absolute rises in NPS show little correlation to gains in market share (Keiningham et al, 2014), but gains relative to NPS measured against a peer group are much more predictive of growth. We knew that our cloud services company was good at its job, but we also knew that it was one of the top service providers in the UK.

Ask why

That second question – 'Why?' – matters, especially for detractors and the middle group who have no strong emotion. You can use simple free text analysis to find common words or phrases in each group and use them to inform decision-making that should be reflected in the score.

Beware of manipulation

You can increase NPS scores by reducing the number of detractors, or converting those who don't care to promoters, but it is possible for teams in the business to target the number rather than a service improvement that aligns with the data and analytics strategy (Recall Goodhart's Law in Chapter 10). For example, offering a discount will raise the NPS, but it's not a good strategy if you are targeting customer satisfaction to improve margins.

Don't over-survey

It is tempting to ask everyone, all the time, to fill in an NPS survey. You've probably done at least one of them this week. Over-surveying reduces data quality because respondents are more likely to enter a random number or look for the number that means they don't have to answer a question. Fred Reichheld of Bain & Co, who was the creator of NPS, told an interviewer that 'the instant we have a technology to minimize surveys, I'm the first one on that bandwagon'.

Integration

Throughout this chapter I have implied that integration is important. The principle of integration is simple enough, but it requires a bit more elaboration: the more sources of data you can provide, the more insight you get. A simple example is that you see data from a finance system that tells you revenue is growing. Then you look at your sales dashboard and you see a breakdown by region and you see growth is good across all regions, but by product you see that some products are generating a lot of revenue, but one is less so. You look at the historical data and you realize that the revenue is in gradual decline over time. You look at the market data and you see that the overall market is in growth. You look at your NPS scores and you see that customer NPS scores are stable. You then look at the competitive environment and you see that a new start-up has launched a product in direct competition with you for lower prices and rave reviews in the press. Overall this is a useful story to tell with data, but you can only tell that story if you integrate multiple data sets: finance data, sales data, customer data, product breakdown data, historic data, and external websites and social media. Any one data set alone would not have given you the insight you needed, and you never know which one will give you the golden nugget.

Hear the bad news

A final warning: I can't stress enough that measurement has to be the basis for action. Too many organizations collect data to validate decisions, not to make them. NPS is a perfect example: its role is not to provide comfort about doing well (though of course you are welcome to do that) but to form a basis for improvement.

That means the important customer voices that the data team discovers and communicates internally are those that deliver bad news. This can be a difficult message to convey. But this is a transformation: the voice of the customer that matters is the one that tells us how to do better. This underpins the ability for an organization to continuously improve. In Chapter 4 we talked about continuous improvement of data science models. One way we can apply NPS is through the example of recommending additional products to clients. Perhaps your data science models recommend to certain customers that have product A that they might also like product B. Let's assume that our overall sales do increase but the NPS scores for those customers go down. This could be an indication that new products were diluting the customers' loyalty, perhaps because they were less reliable or enjoyable. This would be worth further investigation. The point is that it would be naïve to think that just because sales were going up, everything was ok.

SUMMARY

- The data acquired during interactions with customers is a partial picture and may mean a business overestimates loyalty or misses important signals that show up outside the transaction.

- Listening to the voice of the customer requires external data. Surveys and trackers are useful, but only if integrated with existing systems so that they trigger actions.

- One important function of external data is to give early warning of disruptive competitive threats that will not otherwise show up in sales or CRM data.

- Social media is a valuable source of insight and can be used to improve both CRM and strategic planning. But sample bias and behavioural effects mean it must be handled with care.

- The NPS is a powerful tool that can be used on every dashboard. Again, it must be deployed rigorously and linked to strategic action.

References

Baker, T (2019) Fake TripAdvisor reviews push 'world's best' hotels up the rankings, *Which?* https://www.which.co.uk/news/2019/09/fake-tripadvisor-reviews-push-worlds-best-hotels-up-the-rankings/ (archived at https://perma.cc/4WNL-3AUZ)

Forbes (2020) 10 ways to prevent an API data breach, https://www.forbes.com/sites/forbestechcouncil/2020/07/13/10-ways-to-prevent-an-api-data-breach (archived at https://perma.cc/3PX6-D3DD)

Griffin, A and Hauser, J (1993) The voice of the customer, *Marketing Science*, **12** (1), pp 1–27

IBM Services (2019) How Kroger is using data and analytics to improve the customer experience, https://www.ibm.com/blogs/services/2021/07/29/how-kroger-is-using-data-and-analytics-to-improve-the-customer-experience/ (archived at https://perma.cc/MEF9-RCPD)

Keiningham, T et al (2014) The high price of customer satisfaction, *MIT Sloan Management Review*, 18 March

Kenny, C (nd) Web scaping, *Zyte.com*, https://www.zyte.com/learn/what-is-web-scraping/ (archived at https://perma.cc/FUA9-6J8V)

Omnicore (2021) Social media by the numbers: Stats, demographics and fun facts, https://www.omnicoreagency.com/category/statistics/ (archived at https://perma.cc/DUF9-EESY)

RAC Foundation (2012) Spaced out: Perspectives on parking policy, https://www.racfoundation.org/research/mobility/spaced-out-perspectives-on-parking (archived at https://perma.cc/5N6F-N6BH)

UK Government (2012) CE marking, https://www.gov.uk/guidance/ce-marking (archived at https://perma.cc/3RC7-4SHP)

Zhang, Q, Gangwar, M and Seetharaman, P B (2017) Polygamous store loyalties: An empirical investigation, *Journal of Retailing*, **93** (4), pp 477–92

16

Maximizing data science

The way in which data science and data scientists themselves are deployed and managed will determine whether they are a source of value. Embedding data science in the business potentially has high returns, but its value is often wasted, because they need support and prioritization to be successful.

KEY CONCEPTS

- Data science

- Data warehouse

- Data lake

Introduction

Chris Anderson is the person who came up with the *Long Tail* (Anderson, 2006), the idea that in the internet age there are millions of niche markets that can be serviced profitably, and opportunities for the data-rich start-ups that identify them. His vision is an apt description of a remarkable change in what has been possible to sell profitably, and the emergence of the businesses that have been successful by being 'long tail'. So now we have pet cremation jewellery, portion control dinnerware and mermaid swimsuits. We have a lot to thank Chris for.

In 2008 he revealed his vision for what he called the 'Petabyte age', called 'The End of Theory' (Anderson, 2008).

'It calls for an entirely different approach, one that requires us to lose the tether of data as something that can be visualized in its totality. It forces us to view data mathematically first and establish a context for it later...' His idea was that we no longer need a theory, a model, a hypothesis of what is correct, to test with data. If we have enough data we can try everything, and just go with what works. 'Forget taxonomy, ontology, and psychology... With enough data, the numbers speak for themselves.'

This is an alluring idea, and it would make your job a lot easier. Everything we have done on our journey so far has maximized the amount, the relevance and the quality of the data available to the business. If this really is the end of theory, then all that remains to do is hire a couple of data scientists, put your feet up and wait for the good ideas.

This rather makes me suspect that Anderson did not spend much time in conversation with CDOs (who, to be fair, were a new thing in 2008) before writing his article. In my experience, this approach to data science will suck up years of everyone's time, waste millions of pounds, dollars or euros, and destroy any reputation for efficiency that you have earned.

I know: I have inherited these projects more than once.

Data science, not data magic

Our goal is to embed data science in the business in the same way that sales, marketing or finance are embedded. All these functions form an integral part of any workflow, and often the earlier they are involved in a project, the greater the chance of a good outcome. So it is also with data science.

Data science can be transformative, a catalyst for change and a unique route to competitive advantage. For the data science function to succeed it needs to be part of, or at least aligned to, the data team, aligned with the same strategy, working to the same deadlines, and measured by the same criteria for success. The two can create value together: without the data team to ensure that data sources are available, and of high quality, the value of data science is constrained. Without data science to provide insight and innovation, the data transformation never achieves its full transformative potential. Ultimately, it makes sense to create a 'data centre of excellence' that combines these abilities. But, of course, the first task is to be excellent.

The problem with many data scientists is that (not their fault) no one else really understands what they are doing, so they become effectively autonomous, drifting from project to project, always with a transformative insight that they never quite deliver. If they do, the insights can't be replicated and are hard to operationalize.

> ## DATA SCIENCE
>
> The discipline that combines programming skills and knowledge of business, mathematics and statistics to extract meaningful insights from data. Those insights can be turned into value for the business.

We can establish data science as an integral part of the data transformation, but definitely not by letting 'the numbers speak for themselves'.

How *not* to do data science

One of the reasons that your company may finally have become serious about extracting value from data is that a failed data science experiment is extremely costly in both money and time, and no one quite knows why. The downside of this for a data team is that it becomes their job to sweep up the mess.

An example: several years ago I was recruited by an organization that was in precisely this place. It was my job to help everyone climb out of the hole that a failed investment had dug, and into which the entire data function had jumped.

When I arrived, I heard the same thing from many people in the business. In meetings, they would speak in awe of the data scientists. 'They're doing great stuff,' they would tell me, 'really great stuff.'

The data science team was, as I suspected, one director's bet on the future.

The data scientist he hired to lead this initiative also saw this as a great opportunity. He had never led a data programme or team before, and it was an opportunity to develop his career, rather than a data capability for the company. I asked the data scientists what the plan was.

'We will build some data models that will be pretty cool,' they replied, 'and they will change the business.'

The models had been built, this was true. Using data that had been curated for them, the team had created some analytics that predicted which customers would become the VIPs in future.

'Pretty cool,' said the data scientists, raising an eyebrow.

'Great stuff,' agreed their managers, 'really great stuff.'

But no one could actually use the model to do anything useful. The first problem was that it was not connected to any pipeline of input data, so it could not be updated. There is a reason to build a data warehouse or a data lake, and that is precisely to give the people who do this job a source of up-to-date information. Therefore, instead of running the model once, they could run it every day.

DATA WAREHOUSE

A store of structured and filtered data used by data scientists (and report and dashboard developers) to build, test, refine and ultimately run their models. The data has been extracted from operational systems and processed for a specific purpose. Ingestion is done by analysing what's needed, then going to find it.

DATA LAKE

A store of raw data, for example social media data, the purpose of which is not yet defined. This may never be used but will be useful to inform and test data science models, because it can demonstrate the evolution of the variables of interest. Ingestion is done by sucking everything in, and then worrying about structure when it is needed.

The second problem was that even if the model was run every day, it wasn't embedded into any business processes or systems. Many people were excited that they had a data model that predicted which customers were likely to become VIPs, but no one had defined what actions anyone would (have to) take to turn that into revenue.

I had been brought on board partly to build that integration at both ends. But to do that, the data team would have to understand what data to feed it and engineer that, and how to integrate the output. And to do that, we needed to know what the model was doing and how. We needed structure, which implied documentation, and there was none. We also needed a process for improvement and integration.

With respect to the many outstandingly talented data scientists I have met, structure, documentation and embedding into a business process are not things they choose to do well, if at all.

To be fair, the data science team knew that it needed more data. It had obtained funding to pay a third party to build its data warehouse, and that project had cost £1.2 million up to that point. It was 80 per cent ready, and had been 80 per cent ready for six months as the people who were building it came up against unsolved data quality and access problems. The only thing to do was to write off the investment, let the data scientists leave (I encountered them later at a conference presenting about 'lessons learned') and start again.

Task: Integrating data science

That's how not to do it. If you're in that situation, it might be quicker to start again than to attempt a fix. If we are starting a data science project, the first thing to do is to ensure it has the business backing and that it adheres to the data strategy.

Define a leadership hypothesis

How does the leadership of the business believe data science can help? For most businesses, this means the four Cs: generate cash, customer retention, cost management, care of employees. Prioritizing these in line with the data and analytics strategy helps align what the business thinks is 'pretty cool' with something that can deliver value. It may be reducing cost through automation, smarter pricing decisions, or a better return on marketing. But it is a positive statement of direction. Note: this is not a narrow set of plans to deliver. Your data science team should not be completely autonomous, but it must have freedom to solve problems creatively. This prioritization is, in my experience, something that data scientists crave and it will make them more successful.

Evangelize data science to the business

The CDO should explain to the people who may benefit from data science what they may get, and what this can potentially deliver. Use examples and recruit sponsors in the business. Be specific and concrete: use business terms such as 'identification of customers with a propensity to churn, which if we act correctly can increase customer retention'.

Define the data science process

It is the job of these sponsors to work with data science. This means that the head of data science must define a process to do that. Then the business can understand what they can expect, and when. This must be repeatable, scalable and described in non-technical language. Figure 16.1 shows my preferred data science process, which has worked well for me.

Embed analytics into production systems

The biggest challenge is to get the output from the models into production. Most organizations fail at this. This requires that the models are tested and documented, the data inputs must be productionized, and the outputs from the models fed into operational systems. This will require that the data team and the IT team work together. This needs to be discussed and planned well ahead of the date to productionize the first model. When this has been done for one model then the process can be repeated much more easily for subsequent models. However, the first implementation will be a major challenge – not just the time and effort, but the conflict in ways of working between an IT department and a data science team.

FIGURE 16.1 The data science and AI method

Ask a business challenge	• What's the business problem you're trying to solve? • What are the benefits?
Do research	• What's the subject matter detail? • How will it generate value?
Construct hypothesis	• What will we build to solve the problem? • How will it integrate into the business?
Analyse data	• What data do we have and what's the quality? • How will we use the data? (wrangling)
Build and test	• Build it and create results. • Did it perform as expected?
Report results	• Did we create some insights / recommendations? • How can they be improved?
Deploy	• Deploy into business operational environment. • Provide support.

Task: Sustaining data science

Given the strategic direction, it is still not simple to align data science with the broader goals of data transformation. But it can be used as a catalyst for the work that you need to do anyway, and its insights will demonstrate the value of the rest of the data team's work.

Show a quick win

We start where we always start: demonstrating value. This will not be a hard sell, but the trick is to align that quick win to a problem that is a strategic priority. This may seem almost trivial to the smart data scientists you employ, but if it was that easy, the problem would have been solved already. Note that we want to build processes, not projects. But at this stage, that might be a step too far. So the quick win demonstrates value to management and to the whole organization. Because it is aligned with the data and analytics strategy, it is likely to uncover areas in which more data quality and governance investment is needed – which, with a win under your belt, is something you can argue for.

Do the data engineering first

A data scientist, given data and a challenge, will come up with some insight. But problems in the data will have a direct impact on the usefulness of this insight. If the data is incorrect or out of date, the same can be expected from the insights of the model. If there is no golden ID for the customer or no provenance for the data, there can be no confidence in the model's recommendations. If there is no external data, then its external validity can be questioned. Understanding the precise nature of the shortfall is a vital part of the process.

There's always more engineering up-front than you might anticipate

Data engineering is, as we have seen, not a quick fix. This is frustrating for everyone, not least for the data scientist who was promised some shiny data to work with and finds that there is plenty of data, just not yet. Data scientists often have low boredom thresholds and many alternative job offers.

It is also frustrating for the business, which has paid for a service that it is not getting yet. The data team may have a role in acting almost as Sherpas: doing the tough work that sets up the data sources that are needed, evaluating their quality, and making sure this is sustainable. They can also take care of documentation, making it easier to understand what is being done, and how, although, as previously discussed, this is a potential area for automation.

Recognize success

It is important for the data science team to own its successes, not in a vague way ('Great stuff!') but using specifics that are matched to the strategic data and business goals. This both demystifies what the discipline does and builds support and engagement across the business. It also helps to make the case for investment. If you can describe a 5 per cent uplift in sales, you can describe how, if you reach a data quality target, that would be 7 per cent. And how, if you could streamline the process underpinning it, that would be 7 per cent across all businesses, every week.

Encourage executive sponsorship

By far the most valuable engagement is that of the executive team. I have seen far too many situations in which no one is asking the difficult questions, among them, 'what is this actually for?' An executive would routinely ask questions like this to interrogate any other specialist function. This disengagement may seem like freedom to innovate for the data science team but, because of the importance of the problems that team has been tasked to solve, the executive team understands the nature of the commitment it is making, not just how much it costs. This is partly because data science is speculative. It doesn't always turn out the way we want. If there is bad news some way down the line, it should not come as a surprise that this was a possible outcome.

Encourage scepticism about the output

Much of the most valuable data analytics is forward-looking and so it is always speculative. This means there will be confidence intervals on any of the output (these may be explicit, by using different models or different inputs). Encourage the business to consider these forecasts as strong – but not the only – signals, because the model cannot capture every piece of data, and contexts change. Informed debate inspired by the models can improve the decisions, and give signposts to improve the models too.

Embrace the potential for failure

If there are potential misunderstandings between the data science team and the business, that's to be expected. What they do is a little bit 'woo'. The integration process, with the data team in the middle in a supporting role, may take care of much of that. There is another source of potential misunderstanding, and that is between the IT department and the data science team. This potential problem is another reason why it is important to define a leadership hypothesis at the outset, rather than just a product delivery plan.

The IT department has two well-established processes for delivering technology to the business. Most CIOs have been brought up with a waterfall process for development: start with a problem, define the requirements, validate the requirements, deliver the solution, put it into production, support it. The alternative is agile development: define high-level requirements, pick one part of the requirements (a user story), deliver it in short bursts of activity (known as sprints) and then do the next task. Each method has its advantages.

Working with data, especially data science, is different from both of these. Data science is an experiment. Done properly, it is based on the scientific method: make observations, create a hypothesis that might explain them, build a model, test the model using data, see how well it fits your observations, refine the model, use the model to make predictions, use observations to improve the model.

But there is the potential at this stage for the model to demonstrate nothing of any value at all. This has positive aspects. For example, discovering that you cannot identify customers who are in danger of defecting because you don't capture enough data is not a failure, it's a clear sign that you need to improve data quality. Even with that data, your model may not deliver value. An example is the Netflix Prize, awarded to the data science team that could improve the company's recommendation algorithm by 10 per cent. After three years of competition, the prize was won on 21 September 2009 by a team called 'BellKor's Pragmatic Chaos' (Netflix, 2009). The improvements were never implemented because the increased revenue and the time taken wouldn't justify the amount of work. Instead, Netflix found simpler, quicker ways to improve the recommendations, freeing up the investment to improve its programmes instead.

This is a good decision and can only be made if you embed data science into the organization, and do not think of it as a project that has to be implemented come what may.

At one point in my career, I found myself having this conversation with the CIO who, at that time, was my line manager. I was explaining to him that we could not find out what we had until partway through the project, and at that point we didn't have anything of value. He wanted me to resign. He told the CEO I was a maverick, and so not the person to be running data science. The CEO disagreed, because he understood the experimental nature of data science. I was moved to report to the CFO – hardly a soft touch, but someone who understood the nature of the trade-off I was making.

The alternative would have been to carry on regardless in pursuit of an over-defined goal. This would have been no better than carrying on regardless in pursuit of no goal at all. Which shows that nothing in your data transformation will test your business acumen as much as the project to tame data science in the interests of the business.

SUMMARY

- Data science has huge potential if it is embedded in the business – but often teams are left to their own devices.

- First steps of data science are to define a leadership hypothesis and process for data science that will focus the output where it can have the greatest impact.

- Engagement at executive level and practical support from the data team help define an analytical capability that can be optimized in service of the business.

- Data science will always be experimental. It cannot be managed to deliver a pre-determined goal or return on investment.

References

Anderson, C (2006) *The Long Tail: Why the future of business is selling less of more*, Hyperion

Anderson, C (2008) The End of Theory, *Wired*, 23 June

Netflix (2009) The Netflix Prize sought to substantially improve the accuracy of predictions about how much someone is going to enjoy a movie based on their movie preferences, http://web.archive.org/web/20191216233928/http://www.netflixprize.com/ (archived at https://perma.cc/Y499-4UYG)

17

Sharing data with suppliers and customers

If you securely and transparently allow others to access, use and create your data, this can be an efficient way to generate more value, and also improve knowledge and data quality. It also crowdsources innovation. Done well, everybody benefits.

KEY CONCEPTS

- Blockchain
- Asymmetric information
- Subject access request (SAR)

Introduction

In 2002 Jeff Bezos, the founder of Amazon, issued an internal memo (Schroeder, 2016):

1 All teams will henceforth expose their data and functionality through service interfaces,

it began, mandating that

2 Teams must communicate with each other through these interfaces.

Looking back, it is hard to imagine how revolutionary this was, and at the time it would have been hard to imagine that Bezos was setting the tone for how data would be shared two decades later. It was revolutionary because he wasn't just thinking about how the different bits of the rapidly growing Amazon would communicate but how Amazon would share data with everyone else:

3 All service interfaces, without exception, must be designed from the ground up to be externalizable. That is to say, the team must plan and design to be able to expose the interface to developers in the outside world. No exceptions.

4 Anyone who doesn't do this will be fired.

Amazon's developers, as far as we know, kept their jobs. But this mandate set the tone for the widespread use of application programming interfaces today as a way to expose data to customers, suppliers, the public and your market. This has many benefits and some risks, but it is an integral part of the data transformation process.

Widespread exposure

We first encountered the influence of APIs in Chapter 15, referencing their role in how competitors can use them to discover pricing data. Of course, the use of APIs is not the only way to share data, but two decades after the Bezos mandate, the technique is becoming pervasive. *Forbes* found that enterprises with advanced API management processes experience up to 47 per cent better business results compared with enterprises with basic API management, and that 34 per cent of companies use APIs to improve speed to market and innovation (Salyer, 2021).

Among the companies that use APIs, Google's report into the state of the API economy (Google, 2021) asked 700 organizations how they were sharing data using APIs. More than half were 'exposing assets with partners', 36 per cent found them to be a 'strategic asset for creating business value', and 22 per cent reported that their APIs 'are directly leveraged by external customers'. A third were developing new business-to-business partners on the back of the technology, and 10 per cent were leveraging their APIs directly as a revenue stream: access to their data had a monetary value.

We can leave aside the technology questions about whether to use APIs or which type of APIs to use. What we have here is a data transformation process that is happening with or without us: this train is leaving the station.

This is a culture in which software talks unto software, across organizational boundaries (internal and external). If we automate the process of connection, it can turn the process of systems integration, once a project that kept the CIO awake at night and derailed careers, into a strategic rather than a technical issue.

At that strategic level, sharing has many benefits at this point in our transformation:

- Data shared improves the efficiency of the interface between your business, suppliers, partners and customers. It speeds things up, avoids rekeying, and reduces errors and risk.
- Sharing data with the market can help grow and improve the overall efficiency of the market.
- Sharing data with the public can build your reputation.

But this isn't a free lunch. The main risk associated with sharing lies, and this will come as no surprise to you by now, in the quality and governance of the data you share. Quality, because flaws and omissions are now obvious to everyone, and it will have an impact, not just on your efficiency but also on theirs (and on the quality of your relationship). Governance, because your data needs to be secure and shared appropriately, and you have crossed over into new legal and regulatory territory.

So let's not get hung up on technology: the API economy is one manifestation of an inexorable process. The power in the Bezos memo was that he understood that sharing data optimally didn't mean moving it around, that it worked best when it was automated, and that it created entirely new business processes.

Exposing data to business partners and suppliers

In 2016 I briefly worked as a CDO for a private healthcare provider. Part of my brief was to reduce costs.

They had a wide and diverse global supply chain; in plain language, they did business with a lot of hospitals. In the Middle East region, we could see that the many hospitals to which their patients were sent were all billing separately, but we could not see what those bills contained; data was shared as a financial process, not an operational one.

When we shared accessed data from the hospital billing systems in a common format, we realized that there was a huge spread of prices and services between hospitals. Each treatment was charged at a price that aggregated the cost of common items like drugs, as well as unique items like the doctors, nurses and processes involved. When they became aware of this, we realized we could pivot to doing business directly with the drug suppliers, because the savings would be enormous – for our business in this region, it would cut costs by 30 per cent.

Enormous, yes, but not obvious until we integrated billing systems with our data. Innovations like this helped to deliver a £20 million reduction in costs in a matter of months and, because the integration was permanent, the savings were too.

This sharing of data worked in our favour, but think for a minute about the impact on both sides. From the hospitals' perspective, the obvious conclusion is that this delivered a permanent reduction in their margins. From the healthcare provider's perspective, considering the scale of the savings, there's a strong argument that this was an efficiency long overdue, and one that they could pass on to customers in the form of lower premiums. But eliminating inefficiency by exposing data in this way will never be revenue-neutral, and some business partners might resist if they have the choice. Work like this that enables one partner to benefit and the other to lose may require some sort of commercial consideration, not just a data project.

Sharing data will also be a test of the work that the data team has done on quality and governance. The potential benefits include an increase in transparency. But if that data is incomplete, slow to update or inaccurately defined, it will have less value for suppliers or service partners, or be reputationally damaging. An example would be automatic stock replenishment, which needs accurate, disaggregated and timely data on your sales for a supplier's systems to respond.

If partner data teams struggle to achieve meaningful results from shared data, or find it to be inconsistent, this will suck up the data team's time and resources. Ultimately it might also create a competitive disadvantage if suppliers choose to focus on joint innovation with other brands (not least with data-savvy challenger brands) which promise deep integration and can deliver it in a timely way.

Blockchain in the supply chain

One of the most talked-about, if not necessarily implemented, ways of sharing data is on a blockchain. You might have been tasked already by your CEO to look into blockchains or watched an excited conference presentation about their potential to create digital trust through data sharing.

BLOCKCHAIN

A system in which a record of transactions is maintained across several computers that are linked in a peer-to-peer network.

Blockchains are interesting because the record of a transaction is owned by no one in the business process. It is a distributed electronic ledger that records transactions as blocks of data. Each party on a blockchain can see the entire database and its history. When new information is generated, it is added directly by the relevant party to the transaction, not by a central authority. We can't ignore it: IDC, the global market intelligence firm, predicts investment rising from $1.5 billion in 2018 to $19 billion in 2024 (IDC, 2021), with payments and settlements representing the biggest use case.

Blockchain applications in finance are interesting: for example, if your process involves generating shared documents (letters of credit, for example, in international trade), this offers huge potential benefits to processes in which data sharing has been inefficient, manual and expensive due to the need to build in ways for the parties to trust one another. But blockchains need agreement from everyone in the supply chain, which requires consortia to agree to standards, which, in turn, requires everyone in the process to be in the same consortium.

This is not in the spirit of our *Data and Analytics Strategy for Business*. Our entire approach to this point has been to find a manageable project that creates value, incrementally improve the data that supports it, industrialize and strengthen the processes that support it, and expand it. At every stage we have been careful not to take on something over-ambitious, or create projects in which large parts of the implementation are out of the control of the data team. Blockchain has huge promise, but unfortunately does not fit these criteria.

It also bypasses the reality in data-based supply chains: there is always a dominant partner. It may be Amazon, it may be Tesco, it may be the NHS. And that partner can mandate the way in which the data is shared. The theory sounds great, but it's hard to find the right business case where it will work.

Sharing improves markets

In 1970, George Akerlof, then a first-year assistant professor of economics who hadn't yet won the Nobel Prize, struggled to get a paper published in an academic journal. Editors simply could not believe his conclusions in 'The market for "lemons"' (Akerlof, 1970). Akerlof's idea was that if we wanted to buy a used car and we visited the car showroom, and we didn't know whether the car we were looking at had been well maintained or was a clunker (a 'lemon'), we would never offer the price we would happily pay for a well-maintained car. And so the only cars that a salesman would ever agree to sell would be the lemons. All the best cars on the lot would go unsold, because no one could afford them due to the risk that they might be lemons.

He had 'discovered' asymmetric information, in one of those insights about which many people who were not economists would say, yes, I knew that.

ASYMMETRIC INFORMATION

A situation or transaction in which one party has more or better information than the other.

But the consequences of asymmetric information are profound. Most importantly, finding ways to share more information creates a basis of trust that can lead to a more profitable business. It's no coincidence that now there are online car retailers that deliver much more complete information and precise guarantees so that the first time we see the second-hand car we bought is when it is delivered to our house. This process would have filled our grandparents with horror.

In Chapter 11 I showed how a crisis at the investment banks in 2002 over the objectivity of their research led to the development of the RIXML standard for sharing the data and models that financial analysts use. I was working at the investment bank at the time, and this led directly to a project to create transparency and consistency in the rating process.

The data standard, which is still maintained by a consortium, has helped to improve the market as a whole.

CASE STUDY
RIXML (RIXML, 2021)

Challenge: Dissemination of research

The consumers of investment research needed better ways to access the precise research they needed, and the creators of investment research needed a better way to ensure that their research was seen by those who would benefit from it.

Analysis: A confluence of needs

On the one hand, firms on the buy side wanted to search, sort and filter information published by research providers. It had to be easy to use, and they wanted to combine research from different providers. On the other hand, those firms on the sell side wanted to focus on developing and producing content and to dedicate fewer resources to delivering it.

Action: Tagging data in a consistent format

Having researched the needs of both sides of the market, the RIXML consortium in 2001 created an initial list of tags, which became the RIXML schema. There were three guiding principles: standards must provide an improvement for all participants in the process; standards must be able to expand and evolve to adapt to changes in technology and business; end users must be able to benefit from RIXML without even needing to know it exists.

Outcome: Higher-quality data in more places

There are many use cases for RIXML. For example, an asset management firm creates digital content that automatically combines internal information with external information. Translations of financial research can be linked to the source data. Buy-side firms can easily filter data to focus only on what they want to see. There are incentives on both sides to use the standard, which is free and open. Documents tagged using RIXML are used in more places. Consumers of research want to spend more time reading and less time accessing data.

This is not to say that the process of adopting RIXML was straightforward.

By creating the RIXML standard for sharing data with fund management clients, the investment bank was able to share models with investment managers like Fidelity, so its managers could see not only that the conclusions were consistent, and consistent with the data, but also where those conclusions came from. It was a way to demonstrate that the reports created by analysts were not lemons.

But this comes at a price: in one meeting, Fidelity pointed out to us that the airline analyst wasn't using the same arguments about the future price of oil as the commodities oil analyst, both of whom took the optimistic view for their sector. For the oil research it meant the price was going up and for the airline research it meant that the oil price was going down.

This was a small error that we had not spotted. But it was indicative of a larger data problem: if the data going into the models was not consistent, how could clients trust the conclusions? Remediating that problem meant that we, and every other firm employing sell-side analysts, had to improve the data process. This meant standard definitions, naming conventions, consistent formats, data quality checks, cross-checks for inconsistent items (such as fuel costs mentioned above), dependencies between fields. It was a non-trivial exercise, but it meant far more transparency for the buy-side firms which used the research, and ultimately increased the integrity and usefulness of the entire research function.

It also disintermediated some brokers, whose job of helping to interpret and explain research to win business effectively became redundant.

Exposing data to customers

Exposing data creates efficiencies at the other end of the value chain too, by allowing customers to do tasks for themselves: checking order status, changing their address, setting preferences.

Immediately, this is attractive to any executive team, because it implies cost reduction. It also reduces the need to second-guess the customer; instead of debating what they will or will not require, it is sufficient simply to offer the choices and measure which ones are taken up.

But always record and track the actions that customers take. This has two positive outcomes. The first is that you can track shifts in preferences, which may require action – for example, if there is a sudden upswing in preference for click and collect. This is a resourcing challenge, but also might imply that similar customers might prefer it if they knew it existed.

The other impact is that it can effectively crowdsource solutions to data or service problems. Our defining challenge at the outset was to raise data quality. Some of this can be done by combining sources. Some can be done by recontacting customers or using contacts to check and improve data quality. But the most assiduous stewards of customer data are likely to be the customers themselves, who can quickly spot a wrong postal code or phone number and have a motivation to correct it.

You can encourage this by making sure that, when they are logged in, your systems are constantly asking 'is this data correct?'.

This may be uncomfortable, especially if it leads to the realization that data quality is not of the standard that the business assumed. An initiative to encourage customers to make corrections can lead to a sudden rush of improvements, but also some negative feedback too. But crowdsourcing quality is extremely efficient. In my experience, after the rush, the process quickly stabilizes and becomes an engine of quality data.

Task: Prepare to share

As with all the projects in this wave, you have hopefully done much of the hard work already.

Establish a threshold for quality

For new services, built with data in mind, quality may be exemplary. But if, for example, you have struggled to integrate data sources, your suppliers or customers may notice more what they are not able to find, or the errors in what they do discover.

This may be a reason to delay as you invest more in quality, or it may be a reason to go ahead and brace for the feedback. Provided you make these improvements as part of your quality initiative, this has a positive outcome and does not go on forever. Your chosen strategy depends on your risk appetite, and the relationship you have with customers and partners.

No hiding place for governance

Exposing data means exposing your governance systems to inspection. Partners may require provenance (where did this stock record come from and how was it generated?) and customers are driven insane by inaccurate or obsolete data (if you doubt this, download your credit record summary from a credit reference agency and feel your blood boil).

Establish the optimum internal process

Exposing data improves processes by breaking them. An obvious example is giving customers self-service, which requires that you make available all the appropriate data, but also capture the data from their query or action. This also means managing the internal impact on staff roles. Self-service support, for example, disintermediates customer service agents, or changes their role into the support of last resort, requiring higher levels of training.

Provision for remediation and continuous improvement

As above, sharing will reveal problems. These might be individual data points, but it might show up deeper problems of data acquisition, accuracy and availability, which means you need an agile process to remediate it. The first time you may feel like ignoring it. But that may be the reason why your clients now prefer going to a different supplier.

Be prepared for SARs

A subset of customers will also use their right under the GDPR to access the data you hold on them. This is known as a subject access request (SAR). In the UK, the Information Commissioner has decided that businesses should 'respond without delay and within one month of receipt of the request', and that 'You should provide the information in an accessible, concise and intelligible format' (ICO, 2021). Unless these requests are very complex, if you're taking a month to respond, it might be worth creating a project to report this information in a standard format.

SUBJECT ACCESS REQUEST (SAR)

Individuals have the right under the GDPR to request the information that an organization holds on them. They can do this verbally or in writing, including via social media. The organization has the responsibility to disclose this promptly in an easy-to-understand format.

Exposure is inevitable, so do it your way

While the upsides of sharing data are many, this will never be an easy project to take on because of the stress it places not just on your data capability but also on business models. There is, however, an inevitability about this, and so that creates space to be proactive.

Many of us select our insurance, our phone contracts or our next tech gadget purchase through comparison sites. We can even do this when we Google the product name and click on 'shopping'. Even if you sell your product on Amazon, the way in which you expose your data makes it easy for the retailer to create a four-product comparison, whether the customer has asked for it or not. There is no escape from being compared: if you are a retailer, your pricing data is exposed.

These comparisons offer great advantages for the consumer but are not perfect, because the phone contracts or home insurance they are offered from different companies differ in many dimensions, not all of which can be captured in a comparison table. Often those extra services have been bundled in specifically to defeat an easy comparison, potentially even to distract from a weak core offering. In this case, influencing the customer's attention to focus on the attributes of the service or product that you offer is a challenging data problem. The solution to this is cross-functional: the data team has a role, but so does marketing, so does the user experience team who can design the way that information is presented.

An interesting example of creative problem-solving is Progressive Insurance in the United States. Its advertising invites prospective customers to view competitors' prices on its website, telling them before they visit that some competitors will be cheaper. It is voluntarily offering its prices for comparison, while scraping data from rivals. But by running its own site, it means it can control the way in which the comparison is made, offering information about why its services are better, or extra features included in its prices.

One can only imagine the board's initial reaction to this strategy if the data team presented it. But it's a smart move to expose data while retaining control of the context.

SUMMARY

- Data sharing done well improves the efficiency of your business, relationships with suppliers and customers, and the efficiency of the market as a whole.

- Exposing inefficiencies through data sharing is not revenue-neutral, so be mindful of the impact on business partners, or even on parts of your business, and work with business units to manage this.

- Letting customers improve their own data is efficient and creates an engine to improve data quality. But it is one of the many data-sharing processes that disintermediates some job roles.

- There are reputational benefits to sharing data as you become easier to do business with. But there is reputational damage when it exposes shoddy data management or lack of capability.

- Price and product comparison that data sharing makes possible is inevitable, and so the only discussion internally is how to evaluate its impact and respond creatively.

References

Akerlof, G (1970) The market for 'lemons': Quality uncertainty and the market mechanism, *The Quarterly Journal of Economics*, 84 (3), pp 488–500

Google (2021) The state of the API economy 2021, https://pages.apigee.com/api-economy-report-register (archived at https://perma.cc/UT98-R9SH)

ICO (2021) More information on how to prepare from the Information Commissioner's Office, https://ico.org.uk/for-organisations/guide-to-data-protection/guide-to-the-general-data-protection-regulation-gdpr/individual-rights/right-of-access/ (archived at https://perma.cc/2BYN-37DN)

IDC (2021) Global spending on blockchain solutions forecast to be nearly $19 billion in 2024, https://www.idc.com/getdoc.jsp?containerId=prUS47617821 (archived at https://perma.cc/28Q7-VSFN)

RIXML (2021) Research Information Exchange Markup Language, https://www.rixml.org (archived at https://perma.cc/YFR8-3ZM7)

Salyer, P (2021) API Stack: The billion dollar opportunities redefining infrastructure services platforms, *Forbes*, https://www.forbes.com/sites/patricksalyer/2021/05/04/api-stack-the-billion-dollar-opportunities-redefining-infrastructure-services--platforms/?sh=48e9047a43f9 (archived at https://perma.cc/BC98-EBUH)

Schroeder, G F (2016) What year did Bezos issue the API mandate at Amazon? https://medium.com/slingr/what-year-did-bezos-issue-the-api-mandate-at-amazon-57f546994ca2 (archived at https://perma.cc/92GD-5YJC)

PART SIX

Wave 5: Differentiate

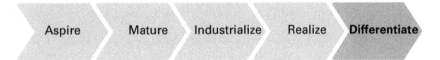

You are now able to *Realize* significant value from data, and measure it, see and feel it every day. The final stage of the data transformation is for your business to become a leader and innovator. It will have the tools to respond to markets changes, competitors and external events, and systematically outperform competitors.

Data has created organizational and behavioural change, but now the potential of artificial intelligence is that it can improve decision-making beyond the capabilities of the people in the business.

The business is fundamentally transformed, as is the function of the data team, which no longer has a project focus but provides the data products that the business uses to thrive. This also changes the role of the leaders of that data transformation, placing focus on strategic insight and creativity. At this stage you will see that you are able to *Differentiate* yourself from your competitors and you'll be seeing that in the margin of the business.

Value, Build, Improve content of this wave

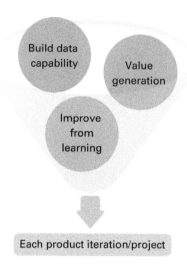

The activities for our VBI model in this wave are:

Value. The focus is no longer on how to create ways for the business to do things better but how to do things that it could not do before. The value of data is expressed in innovation and creativity.

Build. Artificial intelligence has probably been deployed in a variety of ways since early in the process, but now it can be applied to strategic, future-facing processes. A data centre of excellence continuously raises the quality of these innovations.

Improve. The transformation is complete but the process of change, informed by data, is never done. We have created the mechanisms by which innovation becomes business as usual.

18

From data-driven to AI-driven

Artificial intelligence may create profound insights from data and exceed the limitations and bias of the human brain for decision-making. Making AI relevant to everyday business is feasible. However, AI applications need to be built on strong foundations, embedded in business processes, with a clear business case.

KEY CONCEPTS

- Artificial intelligence (AI)
- Machine learning (ML)
- Single supplier view (SSV)
- Forecasting
- Prediction
- Robotic process automation (RPA)
- Natural language processing (NLP)
- Big data
- Black box

Introduction

At a gambling company, they had a lot of invoices in the finance system, but the finance team was struggling to match those to supplier contracts. These supplier contracts each had different terms and conditions across different regions, but the team couldn't match them to the service level agreements the business had with those customers. The finance team monitored budgets for each of the categories of spending in the contracts, but couldn't relate the individual contracts, which often mixed different categories of spending, to the categories. What I would call a 'complete dog's dinner'.

There was a plan to reduce costs across the business. Not easy when it was a headache to even decide what had been spent, by whom, with whom, on what.

This isn't an unusual problem, as anyone in finance will tell you. But it is extremely hard to solve by anything other than dogged, dull, repetitive work.

The business had decided it was going to use artificial intelligence to unpick this knot. It chose a software tool to review the contracts and allocate costs – in principle a wonderful application of AI: a large data set, matching and reconciling data, and, just as importantly, showing what didn't match. Everyone had assumed this was an IT project, and so the IT team set to work.

I got the call when it didn't work. The IT team had combined lots of data sources, but with no common definition of supplier names or details, because the same supplier was spelt differently in different databases, and in some was identified only by a code. So, at first, nearly everything didn't match.

The project manager was puzzled. 'Surely this is what AI is supposed to do?' he asked.

It is, but at this point he was taking a rapid personal journey through the Gartner Hype Cycle (Gartner Inc, 2021), a model invented by the firm of analysts to distil the life of new technology into five phases. First there is what Gartner calls the Innovation Trigger, in which the public hears about exciting new tech that can solve a problem; quickly they climb to the Peak of Inflated Expectations, during which people focus on early success stories, and ignore – or are not told of – the failures. Inevitably, as early users discover that real applications are disappointing, many of us fall into the Trough of Disillusionment. But, as the technology matures and more people figure out what it can and cannot do, the market reaches the Slope of Enlightenment, eventually climbing to the Plateau of Productivity, where the technology pays off. As an experienced CDO I can absolutely relate to this model.

The Hype Cycle was designed to characterize how technology evolves. But it really captures the evolution of our estimation of the ability of technology to solve problems. The project manager was undeniably in the trough.

AI and machine learning (ML), the same as every other tool in this book, rely on good underlying data quality, data governance, and project management. There are no shortcuts. You can't skip the earlier chapters about quality, governance and automation because AI seems like a quick fix (if you did, bad luck: it isn't).

What the gambling company really needed before it jumped to AI would have been a single supplier view (SSV) that could be used by finance and procurement, the equivalent of the single customer view (SCV) that was the subject of Chapter 9. In that chapter I gave some detail on how the gambling company successfully created its SCV. In this case, given an SSV, the AI project would have been a great idea. It would have quickly identified opportunities to reduce cost through better negotiation with suppliers based on terms and conditions; it would have demonstrated to procurement that we were sometimes buying the same products from the same suppliers in different regions, and that we could renegotiate the price as a result. It would even have shown the data team where the gambling company could have benefited from improving its data quality. But the AI tool couldn't do any of these things in this case, because it wasn't fed the data it needed.

ARTIFICIAL INTELLIGENCE (AI)

The ability of a digital computer to perform tasks commonly associated with intelligent beings, such as the ability to reason, discover meaning, generalize, or learn from experience.

MACHINE LEARNING (ML)

An AI discipline that implements computer software that can learn autonomously.

SINGLE SUPPLIER VIEW (SSV)

The process of collecting data from disparate data sources, then matching and merging it to form a single, accurate, up-to-date record for each supplier. It is also known as a '360-degree supplier view'.

What does AI do?

Vannevar Bush, head of the US Office of Scientific Research and Development, wrote an article for the *Atlantic Monthly* in 1945 called 'As we may think' (Bush, 1945). He was one of the few people in the world who knew about a new machine that we would soon call a computer, and it inspired him to write about a machine that could aggregate 'the associated opinions and decisions of [our] whole experience' to help us make decisions. By 1956, the first academic conference on the subject was held, at which the name 'artificial intelligence' was coined.

So we have been hammering away at AI for six decades. Bush and the early AI researchers discovered that the problem of replicating the human brain was much harder than they imagined. They slid into that trough many times. Until recently, the discipline was most actively discussed in science fiction.

Today AI is a powerful tool, and rapidly becoming pervasive, but it pays to be cautious about its application, and rigorous in how a data transformation uses it. This helps to avoid the problems that derail many AI implementations: both a lack of a clear strategy to extract value from an AI model, and a lack of high-quality data to train and feed it.

In 1987, when I was working for a large American bank, at the time the largest bank in the world, I was tasked with automating some of the risk management decisions around its mortgage and credit card products. We used a product called Expertech Xi, a so-called expert system. It was an early AI solution to impute business rules based on the data. This was a smart way of comparing what actually happened after credit decisions with the decisions themselves, and my first foray into AI. Some of the people who advised in this were from Edinburgh University, whose origins in AI date back to 1963 with a small research group established by Donald Michie, who had been a member of the codebreaking group that included Alan Turing at Bletchley Park.

In this chapter we focus on decision support: how AI can improve the way that data provides options and alternatives to human decision-makers. In the next chapter we will focus more on AI's contribution to innovation. These applications blend into each other, but they raise different challenges for the data team.

There are two intractable problems for a would-be data-driven business that can be solved through the use of AI: speed and complexity.

*An AI application can interpret data much more quickly
than a human can*

This is important when the company has to be the quickest with a non-obvious insight, such as being the first to lower or raise a price, to speedily identify someone who is trying to hack into your network, or to make a stock trade before the price changes.

An AI application can interpret much more data than a human can

We quickly reach the limit of our cognitive abilities – or our appetite for complexity – when using data to make decisions. Decisions in business are about trading off, under uncertainty, when there are constraints. Even the smartest data visualizations can only deal with the interaction of three or four variables, and most problems have many more influencing factors than that. Our brains have developed heuristic decision-making to deal with this – personal, often unconscious, mental strategies that cause us to instinctively choose rather than reflect in depth – that habitually ignores the same data that it considers to be irrelevant. In day-to-day life this is a useful way of coping, but in business it can mean ignoring new information. So no matter how good the data quality and governance are in your reports and dashboards, complex decisions sometimes need the support of more powerful tools.

A hierarchy of data value

If we think about a hierarchy of value for how data can be used in the business, it would look something like Figure 18.1.

At the bottom, reporting uses a single source of truth to show what happened in the past (Chapters 9 and 10). Insight is the first step to using data for decision support, by drawing inferences about the past and present from patterns in the data (Chapters 13 and 15).

Forecasting is the first step into the future, using those historical trends to make a judgement about what will happen next, but in a general sense: how many of a product the business will sell next month. If the business prefers to know whether a particular event will occur (a particular customer will buy that product), then this requires predictive modelling.

An example: the distinction between the two is captured by the two types of AI applications used to make policing more effective. On the one hand

FIGURE 18.1   Value from data

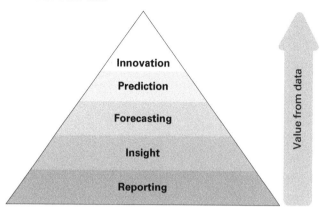

there are location-based algorithms. They match past crime rates to places and events and forecast when and where crimes are more likely to happen. A great example of one used in policing (used widely in the United States, and in some police forces in the UK) is called PredPol (PredPol Inc, 2020), which breaks up locations into blocks and updates the forecast for each block during the day.

On the other hand, predictive tools focus on individuals instead, using data on their age, gender, and history to predict who is more likely to commit a crime. Unsurprisingly, tools that influence decision-making in this way are extremely controversial, because the sort of problems of data governance that your data team encounters every day can, in this context, become matters of life and death (Heaven, 2020). They are also prone to bias – more on this later.

Innovation and redefinition use data to create insight into things that decision-makers don't know that they don't know yet. This offers unconsidered alternatives and helps the business to be more creative and agile.

FORECASTING

A process of estimating future events based on past and present data, most often by analysis of trends.

PREDICTION

Predictive modelling is a form of artificial intelligence that uses probability to estimate the likelihood of specific outcomes.

AI can help us to move up the pyramid. But it has to be implemented with care, and it would be a brave decision (and almost certainly one that any data team would regret) to immediately try to implement AI for sophisticated prediction or innovation.

The AI journey

FIGURE 18.2   Data science and AI maturity model

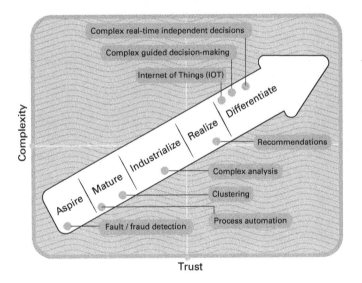

The data science and AI maturity model, Figure 18.2, shows how we might plan a journey in AI implementation. It starts with a very basic decision support process such as detecting faults or fraud, for which the implementation of AI is low risk because there is a process in place already.

As with all the maturity models in the book, this is not simply about increasing levels of complexity but rather about increasing levels of trust in the process. In many cases this is implicit, trust placed in the data team to do the right thing. In this case it is more explicit. At the top right, AI is making decisions for the organization, by implication decisions that a human could not systematically have made. This requires not just trust in the data itself but in the processes that it has created. This is an important responsibility. The chief data officer becomes the focus of future competitive advantage.

So it is important to start from solid foundations, and have a clear business case that aligns with the data and analytics strategy. The table below shows a list of possible applications of AI at each stage of the data transition process.

Task: Detection

Clearly any type of rules-based regulation is the starting point for fraud detection, but clear systems of rules, for example on money laundering, are

AI initiative	Examples
Detection	Customer churn detection Fault detection Anomaly detection Fraud detection
Process automation	Automation of approvals Automation of claims Chatbots Robotics
Clustering	Customer clusters Activity clusters
Complex analysis	Sentiment analysis VIP potential Risk management Facial recognition Voice recognition Deep insight
Recommendations	Forecasting Product recommendation Lead generation and tracking Network security Personalized customer care Predictive maintenance
Guided decision-making	New product development Semi-automated trading
Independent real-time decision-making	Automated trading Automated stock management

also a guide to how anyone who plans to commit fraud can avoid detection: don't do anything that will set off an alert in a deterministic system that looks only for breaches of those rules. The task of detection as driven by AI looks for patterns of behaviour that suggest rule-breaking, to catch it at an early stage. This has several aspects.

Data governance (again)

The minimum requirement for detection systems must be to expose low-level fraudulent behaviour. This clearly relies in turn on your data quality and governance work: are those accounts the same person? Have the ID and credit checks been completed? In a 2016 survey, KPMG International (KPMG International, 2016) found that 61 per cent of frauds benefited from weaknesses in internal controls that allowed criminals to remain undetected, a statistic that was actually increasing.

Automate basic checks and reporting

This clears space to exercise human judgement on those records that fail the test by automating what can be automated. There is plenty of evidence that organizations are not meeting even this standard of diligence. Deloitte's 2018 Global Procurement Officer Survey (Deloitte, 2018), for example, found that 65 per cent of procurement leaders had 'limited visibility' or 'no visibility' of who they were purchasing from beyond their first tier of suppliers. Completing basic profiles and research has the effect that much more is known about who your organization is doing business with, and how.

Employ AI for anomalous patterns

The AI capability in this case will look for anomalous patterns in the data and flag them. Importantly, it neither attempts to remediate the problem nor to provide an explanation. This is only useful if basic fraud detection for rule breaches is effective (for example, preventing customers from making fraudulent e-commerce transactions) and enough is known about the events to enable AI to make a judgement.

Task: Process automation

In Chapter 12 we discussed the standardized, repeatable processes that could be automated. But these are a subset of processes in the business that have a pattern, but are identical every time. This is a powerful opportunity for an AI application, but one that can be wasted if the implementation tries to go too far, too fast.

White-collar robots

Robotic process automation (RPA) is a way to automate common office tasks. It works by its AI observing how those tasks are done and extracting patterns, then replicating them automatically on similar tasks. RPA applications are usually cloud-based and provided by an external specialist, so they can be quick to implement. For processes like forms processing, in which the vast majority of work is repetitive, this has huge potential.

But, again, the underlying data has to be of a good standard. Ernst & Young found that between 30 and 50 per cent of initial deployments of RPA failed (Bhatt, 2019). Among the reasons: confirmations that are supposed to go out to clients were never sent because of missing email addresses; customer complaints were sent to the wrong team because of coding errors. There is a natural route by which processes become more complex: if we start with a task that has a small number of outcomes, eventually an exception will occur. So, to accommodate this, we add a sub-process or another outcome. This requires a workaround that may not be documented or even fully thought through. This becomes another case for continuous improvement.

This becomes a habit, internalized by the team but never fully recognized as a complication of the process that we are expecting RPA to learn, and probably not easy to spot by looking at the data that is being processed. Some organizations have gone as far as to create robotic 'supervisors' to spot flaws in the process, which can quickly alert the data team if more data work needs to be done. But it is always better to understand or simplify the process first.

ROBOTIC PROCESS AUTOMATION (RPA)

A form of business process automation that uses AI to learn and complete data processing applications, usually by observing repeated processes performed by office workers. Also known as software robotics.

Customer service bots

Covid-19 created a boom in bots as contact centres were shut down, creating problems in delivering the correct data and working conditions to agents at home. Even before then, much research and development was directed at creating lifelike, multi-purpose bots. Bank of America invested in a chatbot called Erica (Schwartz, 2021), which is used by some 19.5 million users, answering more than 250 million questions in its first year of service. The idea of creating bots which replicate customer agents is alluring, but the investment is often misdirected.

The problem is with the particular type of AI employed: natural language processing (NLP). This was the obsession of the first generation of AI research in the 1950s, because scientists at that time (and many other people since) naively assumed that if you told a computer the definition of enough words, it would understand meaning. It turns out that intent is much harder to recognize than they assumed. The overall effect the bot has with the customer interaction feels a bit stilted.

It is much more likely that a useful bot will have a defined set of tasks that it can do, reducing the need for it to have a conversation. It recognizes intent, possibly clarifies it as part of the conversation, and completes the task. Complex requests can be turned over to a human.

The bot can also learn more about what its customers want and use this to add to its capability. But if it is getting too many complex requests for help it might be better for the data team and the ops team to work together to fix the underlying problem, which may be as simple as providing better instructions or simplifying a process.

NATURAL LANGUAGE PROCESSING (NLP)

A field of AI that helps computers to recognize the meaning of human language. When successful, a computer may be capable of 'understanding' the contents of messages, documents and speech. NLP is necessary to extract meaning from text for customer service bots and for social media listening.

CASE STUDY
Billy Bot

Challenge: Good barristers' clerks are hard to find

Barristers' clerks match clients with the barristers who are available and do routine tasks to keep the office running efficiently. A clerk needs to use judgement and employ knowledge of who is available and most suitable and must have some industry knowledge.

Analysis: This is a job for a bot

Although the tasks require some interpretation, at their core is a standard set of processes. Clerksroom, which provides clerk services for barristers who work from home, decided in 2017 to create a bot to replicate some of the work.

Action: Billy Bot (Rose, 2017)

Billy was created to perform a subset of the duties of a human clerk, and worked alongside the six clerks employed by Clerksroom. It had access to the case management system and all other IT systems, and was trained to perform 167 tasks including making bookings for mediation, matching clients to the most appropriate barrister, agreeing fees and sending confirmation letters.

Outcome: A permanent increase in productivity

From implementation, Clerksroom calculated that Billy saved the firm 200 hours of work a month.

Task: Improved clustering

When we segment customers, it is natural to do this by observable characteristics, of which demographic characteristics are the most frequent. This creates insights that are useful to a point: high-income customers in the aggregate have different behaviour from low-income customers. This is useful as a way to target activity and can suggest some marketing activity if you know very little about customers, but not insightful and certainly not a source of competitive advantage.

Clusters that have meaning

AI offers the opportunity to discover common changes in behaviour or habits that define a profitable niche, or one that makes sense as a way to target sales. Some of the pioneering work that Tesco did with the analysis of its loyalty card examined this. By focusing on groups of products that were often bought together, it recognized 27 'lifestyles' among its customers that directed its marketing. The caveat is that this can't be fully automated, for two reasons. The AI might find a cluster that makes sense in the (always limited) amount of data but has no external validity. It is important that clusters are reviewed to make sure they are not just spurious correlations in the data. Also, the marketing or sales team must be able to recognize the cluster, to hold a picture of it in their head. This is because they are expected to make decisions and exercise creativity based on the insight. If they don't know who they are doing it for, they can't do it.

Clusters that go beyond behaviour

More recently, O_2, a telecommunications service provider, is one brand that has taken this further, using data and AI to create clusters based on what it calls 'affinities', not just attributes. This gave the business better insight based on customer preferences, so they could create marketing based on what a customer of the mobile network was a fan of or enjoyed. Whatever this analysis finds still has to make sense intuitively. But it raises a question: how do we know what these customers enjoy? By definition, much of this will be discoverable only by using external data or research (Chapter 15).

Data bias

An AI application is not aware of what it does. It finds patterns in the data that feeds it. So what has it been fed?

In Chapter 4, I discussed the benefits of diversity in hiring, something that the technology business in general has struggled with. A few years ago, Amazon created an AI application to avoid bias in hiring. It trained the AI using CVs that it had received in the previous 10 years. The outcome: the AI had inadvertently taught itself to penalize applications from women, because the overwhelming majority of its applicants had been male. Development on the tool was abandoned.

PredPol, the algorithm designed to predict when and where crimes will take place, has the laudable intention to reduce human bias in police work. But the controversy that PredPol has created shows how difficult this is. In 2016, the Human Rights Data Analysis Group researchers applied PredPol's algorithm to drug offences in Oakland, California. It repeatedly sent officers to neighbourhoods with a high proportion of people from racial minorities, regardless of the crime rate in those areas. Researchers at the University of Utah showed that software learns from reports recorded by the police rather than from actual crime rates, potentially creating a feedback loop that increases bias.

If you search YouTube for 'racist faucet' or 'racist soap dispenser', you can now find many videos made by citizen journalists testing no-touch equipment in public or office bathrooms and finding that the light sensors are triggered by white skin but not by black skin.

In 2016, Microsoft created an experiment in 'conversational understanding' called Tay. The more you talked to the AI chatbot, it promised, the smarter it would get. It invited people to message it using 'casual and playful conversation'. The problem was, Tay was released on Twitter, where casual conversation is not always playful. Within a day, Tay was spouting anti-Semitic slurs to its followers.

An AI application knows only about the data it is exposed to and uses the data that trains it to create its view of the world. We create AI applications to make better choices, but they are not intrinsically fair or smart. As AI is employed at the later stages of the data transformation, those reputational and ethical issues will become more important.

HOW TO MEASURE: BIAS IN MACHINE LEARNING

Measuring bias in a model is problematic: we can, of course, never say that there is no bias; we can only evaluate different cases to see if the results contain bias. One way to do this is a test of statistical parity. The point of this test is to create two groups that differ in one aspect that should be irrelevant (a protected attribute) and discover if they have the same probability of a positive outcome.

There is obviously a flaw in this reasoning: we have decided that the attribute should be protected, but the AI might discover that it is statistically relevant. If, for example, we decided that very tall people should not pay more for health insurance, we could test for statistical parity. But very tall people may bump their heads more often, which would mean more hospital visits. In this case it is not the 'fault' of the AI, or even necessarily a 'bad' model. It is that it doesn't reflect the law or our ethical values and will make 'bad' decisions on that basis.

Note that removing bias in AI may also make the algorithm less profitable. But if the original algorithm recommended discrimination that was unfair (or against the law), that's a price worth paying.

Task: Complex analysis and prediction

The point of AI is to tell the business something that it doesn't know and could not easily find out by other means. There are many of these problems, some of which we have dealt with above. As we move from AI applications that support a defined task to those that forecast, predict and even act autonomously on behalf of the business, we need to ask: how does the AI application reach a conclusion? There are several ways to answer this question.

Some tasks do not invite questions

For trivial or mundane tasks, this is unimportant because we are using AI for speed rather than to solve complex problems. For example, as long as RPA has better efficiency than the humans it has replaced, and comparable or better accuracy, there is no point in asking how it discovers patterns. On other tasks, demonstrable efficiency is also the only outcome that matters. For example, BlackBerry no longer makes those phones with keyboards on them but provides 'Unified Endpoint Security' – an AI that protects smartphones by recognizing individual patterns of keystrokes unique to a user, or even the angle at which the phone is held. Interesting for a data geek but for everyone else, it's enough to know that it works.

Some tasks can be validated by a sense check

Some tasks could have been accomplished by skilled staff, but only if they had days to spare. The conceptual step in understanding the insight is not hard to make. For example, the process of discovering sentiment from social listening is not mysterious: the AI is attributing positive sentiment to words and phrases in messages that are like ones that were previously found to be positive. It can output examples of this, showing how strongly it considers those words to be positive. But you can also do a human check: use a sample of these messages and have them rated independently by a group of people, and feed the results into the algorithm. This is also a process that deepens trust.

Some AI applications have learned from external experience

Using cloud-based services to power your bots or analyse sentiment has a huge benefit: they are looking at data aggregated from many sources. This means that much of the learning has been done already to solve similar problems in other domains. The service provider can demonstrate success, building trust that you are making a good decision to use AI for this purpose.

An example is attack detection for computer networks. It's not smart to base your security on an AI application that predicts whether you are under attack using only your past history, because the most dangerous attacks are by definition ones that you haven't seen before. But a shared AI security service can learn from other networks that it protects.

This leaves a subset of AI-driven decisions that affect customers, employees or the business, for which the data team is accountable, and which are complex decisions that we can't understand by a process of reflection. This is the AI as a 'black box'.

Solving the black box problem

When dealing with a regulator, or with risk or safety, or when using AI to support decisions on profitability that need board approval, we are confronted with the problem that someone wants to know or needs to know how the sausage was made, and an AI can appear to be a 'black box': the data goes in, the decision comes out. This is problematic, and may become more so. Although I'm not a fan of the term 'big data', it is the type of data that we consider that can lead to the black box problem, namely high volume, variety and velocity. These are three components of the four 'V's: Variety, Volume, Velocity and Veracity (Williamson, 2021). An AI application works by looking at hundreds of data sources and millions of data points and creating associations between them.

BIG DATA

Data that is high volume, with lots of variety (structured and unstructured) and high velocity. We might consider this to be very complex data that is hard to define and process.

BLACK BOX

A system used to create insight or decisions from data that can only be viewed in terms of its inputs (the data sources) and outputs, without any transparency of its internal workings.

This black box is not a static decision-making frame. For many applications, for example where to allocate advertising online, or how to perform stock trades, it is constantly evolving. You can't draw a simple chart of these interactions, but even if you could, by the time you had drawn it the chart would be out of date.

There are two approaches, given the data and the outcome, that could go some way to solving this problem. This is essential if the data team wants to create trust in AI. The first is an 'explanation by design'. Because an AI application needs to be trained by an ML process, the team can document the data that it was fed, the assumptions made in the design, and some logic of why the outcomes make sense. This helps to create trust that the right ingredients have been used but does not give an insight into the detail of any decision-making process.

A more complete explanation can be made by finding similar inputs for which the outputs varied: customers with similar profiles, for which one was given credit and the other refused. A small set of those records can give insight into how the AI has made its judgement in that part of the data. This can then be done for other cases, which means that the black box will yield a set of decision rules, even though this might be an incomplete one. These are most useful when delivered in plain English, of course. This leads to new roles such as an explainer, someone who articulates and documents how a complex algorithm or AI process works.

The limits of AI as a guide or manager

However much the executive team might want to jump to advanced implementations of AI, there is an unquantified benefit of a gradual approach that will stand both the data team and business in good stead in the long run: it shows how poor your data can be.

At some point an AI implementation will disappoint, just as the attempt at the gambling company to simplify financial reporting did, as explained at the beginning of this chapter. Usually the problem is that the data is not of an acceptable quality to create worthwhile insight. This may be because of:

• **Missing data:** There are relevant fields that are not being captured in data because they are not part of the data acquisition process or would only be accessible in external data.

- **Data leakage:** Data that could have been captured (see Chapter 1), but the business has lacked an incentive to do so until now.

- **Data quality:** The data is out of date, or not measured with the precision or accuracy you need.

It is vital to think about the role of the human in interpreting models based on AI. Making decisions contingent on discovering information or context that the AI does not know is an important learning process. If the guidance from the AI is poor, and is poor for consistent reasons, this is not a reason to throw away the AI, it's an indicator to collect more or better data, and see if that helps.

If your use of AI is deepening into the area of prediction or decision automation, limitations on the usefulness of data will have an even greater impact on how your organization will act. To allow an AI to steer the business, there must be two types of trust invested in the data transformation:

- Employees must trust the AI to make useful decisions for the business.

- Customers must be satisfied that the AI offers them the protection they are promised by law and regulation and that it reflects their concept of fairness and ethics.

Task: Creating commitment to AI for independent real-time decision-making

Neither of these is straightforward to demonstrate, but they are essential if the AI is used for recommendations or decision-making.

Focus on bias in training data

When training, the data team will have used sample data sets. This data may contain bias. If you doubt it, Google 'chief data officer' and see the images it suggests. Take the example of seatbelts, headrests and airbags in cars, which have been designed mainly based on data collected from car crash dummy tests using the physique of men and their seating position. Women's breasts and pregnant bodies don't feed into the 'standard' measurements. As a result, women are 47 per cent more likely to be seriously insured and 17 per cent more likely to die than a man in a similar accident (*Forbes*, 2020).

Prioritize unexpected value

While it is vital to be conservative about the application of AI, once it is used as a recommendation engine, its ability to find unexpected insight is its strength. One previous employer ran a recommendation engine that could be trusted on one level, because its algorithm only recommended the most popular product. It was safe, but not valuable to the business, and so had little commitment from the marketers who were meant to be using it as a tool.

An alternative recommendation strategy may be far more hit and miss, but far more valuable to the business. It is creative to communicate to the customer, 'I know you don't usually go for this, but...' The AI might show only a slightly higher chance than average of success, but this strategy can create confidence that it is performing a valuable role. There has to be an explanation beyond 'the computer told me to do it' or, of course, 'the computer says no'.

Align with the data and analytics strategy

AI can be designed in many ways, to reflect many risk appetites and priorities. So the AI must be responsive to the needs of the business in how it frames decision-making. This means using AI only if there is value or a competitive advantage to do so, not because it is technologically interesting. For example:

- **Do we need real-time data?** If there is a lot of variance in market conditions, then more reliable month-old data might be a competitive disadvantage. If there is not, real-time data is a handicap.

- **How does automating a decision affect customer relationships?** Customers may value not having to interact with a person (for example if they apply for a raised credit limit and want an immediate decision). But this is often not the case.

From data-driven transformation to AI-driven business

We can characterize the data-driven model as a process of making sure that everyone in the organization has the best possible data, in the most appropriate format, at the time they need to make a decision. But this does not solve the problems of information overload or bias in decision-making. Sometimes the data transition fixes everything but the real problem: the limitations of the human who uses the data.

It is tempting to ask AI to do too much, though. The journey with AI goes from it being a simple tool to spot unusual behaviour to a creative catalyst that is innovating processes for the business, perhaps without any human involvement at all.

SUMMARY

- AI is a powerful tool, but it cannot compensate for poor data engineering.

- AI needs to be introduced carefully, with caution. Using external cloud-based applications to improve internal processes is a way to learn about AI capability, but they also may have long-term advantages because these applications are trained on larger data sets.

- Bots to execute tasks or assist customers need to have a clear application that is specific and well defined.

- AI can identify new and profitable opportunities, especially by taking advantage of external data sources.

- As the complexity of an AI application increases, so it is more vulnerable to accusations of being a 'black box', and the problems of data or algorithmic bias. These problems need to be addressed if the goal is to partially or completely automate entire processes.

References

Bhatt, N (2019) Five design principles to help build confidence in RPA implementations, Ernst & Young

Bush, V (1945) As we may think, *The Atlantic*, https://www.theatlantic.com/magazine/archive/1945/07/as-we-may-think/303881/ (archived at https://perma.cc/P3C7-V49B)

Deloitte (2018) Deloitte 2018 global procurement officer survey, https://www2.deloitte.com/content/dam/Deloitte/at/Documents/strategy-operations/deloitte-global-cpo-survey-2018.pdf (archived at https://perma.cc/9KSE-8JE7)

Forbes (2020) AI Bias could put women's lives at risk – a challenge for regulators, https://www.forbes.com/sites/carmenniethammer/2020/03/02/ai-bias-could-put-womens-lives-at-riska-challenge-for-regulators/?sh=2b802d71534f (archived at https://perma.cc/6N2J-F9MY)

Gartner Inc (2021) Gartner Hype Cycle, https://www.gartner.com/en/research/methodologies/gartner-hype-cycle (archived at https://perma.cc/MCY7-5RS7)

Heaven, W D (2020) Predictive policing algorithms are racist. They need to be dismantled, *MIT Technology Review*, 17 July

KPMG International (2016) Global profiles of the fraudster: Technology enables and weak controls fuel the fraud

PredPol Inc (2020) The predictive policing company, https://www.predpol.com/ (archived at https://perma.cc/KCM3-VXFR)

Rose, N (2017) LegalFutures: Exclusive: Here comes Billy, the robot junior clerk, https://www.legalfutures.co.uk/latest-news/exclusive-comes-billy-robot-junior-clerk (archived at https://perma.cc/UV3N-5SJX)

Schwartz, E H (2021) Bank of America's virtual assistant Erica explodes in popularity, https://voicebot.ai/2021/04/21/bank-of-americas-virtual-assistant-erica-explodes-in-popularity/ (archived at https://perma.cc/R6Q3-FR3M)

Williamson, J (2021) *The 4 V's of Big Data*, John Wiley & Sons, Inc. The origin of the 4Vs is unclear but I know from experience it was around in the 1990s and well before the term Big Data was used: https://www.dummies.com/careers/find-a-job/the-4-vs-of-big-data/ (archived at https://perma.cc/79F3-SM43)

19

Data products

Being able to innovate is the most powerful determinant of future success for your business. This process is more likely to succeed if you embed data in each stage of the process. A culture of continuous improvement sustains the momentum of the data transformation.

KEY CONCEPTS

- Data product
- Waterfall development
- Agile development
- Centre of excellence (CoE)

Introduction

In 2015, the Department for Transport (DfT) released its final reports (Department for Transport, 2015) on five years of quantifying a metric called Values of Travel Time Savings, which had been measured and estimated for all major types of transport infrastructure. 'These reports set out the methods used and results from a project to estimate up-to-date national values of travel time for use in transport appraisals,' it declared. 'Travel time savings typically account for a large proportion of the benefits of major transport infrastructure. For this reason they play an important role in policy making and investment decisions.'

One of the ways in which a researcher would do this would be to ask travellers how much they would be willing to pay, hypothetically, for a shorter journey time.

This had been a shift in thinking that had begun in the 1960s with the ability to collate and process large amounts of data, and a new focus on data-driven decisions in the public sector. It is appropriate that we measure whether building a new road or creating a bus lane will be valuable, not least if there isn't money to do both and someone in the ministry has to decide which one to do. But the method may also have been the culmination of a project-based way of thinking: an end, rather than a beginning.

A key term was born: the Value of Travel Time Savings (VTTS), intended to describe the total economic benefits from reduced travel time costs. VTTS gave a number that measured the impact of a policy, and that's what management (policymakers and ministers) could understand and communicate. It was also satisfying to measure, and pleasingly precise.

Today Transport for London (TfL), among many other transport providers, has realized that investment should be motivated by a much wider range of data. Faced with spiralling bills to reduce transport time (even shaving a couple of minutes off a tube journey potentially involves millions of pounds of investment in trains, signalling, safety and staff), it started to ask a wider set of questions more often of the travelling public. Would they prefer a shorter journey or a more comfortable one of the same length? If they had to wait longer, but had better information about when the bus would come, would they mind?

It turns out that we often don't mind a longer journey if we can get work done, or use the internet, or just not be stuffed into someone's armpit. Waiting seems shorter when we know how long we will be waiting for. The insight is that it's much cheaper, and creates much higher satisfaction levels among travellers, if transport providers focus not on making the journey shorter but on making it seem shorter.

'Our team has changed radically in its scope,' says Ian Pring, who is TfL's customer marketing and behaviour change lead. Now, he explains, there is a customer insight team and a staff and stakeholder insight team, both working with the customer directorate, which brings together skills in marketing, planning, technology and data.

The focus on engineering a shorter trip was a goal that is being supplanted by a bigger goal: a better trip. That requires more data, of course, but also a focus on a new type of data-enabled innovation: data products.

What is a data product?

DATA PRODUCT

A process, service or capability innovation that is defined and enabled by data. These products can be delivered internally, to business units, or externally, to partners and customers. Their nature means they can be continuously improved.

When the data team creates the ability to identify VIP customers in the SCV (Chapter 9), or to measure sentiment in social media, or to find anomalies in recharging for photocopying as in Chapter 5, it is delivering a product.

We often consider product development as a project with a deliverable and an endpoint. This is a waterfall approach, and if the DfT wanted to spend £65 billion on a railway line from London to Manchester, that would be the way to go: you need to know what each phase of the project encompasses, what resources are required, exactly what the work is, and how long it will take.

Its weakness for our purposes is that it presupposes that the users of the product know what they want, and that the developers of the product know what problems they might run into along the way. Not, as we have seen, safe assumptions when innovating by using data in fresh ways.

WATERFALL DEVELOPMENT

A development strategy where the project is broken down into phases, and each phase is completed in sequence. Tasks are specialized for each phase. There is a defined deliverable, and a schedule with a completion date. It can be useful in engineering design, and for some types of software development. It is rarely applied to data projects.

The data team creates data products, as we have seen, and this means to some extent that we are speculative:

- we don't know what we have until we look;

- we don't know if it will create business value until we try;
- the people who use it often don't know what they want until they see it.

Products are different from projects in that they don't have a beginning and an end. Once created they are managed, supported and continuously improved.

AGILE DEVELOPMENT

A development strategy in which innovators use a collaborative effort during which smaller teams self-organize to deliver on short-term, specific goals. Its features are adaptive planning and evolutionary development. It is commonly used for software development.

The data transition has led your organization to a point at which it most likely has a portfolio of data products that either individually or together have delivered improvements to the business. The development of those products has mandated work in governance, quality and analytics, and the products embody the benefits of that work. As those products are applied across the organization, they multiply in value. As they are embedded in business processes, their effectiveness improves.

Viewing them as products creates a mental framework that helps the data team to evangelize them to the business, and also to improve the way the products work. We can consider three aspects of how products are created and managed:

1 Data and analytics centre of excellence (CoE).

2 Three functions of research.

3 Continuous improvement life cycle.

A data and analytics centre of excellence (CoE)

Because from day one the data team targeted its data products in places that had the best business case or the most urgent need, there is likely to be uneven knowledge of, or implementation of, best practices. Where that knowledge and learning are at their best, we can establish a centre of excellence (CoE) for data products. This is when the data team has fully grown up and is critical to all aspects of business success.

CENTRE OF EXCELLENCE (CoE)

A team that centralizes know-how about improving and deploying products or services. It has a permanent status, may be cross-functional, and works with all the business units.

CoEs have been successful in recent years at cutting across organizational boundaries and helping to improve and deliver complex products and services. They are expected to use their success to spread insight and actively help other parts of the business to work with data products, and to feed back what they have learned to improve the product itself.

An example of how a CoE can work is demonstrated by WashCo, a US-based organization that sells washing machines to launderettes and supports them. It struggled with support models, first implementing regional support (shorter fix times but lower fix effectiveness) and then specialized support (more first-time fixes by field service teams, but a longer wait for one of them to attend). In 2005 it set up a third structure, with a regional model backed by sector specialists. This led to some improvements, but it was also unclear who was in charge. When it set up a CoE in one region, it solved many of these problems. Engineers in the CoE still made service calls but had a remit to identify common problems and help solve them, as well as to help upskill their colleagues in other departments.

If we apply this to the data function, we begin to move beyond problem-solving into a team that can ensure that the data products are delivered to the highest standard and focus not on their roles but on the products they are delivering. It's a change of mindset. The people within the CoE have deeper knowledge of what data can accomplish, and how to do it, and act as a go-to resource as the rest of the organization becomes more data literate and data hungry.

This means that when your data products have markets in your organization, they are improved and supported. Although it is an elite group, a CoE also breaks down the 'them and us' attitude to data innovations by which operations are passive recipients (or, worst case, victims) of the data and analytics strategy. The data team is constantly working with the CoE to document, standardize and augment the data products it delivers.

Some people have considered embedding different aspects of the data and analytics team across different business teams. This is, in my experience, an unmitigated disaster as it loses the focus and integrated elements of the team.

Task: Creating a data CoE

How does this approach work?

Get buy-in at every level, across disciplines

The CoE is focused on problem-solving in the business. This implies an engagement with the data transition at every level, including executive sponsorship. This has been emphasized by empirical work in the *MIT Sloan Review*:

> It is not enough… to establish centers of excellence to accelerate data initiatives, when only about 1 in 4 executives reported that their organization has successfully forged a data culture. Cultural change and business transformation must be adopted at all levels of an organization for data-driven management to be truly embraced (Bean, 2020).

Two-way communication

When users of data products understand what they have, they may understand how data quality is limiting what they can do, how new data sources or external data could be useful, or how the data does not align to their business processes. At that point the CoE can bridge the gap between what the users have, and what they could achieve. But this is always a discussion between the CoE and the business.

Encourage sharing across the business

As the business scales its data products, the CoE has captured important organizational knowledge and learning that it can pass on to other parts of the business. It is important to build structures to do this, either formal or informal.

Three functions of research

If we want to create successful data products, we need to capture the voice of the customer as an input to the design process. The concept of the 'voice of the consumer' was originally intended to be an input to product design.

This means involving research at every stage of data product design, especially when the product is targeted at an external customer. Therefore our development process needs to encompass the following.

Defining a need

Primary research before any innovation can sketch out a hypothesis for what we need to deliver. What is the most important pain point? This primary research is likely to be incomplete, but it sets a credible first goal. This can be quantitative – for example, if response times are slow for a service, we can measure them. If satisfaction is low or falling, we can establish a baseline level. But it must also investigate what the customer (whether that customer is internal or external) would like to see as an improvement.

Benchmarking improvement

The baseline measure of the effectiveness of a data product can involve data quality or speed, but these are ultimately engineering measurements and can lead to too much focus on this aspect of the product (recall what happened at TfL). Measurement must also seek to capture data on whether the people who should benefit from the product are happier, or feel their job has improved, and track that.

Uncovering new desires

Being confronted with a data product will spark engagement and imagination on how to develop it. If there are new ideas, new parameters of what value is, the development process needs to recognize them. Remember if people are unfamiliar with the potential of data products then they'd only really know what to ask for when they see the data product emerging.

A continuous improvement life cycle

The idea of a data-driven business is often used in a woolly sense, and what this means may be a mystery to anyone who works in any organization;

after all, they use data, there's data everywhere, and their managers talk about data, so isn't that enough?

The ability to create and improve data products, whatever techniques and processes are behind them, is what drives the data transformation. The establishment of feedback mechanisms and CoEs creates continuous improvements. Appropriate measurement and communication create certainty that the transformation is on the right track.

Rolling out data products is not a guarantee of success. They may underwhelm, not match needs sufficiently, or work in one location but be a bad fit elsewhere. This is a message to fix the problem, not to abandon the project. Ultimately the data team is creating satisfaction, not ways to use data. So if the product is not right, negative feedback, properly channelled, is a creative response.

The ability of the data team to continuously uncover business challenges and meet them is unique. It is a process to deliver successful growth, and a process that, thanks to all the work the team has done to this point, can continue to replicate these improvements across the business.

SUMMARY

- Data products use data to create an improvement in the way the business operates. Their users can be internal or external (partners or customers).

- Framing the work of the data team in this way means that it never considers a project complete: what it delivers is constantly reviewed and upgraded in response to user feedback.

- Data centres of excellence help to create a focus for these improvements that can then be copied across the business.

- Research can establish a requirement for innovation, a channel for feedback, and uncover new ideas that users have about how to develop data products.

- This creates a continuous life cycle of innovation that makes the work of the data team self-sustaining.

References

Bean, R (2020) Why culture is the greatest barrier to data success, *MIT Sloan Management Review*

Department for Transport (2015) Values of travel time savings and reliability: final reports, 29 October, https://www.gov.uk/government/publications/values-of-travel-time-savings-and-reliability-final-reports (archived at https://perma.cc/SL64-KYMM)

20

Right leadership, right time

Every transition requires a leader, but this one arguably requires three fundamentally different types of leader. Failure to recognize the required skills can change or derail the transition.

Introduction

In 1908 Henry Ford had the revolutionary idea of creating a production line to create his Model T, and in 1913 he focused on making his technology as efficient as possible. In six months he managed to reduce the time taken to build a Model T from nine hours and 54 minutes to five hours and 56 minutes. He used data to create staggering efficiency in his processes that made a new product that was cheaper and of higher quality than anyone had ever seen. Ford was dominant, unassailable. At one point more than half the cars in the world were Ford Model Ts.

But in 1921 Henry Ford decided to freeze his design so he could optimize his production process. Famously it promised that 'any customer can have a car painted any colour that he wants so long as it is black' (Ford, 1922).

Meanwhile, in 1916, General Motors had also incorporated in Detroit. Alfred Sloan, the general manager, could copy Ford's production line, but he was also interested in the people who drove the cars, and focused his innovation in other areas. GM didn't want to lose customers, so it pioneered the practice of offering credit. While comedians started to make fun of Ford's 'Tin Lizzie', GM used the new discipline of market research to ask what changes its customers wanted in the design, so it could incorporate them into next year's model.

Henry Ford pioneered the production line, but Sloan invented planned obsolescence. By the 1930s, GM was the largest automaker in the world.

Leading a sustainable data culture

In creating a data transition, the job of the CDO has been to drive the organization through the five waves of aspire, mature, industrialize, realize and, finally, differentiate. Each wave requires different skills and techniques, and each one changes the organization, from the data it could employ to the way it makes decisions, remaking processes and raising ambition.

Every team has its leader. If that leader is you, are you a Ford or a Sloan, and can you be both? To create sustainable change, the CDO (or whoever is leading the transition) needs to be different at different times, and this can test the management ability of the most talented executive.

What sort of leader does each wave demand?

Aspire and mature: beat the door down

The key skills at this stage are those of a challenger, because everything will be different. It is usual to inherit work half-finished or failed, and to encounter disappointment and even resistance. The people who went before have tried, and failed, to fix the problems. So at this stage, our data leader must be prepared to evangelize and win friends, make a new business case from the ground up, create a coherent vision, and make hard decisions – break down silos and even kill off projects that can never succeed.

Industrialize: consolidate

This wave is about creating repeatable gains, driving up quality, and scaling solutions. The leader still has to face challenges, but the key skills are attention to detail and process, integration into business processes, automation, and team building.

The key achievement will be to create a stable culture of improvement that achieves the business goals promised at the outset.

Realize and differentiate: innovate

The final two waves in our journey require a different set of skills again. With a toolkit of data products, with management's attention and a track record of success, this requires a deep thinker to create innovative solutions to problems that will give the business an advantage over its competitors, change existing markets and create new ones.

Innovators no longer need to convince executives to buy into the data transition, because it defines the strategic direction of the entire organization. They do not need to break down silos or plead for investment. But as the size of the bets placed on transformative projects increases, so must the leader's ability to think creatively and subtly to stay ahead of the curve.

Which leader are you?

Very few CDOs combine all three attributes and, in my experience, this can derail a transformation. Consolidators may not be prepared to break down silos in the beginning. Innovators may balk at months of work on quality and governance.

The temptation to be the hero means that many of us stay too long or hold on to power when we should delegate. We get side-tracked by our pet projects or stop listening to advice. To succeed at any one of these stages is remarkable; to carry through an entire project from beginning to end would be extraordinary. So, to repeat a final piece of advice: a data transition is a team game.

SUMMARY

- The data transition process is arduous and will require many skills and attributes. It is rare to possess them all.
- The key is finding a CDO with the right leadership skills, not technical ones, to drive the business through the waves.

Reference

Ford, H and Crowther, S (1922) *My Life and Work*, William Heinemann Ltd

EPILOGUE

Data success

As a data leader, you are one of the people who is creating fundamental change for your business. Look back at where we started and see how much has changed and how much value we've created. That's why the struggle is worth it.

I have been through this process many times. Why do I do it? Well, we started the book with 10 questions and by way of symmetry I have 10 answers to this question.

1 Each time I go through this process, with each role, each organization and industry I learn something new, and I bring something new to that organization.

2 Working in data and analytics you have a unique, non-judgemental view across all aspects of a business. That's why it is so powerful and enables you to unlock data assets and increase innovation, which is invaluable to a CEO.

3 Problem-solving for business is a thrill that never goes away.

4 There is a right order to do things in. When you get that right it's powerful and gives a real buzz. You end up avoiding the usual potholes where work gets thrown away, transitions stall, budget is wasted and the business loses confidence.

5 It's a team game. Individually we may make a small difference, but it is the collective that creates a data-first organization. You start as a data team and with maturity you end up with a data centre of excellence that is driving success across the business. The diversity of thinking is a challenge but one that is rewarding too.

6 You're continually being stretched with new developments in the industry, with new products and ways of working. That's exciting as you never stand still. As new AI and ML capabilities develop it means there is a greater dependency on the fundamentals of governance and quality.

7   There are different methodologies of waterfall and agile that are relevant to aspects of our work but data science and AI all require a more scientific, experimental approach. This diversity makes the work more interesting and challenging.

8   Data success is achieved when you can execute all the elements I have described in *Data and Analytics Strategy for Business* – but do them together. Get this working as a well-oiled machine and it's so rewarding.

9   Data isn't something you create. It's out there, waiting for you to discover it and use and reuse it to accomplish fundamental changes that are enormous.

10 It feels like data has now come of age from its early days as a by-product of IT to a fully fledged business capability.

It gets us out of bed in the morning and keeps us up at night until we succeed. And, next morning, we go again. Is it worth it?

Always.

GLOSSARY

A/B tests: Simple tests to establish which of two products or strategies is preferred by customers. Usually one is the control representing business as usual, the other the experiment. Statistically the test is valid only when group A is similar to group B in all relevant ways. If the difference in outcome is large enough, then this is attributable to the treatment.

Adaptability quotient (AQ): The ability to adapt your thinking from one domain to another. For example, if you're an SQL programmer able to program in other languages, such as Python, and you accept that your skill is programming and not SQL. High AQ relates to a high ability to adapt your skills to new problems and not to solve every problem with the same skill.

Agile development: A development strategy in which innovators use a collaborative effort where smaller teams self-organize. Its features are adaptive planning and evolutionary development. It is commonly used for software development.

Application programming interface (API): A set of procedures and communication protocols that provide access to the data of an application, operating system or other services.

Artificial intelligence (AI): The ability of a digital computer to perform tasks commonly associated with intelligent beings, such as the ability to reason, discover meaning, generalize, or learn from experience.

Asymmetric information: A situation or transaction in which one party has more or better information than the other.

Big data: Data that is high volume, lots of variety (structured and unstructured), and high velocity. We might consider this to be very complex data that is hard to define and process.

Black box: A system used to create insight or decisions from data that can only be viewed in terms of its inputs (the data sources) and outputs, without any transparency of its internal workings.

Blockchain: A system in which a record of transactions is maintained across several computers that are linked in a peer-to-peer network.

Business change process: A defined business process achieves value from data for the business. This is a complement to the data process, as it focuses on the actions that users of data can take to realize value. This can be used to communicate the value of a project to all stakeholders, but specifically to those who use the data on a regular basis.

Business dashboard: An information management tool used to present the data points relevant to the performance of a business at a glance. Complex data is simplified and summarized using graphics and visualizations, and users may be able to drill down or filter information to help understanding.

Business report: An analysis of data to evaluate an issue, set of circumstances, or operational goal that relates to the performance of a business. The report may be regular, or a one-off that has been commissioned by the executive leadership. It is used as an aid to decision-making.

Centre of excellence (CoE): A team that centralizes know-how about improving and deploying products or services. It has a permanent status, may be cross-functional, and works with all the business units.

Certified report (or dashboard): A business report that has been 'certified' in terms of its data quality, governance, sources of data, timeliness and knowledge of any transformations, aggregations or calculations in its creation.

Chief data officer (CDO): The person responsible for enterprise-wide governance and use of information as an asset. This involves data collection, governance, processing, analysis, business intelligence, data science and key elements of data-driven AI and other techniques. A CDO usually reports directly to the chief executive officer (CEO).

Cognitive diversity: The differences people have in how they prefer to think, rather than a diversity of genetics or background. There are many models, but Herrmann refers to analytical, practical, relational and experimental skills. Teams may contain members with all four preferences, or some individuals can change their way of thinking depending on context, making them talented problem-solvers.

Data accountability: The principle that the governance of each item of data is someone's responsibility. This means that the person is also able to demonstrate the steps taken to ensure that the data is properly governed. Note that this is part of data regulation, as well as good business.

Data architecture: The design of the logical and physical elements of a company's data assets that includes the data model, rules, storage, integration, access, visualization, performance and security as well as the tools required for data management, which includes data governance, privacy and quality.

Data compliance: Ensuring that data is organized and managed so that organizations meet enterprise business rules and legal and governmental regulations.

Data ethics: The responsible use of data, doing the right thing for people and society, no matter whether they're looking or not.

Data executive: The decision-making and dispute resolution body on how to execute the data and analytics strategy, at which senior representatives of the business interact with the CDO. It should meet regularly, when the data and analytics team can update the business on the progress of the transformation. It reports to the board.

Data fraud: The deliberate fabrication or falsification of data for financial gain.

Data governance: A system of decision rights and accountabilities for information-related processes, executed according to agreed-upon models that describe who can take what actions with what information, and when, under what circumstances, using what methods.

Data inventory: A fully described record of the data assets that you maintain. An inventory should record basic information about a data asset including its name, contents, update frequency, owner and source.

Data lake: A store of raw data, for example social media data, the purpose of which is not yet defined. This may never be used but will be useful to inform and test data science models, because it can demonstrate the evolution of the variables of interest. Ingestion is done by sucking everything in, and then worrying about structure when it is needed.

Data leakage: The failure to take advantage of potentially useful data generated by the business process in a way that can create an advantage for the organization. This can be a failure of acquisition, silos or business processes, but it creates a persistent leak of value that needs to be plugged, or data that is captured with a quality that is too poor to use.

Data model: A visual representation and design of [the] data [in your organization]; showing business components and the data elements within them, the relationships among these data elements, and its formats and attributes.

Data owner: A (non-statutory) role for someone in the business who has decision-making authority for each 'type' of data – people, financial, customer, and so on – who can act as an enabler for projects and process improvements in that area.

Data periodic table: A method to assign strategic business goals to data activities. The table highlights those business activities that can, through the use of data, generate business value. It then links those activities to enabling data activities and the data toolkit, and can be used to align data and organizational strategies.

Data privacy: Determines whether, or how, data is shared with third parties, how data is legally collected or stored, and the regulatory restrictions in which the business operates.

Data process: A defined way to achieve value from data for the business. This includes a definition of the data, where it resides and how to access it, the question it seeks to answer, and the processing and techniques required to find that answer. This can be used to communicate the value of a project to all stakeholders.

Data product: A process, service or capability innovation that is defined and enabled by data. These products can be delivered internally, to business units, or externally, to partners and customers. Their nature means they can be continuously improved.

Data provenance: Metadata that allows us to attribute an item of data to its source. This is used for financial reporting and auditing, for example, but it should be defined for all data that is used to influence business decision-making. Provenance means we can answer why, how, where, when and by which person or process the data has been produced, which means we can make informed decisions about the level of confidence we should put in it.

Data quality: A measure of how well data represents the real-world phenomena it describes for the purpose of the business. The four dimensions of quality are that it should be accurate, valid, accessible and timely.

Data quality leader: The person within the data team tasked with analysing the data in the business, evaluating its quality, and making recommendations on how to create improvements. The role straddles technical improvements (for example, removing duplicates) and process improvements (for example, improving the ways in which data is acquired and entered). The leader also reports on improvements in quality.

Data science: The discipline that combines programming skills and knowledge of business, mathematics and statistics to extract meaningful insights from data. Those insights can be turned into value for the business.

Data security: The practice of protecting data from unauthorized access, corruption, or theft throughout its entire life cycle.

Data steward: A (non-statutory, non-management) role for someone in a department who understands how it collects and uses data. The data steward acts as a two-way conduit of information between the data team and that part of the business.

Data and analytics strategy: The choices and priorities that create a course of action to achieve the high-level goals of the organization. Through the use of all aspects of data – including data generation, data storage, governance, quality, analysis, business intelligence and data science – these goals will create returns or competitive advantage for the business and support its wider goals.

Data warehouse: A store of structured and filtered data used by data scientists to build, test, refine and ultimately run their models. The data has been extracted from operational systems and processed for a specific purpose. Ingestion is done by analysing what's needed, then going to find it.

Digital transition, digital transformation: The process of taking analogue information and translating it to a digital environment. The accompanying transformation involves changing business processes underpinned by data to take advantage of the opportunities.

Disintermediation: A reduction in the use of intermediaries between the origination and execution of a job by automating and reorganizing the data process. This improves efficiency but reduces the need for an employee to complete or monitor the job.

Disruption: A process in which market entrants with novel business models challenge and replace industry incumbents. Because the product or service does not have traditional attributes, the incumbents assume that the entrant's product or service is not a threat until it is too late.

Drill down: Access successively deeper levels of hierarchically ordered data, for example to see the contribution of individual customers, products or regions to a headline statistic.

Firehose API: A stream of data from a source in real time delivered to its subscribers. The volume of data will come in peaks and troughs, but the data continues to flow through the firehose until it is consumed.

Five waves of transformation: A strategy for guiding the data transformation of a business. It posits that you start with projects that are foundational or less complex, and don't require trust from the business or customers. Success in these enables complex activities that generate more value and require more funding or more trust. The waves give a time dimension to a data and analytics strategy.

Forecasting: A process of estimating future events based on past and present data, most often by analysis of trends.

Hackathon: An event at which a lot of people come together to write or improve computer programs. Usually for one very specific purpose or challenge.

Intangible value (of data): Comes from reducing risk and from improving productivity, automation, customer satisfaction and employee satisfaction. Perhaps the business can do something that it could not do before.

Machine learning (ML): An AI discipline that implements computer software that can learn autonomously.

Net promoter score (NPS): The score that you get from subtracting the percentage of detractors from the percentage of promoters when you ask whether a customer would recommend your company to others.

Omnichannel: The term used for providing consistent and seamless customer experience whether the client is shopping in a store, from a smart phone, or through a website (the channels).

Practical quotient (PQ): The ability to think about problem-solving in a way that directly relates to the business, especially the ability to problem-solve using the mindset of other personas, such as an engineer or entrepreneur, without a prescribed solution or approach. High PQ relates to a high ability to conceptualize and solve data problems, and get on and deliver the solution, or get things fixed.

Prediction: Predictive modelling is a form of artificial intelligence that uses probability to estimate the likelihood of specific outcomes.

Quick win: An immediate improvement that delivers obvious value to the business. Because of the short deadline (two to three months), quick wins tend to be easy to implement but limited in scope. The best quick wins can be built on or repeated at a later date.

Quick wins paradox: The problem that the rush to demonstrate tangible value for a leader can often have the opposite effect if project selection or implementation is flawed.

Retention quotient (RQ): The ability to store and recall information easily. Many people who have traditionally done well at exams are good at retaining information but these skills, whilst dominant in CVs, are less useful in a problem-solving environment than PQ, EQ and AQ.

Role-based reporting: A discipline that states that internal reporting is to be done only when it makes a difference to a task or role in the organization. Reports are primarily forward-looking, aligned to the specific challenge, contain only data that is relevant, and clearly state progress or decision options.

Sentiment analysis: The use of natural language processing and text analysis to systematically extract and quantify subjective emotions in data, most often free text.

Shadow data resource: The collection, processing and analysis of data without explicit approval of the data function, usually funded by departmental budgets of corporate credit cards.

Single customer view (SCV): The process of collecting data from disparate data sources, then matching and merging it to form a single, accurate, up-to-date record for each customer. It is also known as a 'Golden ID' or '360-degree customer view'.

Single employee view: The process of collecting data from disparate data sources, then matching and merging it to form a single, accurate, up-to-date record for each employee.

Single product view: The process of collecting data from disparate data sources, then matching and merging it to form a single, accurate, up-to-date record for each product.

Single source of truth: Every data element is stored and edited in only one place, with no duplicates. Updates to the data propagate to the entire system.

Single supplier view (SSV): The process of collecting data from disparate data sources, then matching and merging it to form a single, accurate, up-to-date record for each supplier. It is also known as a '360-degree supplier view'.

Social listening: The process of monitoring social media channels for mentions of your brand, its competitors, your products, or topics in which your brand has a stake.

Straight-through processing (STP): A business process in which data is acquired and used to trigger actions without human intervention. It is most often applied to financial services, and requires complete and accurate data.

Subject access request (SAR): Individuals have the right under the GDPR to request the information that an organization holds on them. They can do this verbally or in writing, including via social media. The organization has the responsibility to disclose this promptly in an easy-to-understand format.

Sunk cost fallacy: When we don't ask, 'For each pound, euro or dollar we spend on this from now on, will it return a pound, euro, or dollar in value?' and instead say, 'Look at all the money we spent and it hasn't generated any value for us yet: we'd better keep going until it does.'

Tangible value (of data): Comes from increasing revenue and reducing costs. Both combine to increase the margin of the business.

Tracking survey: A project to collect consistent information about the market in which a company operates at regular intervals (daily, monthly, quarterly, yearly). The information can cover competitor behaviour, customer feedback or market trends. It allows organizations to spot trends, make comparisons to competitors, and detect threats.

Value, build, improve (VBI): The dimensions that measure the positive impact of each wave of transformation: creating value, building capability, and informing improvements in the business from the learning.

Voice of the customer (VoC): A company-wide effort to capture a customer's expectations, preferences and dislikes, used as a continuous process to create better products and services.

Waterfall development: A development strategy where the project is broken down into phases, and each phase is completed in sequence. Tasks are specialized for each phase. There is a defined deliverable, and a schedule with a completion date. It can be useful in engineering design, and for some type of software development. It is rarely applied to data projects.

ABBREVIATIONS AND ACRONYMS

AI	Artificial intelligence
API	Application programming interface
AQ	Adaptability quotient
AST	Airmen Selection Test
BPO	Business process outsourcing
CDO	Chief data officer
CDR	Core data record
CEO	Chief executive officer
CFO	Chief financial officer
CIO	Chief information officer
CISO	Chief information security officer
CoE	Centre of excellence
COO	Chief operating officer
COUNT	Collect once, use numerous times
CRM	Customer relationship management
DPO	Data privacy officer
EQ	Emotional quotient
FSA	Financial Services Authority
GDPR	General Data Protection Regulation
HR	Human resources
IQ	Intelligence quotient
IT	Information technology
KPI	Key performance indicator
ML	Machine learning
NLP	Natural language processing
NPS	Net promoter score
PQ	Practical quotient
ROI	Return on investment
RPA	Robotic process automation
RQ	Retention quotient
SAR	Subject Access Request
SCV	Single customer view
SFO	Serious Fraud Office

SLA	Service level agreement
SSV	Single supplier view
STP	Straight-through processing
TfL	Transport for London
USA	United States of America
VBI	Value, build, improve
VoC	Voice of the customer
VTTS	Value of travel time savings

INDEX

Page numbers in *italic* indicate figures or tables

360-degree customer view 12

A/B testing 93–94
adaptability quotient (AQ) 58
agile development 240, 281
Akerlof, George 247
Alphabet 3
Amazon 3, 8, 24, 252
   A/B testing 93–94
   Amazon Prime 24, 25, 30
   Amazon Redshift 189
   application programming
      interfaces 242–43
   bias in AI 269
American Express 204
Amstrad 12
Anderson, Chris 232–33
AOL 24
Apple 3, 24
application programming interfaces
   (APIs) 65, 67, 221, 243
   firehose APIs 223
Arthur Andersen 104
artificial intelligence (AI) 4, 19, 66, 171,
   257–76
   bias 262, 269–70
      eliminating 274
   clustering, improved 268–69
   complex analysis / prediction 270–72
      big data 272
      'black box problem', the 272–73
   data quality 260, 273, 274
   definition of 259
   detection 264–65
   forecasting 262
   Gartner Hype Cycle 258
   history of 260
   machine learning (ML) 19, 66, 171, 258,
     259
   maturity model 263
   natural language processing (NLP) 267
   prediction 262
   problems solved by 260–62
   process automation 266–67
      robotic process automation
      (RPA) 266

asymmetric information 247
automation 179–90
   automation tools 180–90
   business process automation, definition
     of 180
   maturity model *181*
   measuring potential for 182
   reasons for 184–86
   scope, manageable 187–89
   spinach case study 186–87
   what can be automated 183–84
Azure 189

bad news, hearing 229–30
Bank of America 267
Bentley, Phil 117
Bezos, Jeff 242, 243, 244
big data 272
Billy Bot 267–68
'black box problem', the 272–73
BlackBerry 271
blockchain 246–47
'bridge to nowhere' 33–34
British Gas 117, 119
BUPA 19
Bush, Vannevar 260
business change process 92
business dashboard 157
business process automation 180
Business Process Outsourcing (BPO) 204–05
business reports *see* reporting

Capital One 53
centre of excellence (CoE) 282–83
certified dashboard 164
certified report 164
chief data officer (CDO) 4–5, 6
   data accountability 106, 108
   data science, supporting 236
   history of role 53
   role of 36–37
   skills required 287–88
   success, seeing 211
   ten questions for 7–19
Chief Information Security Officer
   (CISO) 69

Christensen, Clayton 206, 220
Clay Doss, Cathryne 53
Clerksroom 268
cloud computing 8
cognitive diversity 62–63
competitors, understanding 219–21
Computer Misuse Act 1990 120
Cool, Kenton 192, 193
Corporate Executive Board 75
COUNT (Collect Once, Use Numerous
        Times) 123
Covid-19 pandemic 6, 14, 136, 183
    customer service bots 267
    mortality data 99–101, 103, 106
crisis, handling a 14–15
customer base health dashboard 141
customer behaviour 221–22
customer data sources 217–19
customer loyalty 215–16
customer relationship management
        (CRM) 16, 216
    see also voice of the customer (VoC)
customer service bots 267–68

dashboards 156–66
    certification for 164
    data access 161–62
    data challenges 161
    definition of 157
    designing 158–60, 159
    drilling down 159–60
    insight, gaining 162–63
data accessibility 14–15
data accountability 105–09
    data executives 108–09
    data owners 108
    data stewards 107–08
    definition of 106
data accuracy 103
data and analytics capability model 63–70,
        64
    data architecture 69
    data community 70
    data engineering 66–67
    data operations 68
    data oversight 69
    data product management 65–66
    data science 66
    data security and privacy 67–68
data and analytics strategy, creating a 33–50
    chief data officer (CDO), role of 36–37
    data periodic table 37, 38–44
        compliance 40
        decreased costs 39

        definition of 41
        designing projects with 42–44
        enabling capabilities 40–41
        reduced risk 39
        revenue increase 38
        strategy 40
    definition of 8, 35
    five waves of transformation 44, 45–47
        Aspire 46, 73–74
        definition of 45
        Differentiate 46–47, 254–55
        Industrialize 46, 177–78
        leadership skills required 287–88
        Mature 46, 97–98
        Realize 46, 213–14
    practical use of 35–36
    storytelling 48–50
    sunk cost fallacy 34
    Value, Build, Improve (VBI) 47, 47–48
        definition of 47
data architecture 69, 147
data capture process, the 132–33
data community 70
data compliance 171–72
data consistency 103
data culture 23
data, definition of 4
data engineering 66–67, 238–39
data ethics 170–71
data excellence 114
data executives 108–09
data fraud 172–74
data governance 99–114
    access to data, controlling 170
    Covid-19 mortality data 99–101,
            103, 106
    data accountability 105–09
        data executives 108–09
        data owners 108
        data stewards 107–08
        definition of 106
    data accuracy 103
    data consistency 103
    data provenance 103
    definition of 102
    dimensions of 103
    implementing 111–14
        maturity model 111, 112
    single customer view (SCV) 101, 146–47
    Tesco case study 109–11, 113
    Worldcom case study 102–03, 104
data inventory 26–27
data lake 67, 89, 234–35
data leakage 16–17, 274

data model 138–39
data operations 68
data oversight 69
data owners 108
data periodic table 37, 38–44
    compliance 40
    decreased costs 39
    definition of 41
    designing projects with 42–44
    enabling capabilities 40–41
    reduced risk 39
    revenue increase 38
    strategy 40
data privacy 67–68, 169–70
    data privacy officer (DPO) 68
data process 91
data products 278–85
    agile development 281
    centre of excellence (CoE), establishing
        a 282–83
    continuous improvement 285
    data product management 65–66
    definition of 280
    research, need for 284
    waterfall development 280
Data Protection Act 2018 120
data provenance 103, 238
data quality 27, 116–34
    advantages of 120–21
    in artificial intelligence 273, 274
    data capture process, the 132–33
    data cleansing 132
    data quality auditing 131–32
    data quality team, your 129–30
        data quality leader 129, 130
    definition of 116
    dimensions of 122, 122–24
        accuracy 123–24
        availability 122
        timeliness 123
        validity 124
    examples 125, 126
    improvement, measuring 127, 128
    legal compliance 118, 120
    manual errors, avoiding 133
    maturity model 130, 131
    in reports 153
    risks of 117–19
    when sharing data 250
    single customer view (SCV) 147
    testing for 121
Data Quality International 116
data risk management 168–76
    data compliance 171–72

data ethics 170–71
data fraud 172–74
data privacy 169–70
data security 170
regulators, working with 174–75
data science 66, 232–41
    data lake 234–35
    data warehouse 234–35
    definition of 234
    executive, role of 239
    failure, embracing 240–41
    leadership, role of 236
    'Petabyte age', the 232
    process for 237, 237
data security 67–68, 170
data sharing 242–53
    Amazon case study 242–43
    application programming interfaces
        (APIs) 243
    asymmetric information 247–48
    blockchain 246–47
    control, maintaining 252
    with customers 249–50
        subject access requests (SARs) 251
    with partners 244–45
    risks of 244
    RIXML case study 248–49
data stewards 107–08
data warehouse 67, 89, 234–35
Deloitte 190
Department for Transport (DfT) 278–79
Deutsche Bank 133
digital transition /digital transformation 6
disintermediation 208
disruption 220
disruptive innovation 206
diversity, ensuring 61–63
    cognitive diversity 62–63
drilling down 159–60
Dunning-Kruger effect 154

eBay 25
emotional quotient (EQ) 58
English, Larry 116
Equifax 221
Expertech Xi 260

Facebook 3, 24
    hackathons 199–200, 201
    social listening 222, 223
fallacy of composition, the 206
Fiennes, Ranulph 192
Financial Services Authority (FSA) 175
firehose APIs 223

five waves of transformation *44*, 45–47
    Aspire 46, 73–74
    definition of 45
    Differentiate 46–47, 254–55
    Industrialize 46, 177–78
    leadership skills required 287–88
    Mature 46, 97–98
    Realize 46, 213–14
Ford, Henry 286
forecasting 262
Freedom of Information Act 2000 120
Frey, Carl Benedikt 184

Gartner Hype Cycle 258
General Data Protection Regulation
        (GDPR) 18–19, 67, 68, 207
    data accountability 106
    data relevance 125
    permission 221
    poor quality data 118
    subject access requests (SARs) 251
    value of data 27
General Motors 286
Golden ID 12, 140, 238
Goodhart, Charles 165
Google 3, 8, 24
    A/B testing 93–94
'gut feel' 10–11

hackathons 199–202
    Facebook case study 199–200
heaven and hell problem 59
Herrmann Whole Brain model 62
heuristic decision-making 10–11, 261
Hodges, Andrew 54

Imitation Game, The 54
inaccurate data 11–12
influencers 225
Information Commissioner 251
Information Quality Applied 116
Instagram 222
intangible value of data 29
Intel 24
intuition 10–11
investment in data 8–9, 22–32
    Amazon Prime case study 25
    cost of doing nothing 24
    problems, solving 29
    quality of data 27
    return on investment (ROI) 28
    scepticism 23–24
    value of data 27
        tangible vs intangible 29

Johnson, Boris 100

Kahneman, Daniel 10
Kerviel Jérôme 171–72
Keynes, John Maynard 179
Klein, Geary 10
Kroger 222

Lee, William 179, 180
Lewis, Phillip V 171
Linden, Greg 94
LinkedIn 223
Lloyd's of London 19
Long Tail 232

machine learning (ML) 19, 66, 171, 258
    bias, measuring 270
    definition of 259
MacroCognition 10
market research 220
Michie, Donald 260
Microsoft 3, 24
    Azure 57, 189
    SQL Server 189
    Tay 270
Moltke the Elder (Helmuth Karl Bernhard
        Graf von Moltke) 36

natural language processing (NLP) 267
Net Promoter Score (NPS) 226–28, 229
Netflix Prize 240

O₂ 269
optimization 204–11
    Business Process Outsourcing
        (BPO) 204–05
    disintermediation 208
    fallacy of composition, the 206
    Pragati 205
    resistance, handling 208–09
    silos, overcoming 207
    straight-through processing (StP) 210
Oracle 189
Osborne, Michael 184

Pepsi challenge 94, 223
pet projects 78
Petabyte age 232
Pointillist 12
Power BI 57
practical quotient (PQ) 58
Pragati 205
prediction 262
PredPol 262, 269

Pring, Ian 279
process automation 266–67
   robotic process automation (RPA) 266
Progressive Insurance 252

Quatrro Global Services 204
quick wins 18, 75–85
   anatomy of 77–78
   data science 238
   data transformation quick wins 83–84
   definition of 76
   identifying 79, 79–80
   photocopier case study 81–83, 86–78
   quick win dashboards 160–61
   quick wins paradox 83
   see also repeat-and-learn culture, building
      a; scaling

Rackspace 19
Rank Group 19
recruitment, for data teams 51–71
   adaptability quotient (AQ) 58
   data and analytics capability
      model 63–70, 64
   data architecture 69
   data community 70
   data engineering 66–67
   data operations 68
   data oversight 69
   data product management 65–66
   data science 66
   data security and privacy 67–68
   'describe a car' challenge 59–60
   diversity, ensuring 61–63
      cognitive diversity 62–63
   emotional quotient (EQ) 58
   heaven and hell problem 59
   practical quotient (PQ) 58
   problem-solving 56–57
   ready-made teams 60–61
   résumés, issues with 55–56
   retention quotient (RQ) 57–58
   skills, required 53–55
regulators, working with 174–75
Reichheld, Fred 228
repeat-and-learn culture, building a 86–95
   A/B testing 93–94
   benefits of 87–89
   business change process 92
   customer churn case study 92–93
   data process 91–92
   data, understanding the 89–91
   documentation 88–89
reporting 151–66
   business report 152

dashboards 156–66
   certification for 164
   data access 161–62
   data challenges 161
   definition of 157
   designing 158–60, *159*
   drilling down 159–60
   insight, gaining 162–63
   maturity model 164, *165*
   report auditing 152–54
   role-based reporting 154–56
   short-term thinking, avoiding 165–66
resource multipliers 197–99
retention quotient (RQ) 57–58
returns, measurable 9–10
RIXML standard 247–49
Robbins, Tony 194
robotic process automation (RPA) 266
Rockingham County v. *Luten Bridge*
   Co. 33–34
role-based reporting 154–56
Roy, Raman 204–05

'salami slicing' 82
Salesforce 24
scaling 192–203
   definition of 194
   hackathons 199–202
      Facebook case study 199–200
   resource multipliers 197–99
   scaling out 196–97
   scaling up 195–96
   suitability for, measuring 194–95
   when not to scale 197
Seetharaman, PB 216
sentiment analysis 224
shadow data resources 15–16, *148*, 148–49
silos, overcoming 207
single customer view (SCV) 12–13, 101,
      135–50, *138*, *259*
   benefits of 143–44, *144*
   building a 146–47
   customer base health dashboard 141
   customer business rules 140–41
   customer data 360 139–40
   data model 138–39
   data science models 141
   data sources 137–38
   definition of 12, 137
   gambling company case study 142–43
   Golden ID 12, 140
   ownership of 149
   shadow data resources *148*, 148–49
   value, deriving 142
single employee view 13, 145–46

single product view 146
single source of truth 11–12, 13, 109
single supplier view (SSV) 13,
        145, 259
Sloan, Alfred 286
Smith New Court 51–53
Snowflake 189
social listening 222–26
    emotion, role of 225
    influencers 225
    sentiment analysis 224
Société Générale 171–72
straight-through processing (StP) 210
Strano, Michael 187
subject access requests (SARs) 251
Sugar, Alan 12
sunk cost fallacy 34

tangible value of data 29
Teradata 189
Tesco 19, 109–11, 112, 113, 117
    Clubcard 110, 268
tracking survey 218
Transport for London (TfL) 279, 284
TripAdvisor 223
Turing, Alan 53–55, 260
Twitter 24, 270
    social listening 222, 224–25

Uber 24
    Uber Eats 24

Value, Build, Improve (VBI) 47, 47–48
    Aspire activities 74, 74
    definition of 47
    Differentiate activities 256, 256
    Industrialize activities 178, 178
    Mature activities 98, 98
    Realize activities 214, 214
voice of the customer (VoC) 215–30
    bad news, hearing 229–30
    competitors, understanding 219–21
    customer behaviour 221–22
    customer data sources 217–19
    customer loyalty 215–16
    customer relationship management
        (CRM) 16, 216
    definition of 217
    Net Promoter Score (NPS) 226–28, 229
    social listening 222–26
        emotion, role of 225
        influencers 225
        sentiment analysis 224

WashCo 282
waterfall development 240, 280
web scraping 220–21
WhereScape 189
Wipro Spectramind 205
WorldCom 11–12, 102–03, 104, 185
Wright, David 190

Yahoo 53

CPSIA information can be obtained
at www.ICGtesting.com
Printed in the USA
JSHW010943280522
26497JS00005B/26

9 781398 606050